Forbidden Signs

Douglas C. Baynton

FORBIDDEN SIGNS

AMERICAN CULTURE AND
THE CAMPAIGN AGAINST
SIGN LANGUAGE

THE UNIVERSITY OF CHICAGO PRESS
Chicago & London

DOUGLAS C. BAYNTON is visiting professor of history
and American Sign Language at the University of Iowa.

The University of Chicago Press, Chicago 60637
The University of Chicago Press, Ltd., London
© 1996 by The University of Chicago
All rights reserved. Published 1996
Printed in the United States of America
05 04 03 02 01 00 99 98 97 96   1 2 3 4 5

ISBN: 0-226-03963-3 (cloth)

Library of Congress Cataloging-in-Publication Data

Baynton, Douglas C.
    Forbidden signs : American culture and the campaign
against sign language / Douglas C. Baynton.
        p. cm.
    Includes bibliographical references and index.
    ISBN 0-226-03963-3 (cloth)
    1. Deaf—Means of communication—United
States—History. 2. Sign language—Study and
teaching—United States—History. 3. Deaf—United
States—Social conditions. I. Title.
HV2471.B39   1996
419—dc20   96-12889
                                                    CIP

◎ The paper used in this publication meets the minimum
requirements of the American National Standard for Information
Sciences—Permanence of Paper for Printed Library Materials,
ANSI Z39.48-1984.

For my parents

CONTENTS

Acknowledgments *ix*

Introduction *1*

ONE   Foreigners in Their Own Land: Community *15*

TWO   Savages and Deaf Mutes: Species and Race *36*

THREE   Without Voices: Gender *56*

FOUR   From Refinement to Efficiency: Culture *83*

FIVE   The Natural Language of Signs: Nature *108*

SIX   The Unnatural Language of Signs: Normality *132*

Epilogue: The Trap of Paternalism *149*

Notes *164*

Index *217*

A gallery of photographs follows page 82.

Historians cannot do their work unless librarians and archivists do theirs. I want to thank Michael Olson, Marguerite Glass-Englehart, and Ulf Hedberg of the Gallaudet University Archives in Washington, D.C., not only for doing their jobs well, but for offering their friendship and encouragement. At the American School for the Deaf in Hartford, Connecticut, thanks to Winfield McChord, executive director, Denise Bransford, administrative assistant, and David Halberg, former teacher and archivist, for helping me to use their archives. Dennis Gjerdingen, president of the Clarke School for the Deaf in Northampton, Massachusetts, generously permitted me access to the records and files stored in his office dating back to the nineteenth century. Also at the Clarke School, thanks to Linda Callahan, administrative assistant, and Donna Meehan, librarian, for their help, and to Marjorie Magner, library assistant and former teacher, for sharing with me experiences and insights from her over forty years of experience teaching in schools for the deaf.

This book began as a Ph.D. dissertation. Financial support from the University of Iowa made completion of the dissertation possible. My first four years of graduate study were supported by a University of Iowa Fellowship, with the final year free of teaching duties so that I could begin my research. An Elizabeth Bennett Ink Fellowship from the history department and an Ida Louise Ballard Fellowship from the Graduate College provided me a full year to complete the writing of the dissertation. The Graduate Student Senate and the Sims Riddle *ix*

Fund of the Graduate College helped out with travel funds for the presentation of research at scholarly conferences.

Portions of chapter 1 appeared in *American Quarterly* 44 (June 1992): 216–43. Portions of chapter 2 appeared in John Vickrey Van Cleve, ed., *Deaf History Unveiled: Interpretations from the New Scholarship* (Washington, D.C.: Gallaudet University Press, 1993). Thanks are due to both for permission to reprint this material, and to the editors of both—Gary Kulik and John Van Cleve—for their editorial expertise.

A number of people have read part or all of the book and made valuable suggestions and criticisms. About Kenneth Cmiel, who directed my dissertation work at the University of Iowa, I cannot say enough good things. Many of the ideas I pursue here grew out of classes or informal discussions with him. Always generous with both his time and knowledge, his readings of the dissertation were critical and insightful. Shelton Stromquist, the second reader on my dissertation committee, was as thorough and helpful as anyone could ask for, during not only this project but throughout my graduate school career. The first chapter of the book began in a women's history seminar with Linda Kerber, who offered painstaking and astute criticisms on several of the chapters, going—as she unfailingly does with Iowa students—well beyond the call of duty. Thanks also to Charles Anderson and Ellis Hawley, who also served on my committee, for their comments and criticisms on the final draft of the dissertation.

Others have also read and commented upon portions of the book at various stages. Sue Peabody, Allan Megill, Christie York, Dan Goldstein, Robert Burchfield, Teresa Faden, and Bryan Eldredge have all given helpful advice. Colleagues in the small world of deaf history have offered invaluable assistance. John Vickrey Van Cleve of Gallaudet University has been both a generous colleague and a good friend. As one of the pioneers of deaf history, he is owed a debt of gratitude from those of us working in this field. I owe him a particular debt for reading the manuscript in its entirety and giving detailed suggestions that have greatly improved the book. Robert Buchanan has generously shared both research and ideas; his comments and suggestions on chapter 3 much improved it. John Schuchman of Gallaudet University made helpful comments on an earlier version of chapter 1. Conversations with Phyllis Valentine, Brenda

Farnell, Kate Gfeller, and Kimela Nelson have helped to clarify important issues for me.

I would never have embarked on this project were it not for deaf friends and teachers who have shared their language and culture with me over the years. Thanks to all of them and especially to Marian Lucas, who first introduced me to American Sign Language and the deaf community and who has remained, across many years and miles, a good friend ever since.

Thanks are due also to my parents and siblings, who have all been unfailingly generous with emotional and financial support in whatever mix or measure was needed. My sister in Oklahoma, Nancy von Bargen, even contributed research skills by tracking down some valuable information for me about the history of deaf education in her state.

Finally, I want to express my gratitude to my medievalist friend, Nancy Turner, for astute advice at every stage of the writing of this book, but especially for her friendship, love, and encouragement.

Introduction

This book is an exploration of American culture through the medium of the history of sign language and deafness. I have two aims. The first is to explain why sign language enjoyed great popularity and esteem among hearing Americans through most of the nineteenth century and then, near the end of the century, fell into such disrepute that hearing educators and reformers waged a campaign to eradicate it by forbidding its use in schools for the deaf. My second aim is to illuminate the landscape of American cultural history from the mid nineteenth century to 1920 from a new and revealing perspective. Thus I hope this book will find an audience among scholars interested in American cultural history as well as those with a special interest in sign language and the American deaf community.

The debate over sign language called upon and expressed the central debates of the time, involving such fundamental issues as what distinguished Americans from non-Americans, civilized people from "savages," humans from animals, and men from women; what purposes education should serve; and what "nature" and "normality" meant and how they were related to one another. Because deafness is in good part a cultural construction, as I will argue, the shape of its construction is an expression of broader cultural values. And since deafness is usually conceived by hearing people as merely a lack, an emptiness where hearing and sound ought to be, the effect is that deaf people and their means of communication become blank screens for the projection of cultural prejudice, fear and hope, faith and ideology. The ever-changing meanings of deafness, the shifting contours of its construction over time, and the images that deaf people and their language have inspired offer a unique point of access into the history of American culture.

Deafness is a cultural construction as well as a physical phenomenon. The difference between hearing people and deaf people is typically construed as simply a matter of hearing loss. For most, this is the common sense of the matter—deaf people cannot hear, and all else about them seems to follow naturally and necessarily from that fact. The result is that the relationship between hearing and deaf people appears solely as a natural one. The meanings of "hearing" and "deaf" are not transparent, however. As with gender, age, race, and other such categories, physical difference is involved, but physical differences do not carry inherent meanings. They must be interpreted and cannot be apprehended apart from a culturally created web of meaning. The meaning of deafness is contested, although most hearing and many deaf people are not aware that it is contested, and it changes over time. It has, that is to say, a history.

While social scientists have taken an increased interest in the cultures and languages of deaf people since the 1960s, deafness as a cultural phenomenon is an area still unfamiliar to most scholars. Gordon Allport was able in 1954 to state unequivocally: "There is one law—universal in all human societies. . . . *In every society on earth the child is regarded as a member of his parents' groups.* He belongs to the same race, stock, family tradition, religion, caste, and occupational status."[1] He was wrong, but it is hard to fault him. Deaf people occupy a unique position. They make up the only cultural group where cultural information and language has been *predominantly* passed down from child to child rather than from adult to child, and the only one in which the native language of the children is different from the language spoken by the parents. In schools for the deaf, children whose parents are deaf (about 10 percent of the total) teach the other children American Sign Language (ASL) and pass on the culture of American deaf people. Deaf teachers and staff also do so, when present; as we shall see, however, deaf adults were increasingly excluded from the schools in the late nineteenth and early twentieth centuries. This process has been going on for nearly two hundred years in America, and for somewhat longer in Europe.[2]

Deaf people are commonly placed in that large, amorphous category labeled, most commonly today, "disabled." What they have in common with others in this category is that their differences from the majority are caused by disease, trauma, or unusual genes. Deaf people, however, differ in an important way: in certain circumstances they have the propensity to invent languages and cultures distinct from those of the hearing societies surrounding them. Like the blind and others with individual physical differences, their difference is not in most cases passed on to their children; like ethnic groups, however, they form cohesive, culturally and linguistically distinct groups.

All histories of the deaf—including those in the lively oral tradition of the American deaf community (if we can call a tradition literally *handed down* by means of sign language an "oral" tradition)— emphasize two turning points for the education of American deaf people in the nineteenth century. One was the creation of the first school for the deaf in 1817 by Thomas H. Gallaudet and Laurent Clerc, the American Asylum for the Deaf at Hartford, Connecticut. With the creation of the first residential school—and the others that soon followed—individuals who shared a sensory world that differed from that of the majority began to coalesce into a community that shared a language and a culture.[3] To be sure, wherever sufficient numbers of deaf people have congregated, a distinctive community and language has come into existence; urban societies, by bringing numerous deaf people into contact with one another, always have deaf communities. We know of one such community in eighteenth-century Paris. A deaf Parisian, Pierre Desloges, wrote in 1779 that while the communication ability of a deaf person living isolated in the provinces was "limited to physical things and bodily needs," this was not the case in Paris; through "intercourse with his [deaf] fellows he promptly acquires the supposedly difficult art of depicting and expressing all his thoughts" using sign language. Deaf Parisians, Desloges contended, expressed themselves "on all subjects with as much order, precision, and rapidity as if we enjoyed the faculty of speech and hearing." As a result, "No event—in Paris, in France, or in the four corners of the world—lies outside the scope of our discussion."[4] And on Martha's Vineyard from the seventeenth century to the nineteenth, an unusually high rate of inherited deafness resulted in a community in which both hearing and deaf islanders knew and used sign language.[5]

In America, however, the schools for the deaf gathered together larger numbers of deaf people than ever before, placed them in communal living situations, and taught them not only formally about the world at large but informally about themselves. Those from small towns and the countryside—the great majority in early nineteenth-century America—met other deaf people for the first time and learned, also for the first time, how to communicate beyond the level of pantomime and gesture. They encountered the surprising knowledge that they had a history and an identity shared by many others. From this common language and common experience, they began to create an American deaf community.[6]

The second turning point in the history of the deaf was the attempt by another group of reformers, in the late nineteenth century and continuing into the twentieth, to unmake that community and culture. Central to that project was a campaign to eliminate what was called "manualism"—the use of sign language in the classroom—and to replace it with the *exclusive* use of lip-reading and speech, which was known as "oralism." Residential schools had been manualist from their beginnings, conducting their classes in sign language, finger-spelling, and written English. Lessons in speech and lip-reading were added to the curricula in most manualist schools by the latter decades of the century, but this was not the crux of the issue for the advocates of oralism. They opposed the use of sign language in any form for any purpose.

The larger goals of the oralist movement were not achieved—the deaf community was not unmade, and sign language continued to be used within it. The great majority of deaf people rejected the oralist philosophy and maintained an alternative vision of what being deaf meant for them. Leaders in the deaf community such as Olof Hanson, president of the National Association of the Deaf, sent an unending stream of letters to hearing educators protesting that, while most deaf people were "not opposed to oral instruction," they were deeply "opposed to the *exclusive* use of the oral method for all the deaf, and . . . to the abolition of the sign language."[7] The deaf community had little influence within the educational establishment, however, and the campaign to eliminate sign language from the classroom was largely successful. In 1860 almost no deaf students were being taught by exclusively oral methods. In the late 1860s the first oral schools were founded, and in the 1870s and 1880s most schools began to experiment with oral methods of teaching. By the turn of the century, nearly 40 percent of American deaf students were taught without the use of sign language, and more than half were so taught in at least some of their classes.[8] The number of children taught entirely without sign language was nearing 80 percent by the end of the First World War, and oralism remained orthodox until the 1970s.[9]

Why did educators of the deaf take this road? Oralists themselves most often explained it simply as a matter of progress.[10] If sign language had ever served any good purpose in deaf education (which most of them doubted), they believed that improved techniques and new knowledge in teaching speech and lip-reading made the use of sign language obsolete. Indeed, this remained the dominant view in the field until the 1960s and 1970s, when the efficacy of oral educational methods began to be seriously questioned once again. Most recent research has concluded that the oralist approach was devastating for generations of deaf people. Although most deaf children eventually would learn sign language on their own, their early language development and their education in the classroom was often severely stunted. The difficulty of learning spoken English for a person profoundly deaf from an early age has been likened to a hearing American trying to learn spoken Japanese while locked within a soundproof glass cubicle. A few gifted individuals succeed, but the majority face years of frustration and failure. Since most researchers and educators have rejected oralism in favor of an eclectic approach that includes the use of sign language—as an orally trained deaf writer said recently, the "Old Orthodoxy of oral-or-nothing paternalism has died a richly deserved death"—the progress model has become rather less tenable.[11]

Most deaf adults and their organizations strenuously opposed the elimination of sign language from the classroom and had their own explanations for the rise of oralism.[12] At a convention of teachers of the deaf in 1890, an angry deaf member noted that "Chinese women bind their babies' feet to make them small; the Flathead Indians bind their babies' heads to make them flat." Those who prohibit sign language in the schools, he declared, "are denying the deaf their free mental growth . . . and are in the same class of criminals."[13] Olof Hanson wrote in 1912 that "most of us [deaf people] are poor and have to earn our living by our work, and we realize that we have a large task to combat the oralists, backed as they are by ample funds, and advocating a method which in the very nature of things appeals strongly to the hearing public."[14] Robert P. McGregor, a deaf man, school principal, and first president of the National Association of the Deaf, in 1896 posed the question, "By whom then are signs proscribed?" His answer was this: "By a few educators of the deaf whose boast is that they do not understand signs and do not want to; by a few philanthropists who are otherwise ignorant of the language; by parents who do not understand the requisites to the happiness of their deaf children and are inspired with false fears by the educators and philanthropists."[15]

Scholars today in the new and still very small field of deaf history have in general agreed with these assessments and have been uniformly critical of oralism. Oralists, it has been argued, were in many cases woefully ignorant of deafness. Their faith in oralism was based more upon wishful thinking than evidence, and they were often taken in by charlatans and quacks.[16] Others, such as Alexander Graham Bell, were perhaps more knowledgeable but motivated by eugenicist fears that intermarriage among the deaf, encouraged by separate schools and the use of sign language, would lead to the "formation of a deaf variety of the human race." The resonance of this sort of language among late nineteenth-century Americans, as well as Bell's prestige, leadership abilities, and dedication to the cause, gave a tremendous boost to oralism.[17] Opponents of sign language believed that its use discouraged the learning of oral communication skills; hearing parents, eager to believe their deaf children could learn to function like hearing people, supported its proscription. State legislators were persuaded by claims that oral education would be less expensive.[18] Finally, "on the face of it, people are quite afraid of human diversity." The "fear of diversity leads majorities to oppress minorities"; the suppression of sign language, according to this view, was yet another example of the suppression of a minority language by an intolerant majority.[19]

The question of why schools adopted and continued to practice manualism for the better part of the nineteenth century has been given less attention. Manualism has seemed less in need of explanation than oralism; since it is closer to current practice, the manualist philosophy of the nineteenth century has simply come to seem more sensible. With oralism now widely rejected, the focus has been upon explaining how and why such a philosophy gained ascendance.[20] Why manualism took root so readily in the first half of the nineteenth century, however, and why attempts to establish oral schools were unsuccessful until the decades after the Civil War are questions that have not been adequately treated. Rather than treating manualism as merely sensible and oralism as an unfortunate aberration, seeing both as reform movements embedded in particular historical moments and expressing historically situated constructions of deafness can illuminate both them and the reform eras of which they were a part.

Opponents of sign language in the latter half of the nineteenth century were apt to argue that the age of manualism in American schools was merely the result of a historical accident. In 1815 Thomas H. Gallaudet had traveled to England and Scotland to learn the methods of teaching the deaf in use there. These methods—which were based upon oral communication rather than sign language—were treated as proprietary secrets by their practitioners, however, and he was unable to gain access to them. While in London he happened to meet the eminent French teacher of the deaf, the Abbé Sicard, who was traveling with two of his former pupils, Laurent Clerc and Jean Massieu, exhibiting his own method of teaching the deaf through sign language. Sicard invited Gallaudet to come to Paris to study with him, and Gallaudet accepted the offer. Gallaudet was impressed by the work of the Paris school and some months later asked Clerc if he would accompany him to Hartford, Connecticut, to establish the first school for the deaf in America. Clerc assented, became head teacher of the fledgling school, and thus was deaf education established in America. The story of Gallaudet's meeting with Sicard and Clerc was told and retold in succeeding years by teachers of the deaf as the story of the birth of their profession in America. It was a kind of origin myth.

While the manualist teachers saw the London encounter between Gallaudet and Clerc as serendipitous, even providential, oralists gave the story a different twist. They saw in it evidence that the use of sign language was not a result of reasoned or empirical investigation but merely an accident. T. H. Gallaudet was, in this version of the story, an innocent abroad, ready to uncritically accept the first method of teaching the deaf that anyone would be willing to provide him. The meeting with Sicard, oralists said, was a mischance with unfortunate and long-standing ramifications, the damage from which they were now setting about in a rational and orderly way to undo.[21]

Edward Miner Gallaudet, son of Thomas H., attempted to

counter this version of the story on numerous occasions, arguing that the belief that "sign language obtained a foothold in this country merely through an accident" was one of "several errors which have of late attained popularity and credence, as supposed truths."[22] He told a conference of school principals in 1868 that the fact that nearly all the schools for the deaf in America founded over the past fifty years used sign language was evidence of his father's good judgment. "A harmony so widespread and long continued," he insisted, "could scarcely have resulted from the accidental transplanting of an inferior system from Europe."[23]

Although historians rightly would be skeptical of Gallaudet's conclusion that "much of truth and reason must dwell where such a coincidence of opinion and practice was found," he was surely right that the reign of manualism for more than half a century was no accident.[24] It was, instead, a practice that was consonant with the culture of the day. Nor did oralism result simply from the actions of a few dedicated and powerful individuals, such as Alexander Graham Bell and Samuel Gridley Howe, as was often claimed by manualists and is often assumed today. Oralism, rather, was an outgrowth of fundamental changes in American culture after the Civil War. In the 1840s Samuel Gridley Howe was a dedicated and powerful proponent of oral education, and even Horace Mann, America's preeminent educator, wrote in favor of oralism, yet the results of their efforts were negligible.[25] In the decades after the Civil War, similar efforts bore fruit. In the following chapters, I conclude that the 1840s were not conducive to oralism and that the years after the 1860s were, for reasons generally unrelated to either pedagogy or the needs and desires of deaf people.

In one sense, however, the oralists were right that manualism was an accident. Manualism—and oralism as well—was the result of a fortuitous confluence of various related and unrelated cultural and social factors which created a context, a *climate,* conducive to it. Oralism did not replace manualism because in any absolute sense it "worked" better. Oralism was adopted not because it accomplished more but because it seemed to better answer the anxieties and concerns of the time. The accomplishments of oralism carried cultural meanings of greater importance to the hearing people of the era than the accomplishments of manualism, while its failures (however great they were for deaf people) were of lesser cultural weight.

Individuals always comprise multiple roles and points of view; their beliefs and attitudes inevitably are built from complex mosaics of various aspects of the self. The dramatically different attitudes toward sign language held by the manualist and oralist generations were such mosaics. Manualist teachers were evangelical Protestants attracted to sign language as a means of converting souls previously cut off from the gospel; it was the special gift of God to deaf people. They were also products of a Romantic era in philosophy, art, and literature and saw in this "original language of mankind," as they believed it to be, a language closer to God and nature than speech, uncorrupted and pure, more honest because more direct as a means of emotional expression. They were college graduates who spent a good portion of their youths absorbing the literature of antiquity and, for several curious reasons that I will later explore, linked sign language with the ancient world and saw it as a high-culture, genteel, even heroic language.

Oralists, on the other hand, were of a generation frightened by growing cultural and linguistic diversity and more immediately concerned with the national community than the Christian one. They thought in the terms of scientific naturalism, especially evolutionary theory, more than those of religion; they associated sign language not with God and nature nor with gentility but with "inferior races" and "lower animals." While manualist teachers were predominantly men, most oralist teachers were women, which, in the context of the nineteenth-century suffrage movement and the struggle for the right to speak in public, gave them different perspectives on the relative worth of "possessing a voice." They were professional teachers who saw one of their tasks as the production of efficient workers and worried that the continued use of sign language impaired efficiency in the workplace. Like others of their generation, they believed "normality" to be a goal of great significance, and they worried about the effects on deaf children of being different. In good part, the fight over sign language was a play in miniature of the late nineteenth-century fight between the upholders of an older romantic, genteel, and pastoral vision of life and the proponents of an efficient and rational modernity.

I identify here what I believe to be some of the major factors in the rise of oralism, but it should go without saying that I do not identify all. Historians have in recent years become inordinately fond of the easy criticism that "it (that is, whatever historical subject they are addressing) is more complex than that." Of course "it" is. Reality is inevitably more complex than we can possibly capture in words or by any other means. By choosing to focus on the very disparate strands of thought and culture that I have, I hope to suggest the complexity of the reality that extends beyond my description of it, and the accidental nature of the particular constellations of factors that go into the creation of historical "events."

Yet I will not leave it at that, claiming merely that both oralism and manualism were matters of cultural construction, that there was nothing solid or essential beneath all of this superstructure. Deafness is, as I hope to demonstrate in the following pages, very much a cultural construction that changes over time. But it is also a physical reality. The hearing people who have traditionally made most of the decisions concerning the education of deaf children can spend entire careers contented within these constructions of deafness, unconstrained by physical reality, but deaf people cannot. When the cultural climate of the nineteenth century changed to make sign language objectionable, hearing people could simply say, "Away with sign language" and imagine that this could be accomplished. Deaf people could not, for they are both members of a species that by nature seeks optimal communication, and inhabitants of a sensory universe in which that end cannot be achieved by oral means alone. Thus, it is also no accident that deaf people continued to use sign language throughout the long years of its proscription in the schools, and that the living language today called American Sign Language has been handed down, generation to generation, for nearly two hundred years without interruption.[26] As George Veditz, president of the National Association of the Deaf, argued in 1910, deaf people could never abandon sign language: "they are facing not a theory but a condition, for they are first, last, and all the time *the* people of the eye."[27]

Finally, it needs to be stressed that this is chiefly a history of hearing people rather than of deaf people. While I have included the words of deaf people to show where and how they disputed the claims of hearing people, how they created independent constructions of the meaning of deafness, and how their valuation of sign language was distinct and often very different from that of both manualists and oralists, my primary object has been to trace attitudes toward

sign language and the deaf community among hearing people. Some
might object that deaf people should be at the center of this story.
This is a serious objection and one I have much sympathy with. I
have made hearing people my focus for several reasons. First, hearing
people had, and have, much power over the lives of most deaf people;
what they think about deafness and sign language has tremendous
consequences for the lives of deaf people. More to the point, I focus
on the ideas of hearing people because I want to illustrate the dangers
that arise when any powerful group makes important decisions on
the behalf of a less powerful one, and to demonstrate how those
decisions tend to be based on metaphorically constructed fantasies
rather than experience. This is a case study in the decision-making-
by-metaphor that inevitably occurs in paternalistic relationships.

I have also investigated hearing peoples' images of deafness in
the nineteenth century in the hopes of inoculating against similarly
derived views in the present, as a way of cautioning against a way
of thinking about deafness that is still endemic. Hearing people think
in metaphors about deaf people no less today than they did a hundred
years ago, and their decisions concerning deaf people, especially deaf
children, are based upon them. These metaphors are derived from
extraneous cultural concerns with little direct relevance to the lives
of deaf people. I contrast the views of deaf people with those of
hearing people to show how constant they are on the subject of sign
language, and how much more grounded in concrete experience their
opinions are. In a sense, I attend more to what hearing people said
about deaf people in the past to make the point that, in the present,
we should attend to them less.

A note on terminology. The deaf people over whom manualists and
oralists fought did not include all those who were audiologically deaf.
Many people lose their hearing in adulthood as a result of illness or
age and never see deafness as a fundamental part of their identity.
The deaf people they were concerned with were the smaller number
of people for whom deafness came early enough in life to warrant
some kind of special educational measures, and who tended to
become members of the Deaf community—that is, people who
shared a historically created language and culture different from that
of the hearing majority, and who consciously identified themselves
as part of that community. The linguist James Woodward proposed

in 1972 the now common practice of using the lowercase *deaf* when referring to the audiological condition, and the uppercase *Deaf* when referring to the Deaf community and its members. The distinction, while useful and important, is often difficult in practice to apply, especially when dealing with historical figures. At what precise point do deaf people become Deaf? I have not tried to make the distinction here and have used the lowercase in most cases. It should be understood, however, that while precise definitions are not practical, this book concerns people who tended to identify themselves as members of the signing Deaf community (or who, if not exposed to that community as children, were likely to do so upon reaching adulthood).

The term "sign language" likewise needs clarification. American Sign Language (ASL)—known in the nineteenth century as "the natural language of signs"—is a language in which the shapes, positions, and movements of the hands are combined with complex uses of nonmanual signals, such as facial expressions and movements of the head and body, to create a variety of linguistic possibilities as diverse as the combinations of sounds used in oral languages. It is neither an invented nor a universal language but rather has evolved within a linguistic community, like any spoken language, over many years. Descriptions of ASL from the mid-nineteenth century indicate that the sign language of the deaf community today has not essentially changed since then. Films made by the National Association of the Deaf in the second decade of this century show deaf people using a sign language that, while it differs in some particulars, is largely understandable and familiar to ASL users today. This in spite of sign language having no written form and having endured nearly a century of suppression by hearing educators.

The sign languages of different countries differ from one another just as spoken languages do, and are mutually unintelligible. In addition, they do not correspond to the spoken languages of their respective countries, having developed separately within deaf communities. Some countries, such as Germany, have one spoken language but several regional sign languages. Just as the American Deaf community has a cultural history distinct from that of hearing Americans, ASL has a linguistic history distinct from that of the English language. It has roots in the Parisian sign language brought to the United States by Laurent Clerc in 1817, which combined with indigenous local sign languages such as that used on Martha's Vineyard, to form modern ASL. Because sign languages are living languages, French Sign Language and ASL have diverged considerably over the years; nevertheless, the two languages are to a limited extent mutually intelligible—somewhat like modern Spanish and Italian. Unlike the spoken languages of the United States and Britain, British Sign Language and ASL have little historical relation and are mutually unintelligible.[28]

ASL should not be confused with those sign systems that attempt to represent English vocabulary and grammar, and which were invented for the purpose of teaching English to deaf children in school. Several varieties of these "Manually Coded English" systems have been developed in recent years; in the nineteenth century, a system called "methodical sign language" was at times used in some schools. These signed English systems are not true languages (as linguists define the term), but rather are invented, artificial codes. Manualist teachers in the nineteenth century at different times used both forms of sign language, and oralists opposed both.[29]

While oralists rarely made any distinction between them, indiscriminately condemning any form of sign language, the distinction was a significant one for the manualists, and they usually made it quite clear in their writing and speeches whether they meant one or the other. Unless "methodical" signs were specifically mentioned, "sign language" by itself usually meant "natural" signs. For reasons I explain in chapter 5, however, neither nineteenth-century deaf people nor their teachers distinguished between the sign languages of various countries, referring to all generically as simply "sign language." It is the custom today to recognize the diversity of sign languages (or, as some linguists today prefer, "signed languages," a usage that makes the term parallel with "spoken languages") by always attaching a qualifier, as in French Sign Language and American Sign Language. To avoid anachronism and confusion, I use the term "sign language" as it was used by my subjects. Similarly, I use the term "sign" as they did, to mean a gesture-sign, the basic morphemic unit of sign language and the equivalent of a "word" in spoken language.

By "oralism" I do not mean simply the provision of oral instruction but rather the insistence that all or most deaf children should be taught this way exclusively. Most manualists by the 1870s and 1880s advocated providing instruction in oral communication to all who could benefit from it. They began to call themselves advocates of a "combined system," or "combinists," to reflect the eclecticism of their approach. I have avoided, for the most part, using this term because of its ambiguity. The combined system meant so many different things to different people and changed meaning so dramatically over the years that it confuses much more than it clarifies. I will address the question of the combined system again in subsequent chapters. Suffice it to say for now that manualists supported the use of sign language and that oralists for a variety of reasons opposed its use. The question was not, for them or for most deaf people, whether oral communication should be taught. The fight was over sign language.

ONE

Foreigners in Their Own Land: Community

The meaning of deafness changed during the course of the nineteenth century for educators of the deaf, and the kind of education deaf people received changed along with it. Before the 1860s, deafness was most often described as an affliction that isolated the individual from the Christian community. Its tragedy was that deaf people lived beyond the reach of the gospel. After the 1860s, however, deafness was redefined as a condition that isolated people from the national community. Deaf people were cut off from the English speaking American culture, and *that* was the tragedy. The remedies proffered for each of these kinds of isolation were dramatically different. During the early and middle decades of the nineteenth century, sign language was a widely used and respected language among educators at schools for the deaf. By the end of the century, it was widely condemned and banished from many classrooms. In short, sign language was compatible with the former construction of deafness but not with the latter.

Manualism and oralism were the products of two very different reform eras in American history. The first schools for deaf people—such as the American Asylum for the Deaf and Dumb at Hartford, Connecticut, founded in 1817 by the Reverend Thomas H. Gallaudet—were established in the United States by evangelical Protestant reformers during the Second Great Awakening. The early teachers of the deaf learned sign language much as other missionaries of the time learned American Indian or African languages, and they *15* organized schools where deaf people could be brought together and given a Christian education. Manualism, then, came out of the evangelical, romantic reform movements of the antebellum years, movements that emphasized moral regeneration and salvation. Reformers of this period, who were attracted to such issues as temperance, the rehabilitation of criminals, and health reform, usually traced social evils to the weaknesses of individuals, believing that the reformation of society would come about only through the moral reform of its individual members. The primary responsibility of the evangelical reformer was to educate and convert individuals. Each successful conversion brought the Christian nation they desired and the millennial hopes they nurtured one step closer to fruition.

Oralism was the product of a much changed reform atmosphere after the Civil War. While Protestantism continued to be an important ingredient, the emphasis shifted from the reform of the individual to, among other things, the creation of national unity and social order through homogeneity in language and culture. Oralists likened the deaf community to a community of immigrants. They charged that the use of sign language encouraged deaf people to associate principally with each other and to avoid the hard work of learning to communicate in spoken English. They believed that a purely oral education would lead to greater assimilation, and they believed that to be a goal of the highest importance. Much reform of the time, oralism included, reflected widespread fears of unchecked immigration and expanding, multi-ethnic cities. Deaf people in both eras served as convenient, and not always willing, projection screens for the anxieties of their times.

While oralists and manualists are generally portrayed as standing on opposite sides of an ideological fault line, this formulation obscures important similarities between them. Both created images of deaf people as outsiders, with the implicit message that deaf people depended upon hearing people to rescue them from their exile. Both furthermore based their methods of education upon the images they created. Where they differed was in their definition of the "outsider," of what constituted "inside" and "outside." For the manualists, the Christian community was the measure, while for the oralists it was an American nation defined in the secular terms of language and culture. Deafness, constructed as a condition that excluded people from the community, was defined and redefined according to what their hearing educators saw as the essential community.

The manualist image of deafness can be seen in the pages of what was in 1847 a remarkable new journal. Published by the American Asylum for the Deaf and Dumb at Hartford, Connecticut, and proclaiming itself the first of its kind in the English language, the *American Annals of the Deaf and Dumb* was intended to be not only a journal of education but a "treasury of information upon all questions and subjects related, either immediately or remotely, to the deaf and dumb." The editors believed that "the deaf and dumb constitute a distinct and, in some respects, strongly marked class of human beings," and that they also "have a history peculiar to themselves . . . sustaining relations, of more or less interest, to the general history of the human race." The implication of this, and of the editors' suggestions of topics for investigation such as the "social and political condition in ancient times" of the deaf, and "a careful exposition of the philosophy of the language of signs," was that they saw deaf people not only as *individuals* but also as a collectivity, a *people*— albeit, as we shall see, an inferior one, and one in need of missionary guidance.[1]

The Reverend Thomas H. Gallaudet, an evangelical minister with a degree in theology from Yale, wrote in this first volume of the new journal that there was "scarcely a more interesting sight than a bright, cheerful deaf-mute, of one or two years of age" in the midst of its hearing family. "The strangeness of his condition, from the first moment of their discovering it, has attracted their curiosity. They wonder at it." Gallaudet and others of his generation also wondered at the deaf. The source of their wonderment and of the "greatest delight" for the family was the child's efforts "to convey his thoughts and emotions . . . by those various expressions of countenance, and descriptive signs and gestures, which his own spontaneous feelings lead him to employ." For Gallaudet, "substantial good has come out of apparent evil," for this family would now have the privilege of learning "a novel, highly poetical, and singular descriptive language," the language of signs.[2]

As used by a deaf child isolated within a hearing family and community, this language of signs was necessarily limited and rudimentary. But it need not be. Gallaudet knew that the halting and imprecise gestures of most deaf children before they came to school would soon flower into a language not only rich and complex but possessed of a beauty, a "picture-like delineation, pantomimic spirit, variety and grace" that no "merely oral language" could equal. This language was valuable to the deaf, but it could be of great benefit to the hearing as well, for if widely cultivated it could "supply the deficiencies of our oral intercourse [and] perfect the communion of one soul with another." Superior to spoken language in its beauty and emotional expressiveness, sign language brought "kindred souls into a much more close and conscious communion than . . . speech can possibly do."[3]

Most important for Gallaudet, sign language resolved what he saw as the overriding problem facing deaf people: they lived beyond the reach of the gospel. They knew nothing of God and the promise of salvation nor had they a firm basis for the development of a moral sense. An essential aspect of education for Gallaudet and his colleagues was to teach "the necessity and the mode of controlling, directing, and at times subduing" the passions. Gallaudet emphasized the need to develop the conscience, to explain vice and virtue, and to employ "the sanctions of religion" in order to create a moral human being.[4] The "moral influence" with which Gallaudet was concerned could not "be brought to bear . . . without language, and a language intelligible to such a mind." Learning to speak and read lips was a "long and laborious process, even in the comparatively few cases of complete success." Communication between student and teacher, furthermore, was not sufficient. A language was needed with which "the deaf-mute can intelligibly conduct his private devotions, and join in social religious exercises with his fellow pupils."[5]

Prayer, seen as both the means to and the evidence of conversion, held crucial significance for nineteenth-century evangelicals; bringing the unregenerate to prayer was their cardinal challenge. Toward this end, "nothing is more calculated to beget a spirit of prayer," wrote evangelist Charles Finney, "than to unite in social prayer with one who has the spirit himself." As Paul E. Johnson has pointed out, "that simple mechanism is at the heart of evangelical Protestantism." This was the essential point for Gallaudet: he and his fellow teachers had to be able to pray with deaf people.[6]

Manualists sometimes described sign language as inferior for conveying abstract thought, but abstract thought was not necessary for an understanding of God, the cultivation of morality, or the experience of conversion. Education for Gallaudet was therefore not primarily directed to the mind through abstraction; rather, he believed that "the heart is the principal thing which we must aim to reach" to save the souls of the deaf. While manualists differed on the question of whether oral language better communicated abstraction, however, all agreed that sign language was superior for the expression of the emotions. Gallaudet spoke for them all when he wrote that "the heart claims as its peculiar and appropriate language that of the eye and countenance, of the attitudes, movements, and gestures of the body."[7] He described the progress of the student with the use of sign language: "Every day he is improving in this language; and this medium of moral influence is rapidly enlarging. His mind becomes more and more enlightened; his conscience more and more easily addressed; his heart more and more prepared to be accessible to the simple truths and precepts of the Word of God."[8]

The interdependence of the mind, the heart, and the conscience, of both knowledge and morality, run through the writings of Gallaudet and his fellow teachers. Morality, and the self-discipline it required, depended upon a knowledge of God's existence as well as a heartfelt conviction that the soul was immortal and that the promise of its salvation was real. What was more, the proper development of the moral nature not only depended upon knowledge, but in its turn stimulated the higher faculties to yet greater learning.[9] Harvey P. Peet, principal of the New York Institution for the Instruction of the Deaf and Dumb, told the 1853 meeting of the Convention of American Instructors of the Deaf (a professional association founded in 1850) that while their pupils' "intellectual instruction . . . should be subordinate to their moral and religious instruction," there was in fact no conflict between the two aims, "for the most harmonious moral development is not merely perfectly consistent with, but favorable to the highest intellectual cultivation." Indeed, "great as is the influence of the teacher's mind on the mental development of his pupils, the influence of his moral character on their mental development is far greater."[10]

Achieving inner self-discipline was important for evangelicals, not just for the sake of morality, as David Walker Howe has pointed out, but for the liberation of the self. Liberation and morality were seen by antebellum evangelicals as "two sides of the same redemptive process." Evangelicals, according to Howe, "were typically concerned to redeem people who were not functioning as free moral agents: slaves, criminals, the insane, alcoholics, children."[11] The contributors to the *Annals* placed deaf people in this same category.

Outsiders to the Christian community, their liberation depended upon being brought within the fold. Teachers at the Asylum at Hartford, "preeminently a Christian institution" dedicated to teaching those "truths which are received in common by all evangelical denominations," bemoaned the fact that "in this Christian land" there were still deaf people living "in utter seclusion from the direct influences of the gospel."[12] These deaf people "might almost as well have been born in benighted Asia, as in this land of light" and were "little short of a community of heathen at our very doors."[13] The central task of the teacher was to make the "light and intelligence" of the "Christian community" accessible to deaf people.[14] The importance of this work was by no means confined to the salvation of deaf individuals, as crucial as that was. It possessed a clear social significance as well. A community was bound together by its religion—"What would become of the laws of God and of the laws of man, of the good order," T. H. Gallaudet asked, "or even of the very existence of society, if men did not come together to bow before their common Lord, and collectively learn his will?"[15]

Throughout this first year of the journal, images of imprisonment, darkness, blankness, and isolation were repeatedly used to describe the condition of deaf people without education. The interconnectedness of these metaphors was made plain by the Reverend Collins Stone, a teacher at the Hartford school, who described the plight of the uninstructed deaf person: "scarcely a ray of intellectual or moral *light* ever dawns upon his *solitude*"; if "he dies unblessed by education, he dies in this utter moral *darkness*"; "open the doors of his *prison,* and let in upon him the *light* of truth"; "even in the midst of Christian society, he must grope his way in *darkness* and *gloom . . .* unless some kind hand penetrates his *solitude*" (emphases added).[16]

Such metaphors were the common coin of teachers of the deaf. The Reverend Luzerne Rae, speculating upon the "Thoughts of the Deaf and Dumb before Instruction," asked the reader to imagine a child born with no senses, to imagine that "the animal life of this infant is preserved, and that he grows up to be, in outward appearance at least, a man." Rae wondered, "can we properly say that there would be any mind at all" and "could there be any conscious self-existence or self-activity of a soul imprisoned within such a body?" He concluded that to answer in the affirmative would be to succumb to "the lowest form of materialism." While no such person had ever existed, uneducated deaf people living "in a state of isolation the most complete that is ever seen among men" came close.[17] Henry B. Camp similarly lamented the "darkness and solitude" of the person who possessed "no key to unlock the prison of his own mind."[18]

For the manualists, then, the "real calamity for the deaf-mute" was "not that his ear is closed to the cheerful tones of the human voice" and "not that all the treasures of literature and science, of philosophy and history . . . are to him as though they were not"; the calamity was that "the light of divine truth never shines upon his path."[19] The darkness, the emptiness, the solitude were all of a particular kind: uneducated deaf people were cut off from the Christian community and its message.

A peculiar duality that runs throughout their writings, derived from a duality in their Christian theology, illuminates the meaning of deafness for these teachers. In Christianity, knowledge is necessary for salvation—knowledge of God, of the message Christ brought to the earth, of the nature of sin. Yet innocence—the innocence of the child, of the untutored, of the unworldly and cloistered—is also valued and was especially so in the romantic, evangelical Christianity of this era. Deafness, then, was often described by these teachers as both an affliction and a blessing. Lucius Woodruff, for example, explained that the only unusual aspect of educating deaf people in moral and religious matters was that they had "a *simplicity* of mental character and an *ignorance* of the world, highly favorable to the entrance and dominion of this highest and best motive of action" (emphasis added). The properly educated deaf person, he believed, would exhibit "a pleasing combination of strength and simplicity." The strength would come from education but the simplicity was inherent in deafness; it "flows naturally from that comparative isolation of the mind which prevents its being formed too much on the model of others."[20] J. A. Ayres, expressing the same duality, explained this "beautiful compensation" for deafness by noting that even though the deaf person was "deprived of many blessings, he is also shut out from many temptations." For this reason, it was "rare indeed that the claims of religion and the reasonings of morality fail to secure the ready assent both of his heart and his understanding."[21]

Deaf people were thought to have a moral advantage in having been relatively unscathed by a corrupt world. They were in this case innocent rather than in darkness, and their deafness was a sanctuary rather than a prison. Deafness, then, conferred both the benefit of innocence and the burden of ignorance, two sides of the same coin. The state of innocence in which deaf people lived was sublime only when temporary and shaped by teachers of good intent, but potentially evil when neglected and left uncultivated. Constructions of virginity and barrenness (whether of women or of land) are analogous—the first is usually cast as a blessed state, the second as a calamity. Deaf people were blessed if virginal, innocent, and fertile but accursed if left forever in that state. They would then be barren. Innocence held within it the seed of knowledge and salvation. Ignorance was darkness.

The dark side was expressed in 1847 by John Carlin, a former student at the Hartford school, in a poem lamenting his deafness (emphases in original):

> I move—a silent exile on this earth;
> As in his dreary cell one doomed for life,
> My tongue is mute, and closed ear heedeth not;
>
> . . . .
>
> Deep silence over all, and all seems lifeless;
> The orators exciting strains the crowd
> Enraptur'd hear, while meteor-like his wit
> Illuminates the dark abyss of mind—
> Alone, left in the dark—*I hear them not.*
>
> . . . .
>
> The balmy words of God's own messenger
> Excite to love, and troubled spirits soothe—
> Religion's dew-drops bright—*I feel them not.*[22]

Some months later, however, a poem titled "The Children of Silence" was published in response "to show that there are times and circumstances," in the editor's words, "when not to be able to hear must be accounted rather a blessing than a misfortune":

> Not for your ears the bitter word
> Escapes the lips once filled with love;
> The serpent speaking through the dove,

Oh Blessed! ye have never heard.
Your minds by mercy here are sealed
From half the sin in man revealed.[23]

The use of "silent" and "silence" in these poems embodies the contradictions in the innocence/ignorance metaphor. It was (and is) a common description of the world of deafness, and at first glance would seem a common sense description as well. Deaf people have used it as well as hearing. In the nineteenth century, for example, periodicals by and for the deaf had such titles as the *Silent Worker* and *Silent World*. There are still newspapers and clubs today with names such as the *Silent News* and the Chicago Silent Dramatic Club.

"Silence" is not a straightforward or unproblematic description of the experience of deafness, however. First, few deaf people hear nothing. Most have hearing losses that are not uniform across the entire range of pitch—they will hear low sounds better than high ones or vice versa. Sounds will often be quite distorted but heard nevertheless. And second, for those who do not hear, what does the word silence signify? Unless they once heard and *became* deaf, the word is meaningless as a description of their experience. (Even for those who once heard, as the experience of sound recedes further into the past, so too does the significance of "silence" diminish.) Silence is experienced by the hearing as an absence of sound. For those who have never heard, deafness is not an absence.

As used by hearing people, "silence" is a metaphor rather than a simple description of the experience of deaf people.[24] Deaf people may use the analogy of visual clutter to understand noise, and blind people may use tactile sensations of heat and coolness to approach the idea of color. Such *analogies,* in the absence of direct experience, can promote understanding because they juxtapose equally complex phenomena; neither is reduced by the comparison. On the other hand, hearing people may plug their ears and sighted people may close their eyes and then, speaking of silence and darkness, use these experiences to try to understand deafness or blindness. But these *metaphors* are less helpful. Speaking of deaf people as inhabiting a world of silence is metaphorical rather than analogous because it is an attempt to understand the complex and abstract in terms of the simple and concrete. When hearing people think of the world of the deaf as silent, they are comparing and reducing an identity, a way of life, an infinitely complex set of social and cultural relationships to a simple and concrete phenomenon: a temporary absence of sound.

What then did deaf people mean by their use of the word "silent"? Rather than the experience of soundlessness, most often their use of the word seems to point in a different direction and to call up different associations. Deaf people only rarely used it as hearing people did in such phrases as "living in silence." Instead, "silent" usually seems to have referred more to not speaking than not hearing, meaning *mute* more than *deaf,* and pointing to a social relation rather than a state of being. It indicated a social identity, setting "mutes" off from "speaking people"—both common terms among nineteenth-century deaf people. The *Silent Worker* and the *Silent Courier,* for example, like the *Nebraska Mute Journal* and the *Deaf Mute Times,* were identified as newspapers of the deaf community by their titles. Such usages do not call up the same associations as the phrase "living in silence"; only rarely does one find deaf people using "silence" as John Carlin does above, to describe a state of being and a lack.

To be deaf is *not* to not hear for most profoundly deaf people but a social relation—that is, a relation with other human beings, hearing and deaf. What the deaf person sees in these other people is not the presence or absence of hearing, not their soundfulness or their silence, but their mode of communication—they sign, or they move their lips. That is why deaf people in the nineteenth century typically referred to themselves not as deaf people but as "mutes." That is why the sign still used today that is translated as "hearing person" is made next to the mouth, not the ear, and literally means "speaking person."

Deafness is a relationship not a state, and the way that the "silence" metaphor is usually understood by hearing people is one indication of how they view the relationship. To hearing people, deaf people are incomplete. They are different but not merely different: their difference is also a deficiency (which is probably the shared characteristic of all perceived as "other"). Hearing is defined as the universal, and deafness, therefore, as an absence, as an emptiness, as a silence. Silence can represent innocence and fertility, and it can represent darkness and barrenness. In both cases it is empty. In both cases it needs to be filled. Images such as these—images of light and darkness, of society and isolation, of soundfulness and silence— construct a hierarchical relationship in which deaf people are said to lack what hearing people alone can provide.

The absence that defined deaf people was framed as a place in which they lived: a "Ghetto of Silence," a prison from which they could not without help escape, a blankness and ignorance that denied them humanity.[25] Deaf people were trapped within this place of darkness, but the problem was not only that the deaf could not see *out* but that the hearing could not see *in*. The minds of deaf people represented impenetrable dark spaces within Christian society—or better, *without* Christian society—of which the hearing had little knowledge. Sign language was the light that could illuminate the darkness.

In 1899, half a century after the founding of the *Annals,* the *Association Review* was established as the journal of the American Association to Promote the Teaching of Speech to the Deaf, an organization with Alexander Graham Bell as its first president. In the introduction to the first issue, the editor, Frank Booth, was able to state confidently that "the spirit prevalent in our schools is one entirely favorable to speech for the deaf, and to more and better speech teaching so soon as more favorable conditions may warrant and permit."[26] The times were not only favorable to speech but quite hostile to sign language. Nearly 40 percent of American deaf students now sat in classrooms from which sign language had been banished. Within twenty years it would be 80 percent.[27] Deaf teachers were rarely hired by the schools anymore and made up only 16 percent of the teaching corps, down from 40 percent in the 1850s and 1860s.[28] Those who remained were increasingly confined to teaching industrial education courses, to which students who were "oral failures" were relegated. The new teacher-training school established in 1891 at Gallaudet College, a liberal arts college primarily for deaf students, itself refused, as a matter of policy, to train deaf teachers.[29] Booth himself would forbid the use of sign language at the Nebraska School for the Deaf when he became its superintendent in 1911. "That language is not now used in the school-room," he wrote to Olof Hanson, president of the National Association of the Deaf, "and I hope to do away with its use outside of the school-room."[30]

Booth was certainly correct that the "spirit now prevalent" was much changed. The *American Annals of the Deaf* at the turn of the century reflected the changed climate as well. Educational philosophy had shifted ground so dramatically that unabashed manualism had nearly disappeared from its pages, with the majority of opinion ranging between oralism and what was called the "combined system." The definition of the latter varied widely and changed over time. In some cases it meant supplementing speech with fingerspelling but forbidding sign language; in others, speech alone was used in the classroom, with sign language permitted outside; in many cases it meant using speech with all young students and resorting later to sign language only with older "oral failures." To Edward M. Gallaudet, son of Thomas and first president of Gallaudet College, the combined system meant preserving sign language but using it in the classroom "as little as possible." He defended this tiny remnant of his father's world in an article bearing the plaintive title "Must the Sign-Language Go?"[31]

The new aversion to sign language accompanied an important change in the images and meaning of deafness during the latter decades of the nineteenth century. The ardent nationalism that followed the Civil War—the sense that divisions or particularisms within the nation were dangerous and ought to be suppressed—provided most of the initial impetus for a new concern about what came to be termed the "clannishness" of deaf people. Even some of the hearing educators who had long supported sign language began in the years following the war to voice criticisms of the deaf community. In 1873, for example, Edward M. Gallaudet condemned the conventions, associations, and newspapers of deaf people, as well as their tendency to intermarry, arguing that these discouraged intercourse between them and "the world." It was injurious to the best interests of deaf people when they came to consider themselves "members of society with interests apart from the mass, . . . a 'community,' with its leaders and rulers, its associations and organs, and its channels of communication." Gallaudet's concerns were similar to those voiced by oralists, except that he thought sign language to be nevertheless necessary—a "necessary evil"—since oral communication could never provide most deaf people with full participation in the classroom or the chapel.[32] Oralists soon escalated the charge of "clannishness" to "foreignness," however, a more highly charged term, and one with more ominous connotations.

The opening article of the first issue of the *Association Review* is revealing. Reprinted from an address delivered before a meeting of the association by John M. Tyler (president of Amherst College), "The Teacher and the State" concerned what teachers could do about two related national problems: the new immigration and the decline in law and order. There was a "struggle between rival civilizations" within America. "Shall her standards and aims, in one word her civilization, be those of old New England, or shall they be Canadian or Irish, or somewhat better or worse than any of these?" The burden rested upon the teachers, for "'Waterloo was won at Rugby' [and] it was the German schoolmaster who triumphed at Sedan." Furthermore, teachers could no longer focus on "purely intellectual training," for "the material which we are trying to fashion has changed; the children are no longer of the former blood, stock, and training." Teachers must make up for the new immigrants' deficiencies as parents, he warned: "the emergency remains and we must meet it as best we can." Otherwise, the "uncontrolled child grows into the lawless youth and the anarchistic adult."[33]

Tyler's speech was not directly about deaf people, but it must have resonated with his audience of educators of the deaf. Metaphors of deafness by the turn of the century were no longer ones of spiritual darkness but instead conjured images of foreign enclaves within American society. Articles about deaf people during this period, with the substitution of "German" or "Italian" for "deaf" here and there, might just as well have been about immigrant communities. The central problem for deaf people and deaf education was what was now commonly referred to as "the foreign language of signs." Educators worried that if deaf people "are to exercise intelligently the rights of citizenship, then they must be made people of our language." They insisted that "the English language must be made the vernacular of the deaf if they are not to become a class unto themselves—foreigners among their own countrymen." An article in *Science* magazine lamented that sign language in the schools made the deaf child a "foreigner in his own land."[34]

A parent who wrote to the superintendent of the Illinois Institution for the Education of the Deaf and Dumb to request information about methods of deaf education was answered that there were two: "the English language method" and the method in which "the English language is considered a foreign language" taught through "translation from the indefinite and crude sign language."[35] A teacher insisted that a deaf person who does not use English as a primary language "can never acquire that command of it that would make him an American." Indeed, "no gesturer can become an American" when sign language is the primary language; "the gesturer is, and always will remain, a foreigner."[36] A teacher from a small day school in Los Angeles who wrote to Alexander Graham Bell for information on sign language was told by him that sign language was "essentially a foreign language" and furthermore that "in an English speaking country like the United States, the English language, *and the English language alone,* should be used as the means of communication and instruction—at least in schools supported at public expense."[37] In another letter, drafted to send to a journal of deaf education, Bell objected that the use of sign language "in our public schools is contrary to the spirit and practice of American Institutions (as foreign immigrants have found out)." He added it was "un-American" but apparently thought better of it and crossed the word out.[38] Oralism was about much more than just speech and lip-reading. It incorporated and symbolized the larger argument about language and national community that was occurring in the wake of civil war and in the face of massive immigration.

For some, the oralist argument shaded into jingoism and xenophobia. "Sign language is an evil," avowed J. D. Kirkhuff, a teacher at the Pennsylvania Institution for the Deaf and Dumb (one of the first state schools to adopt the oralist philosophy), in 1892. The mastery of English was not by itself the point, he argued. Sign language made deaf people "a kind of foreigners in tongue," and this was so whether or not they also mastered English. Deaf people who signed were not bona fide members of the American community but rather "a sign making people who have studied English so as to carry on business relations with those who do not understand signs." Using another language was the offense, for "English is a jealous mistress. She brooks no rival. She was born to conquer and to spread all over the world. She has no equal."[39]

Most oralists did not, however, exhibit this kind of overt xenophobia, insist upon Anglo-Saxon superiority, or advocate one worldwide language. Rather, they most often contended that sign language isolated deaf people, made the deaf person an outsider who was "not an Englishman, a German, a Frenchman, or a member of any other nationality, but, intellectually, a man without a country."[40] They were convinced, and deeply troubled by the conviction, that signing deaf people existed apart and isolated from the life of the nation. An earlier generation of educators had believed that sign language liberated deaf people from their confinement; for this generation it was the instrument of their imprisonment.

Foreignness was a metaphor of great significance for Americans of the late nineteenth century. References to deaf people as foreigners coincided with the greatest influx of immigrants in United States history. The new immigrants were concentrated in urban areas, and no major city was without its quilt pattern of immigrant communities. Many came from eastern and southern Europe, bringing with them cultural beliefs and habits that native-born Americans often regarded as peculiar, inferior, or even dangerous. Frederick E. Hoxie has noted in his study of the Indian assimilation movement (a movement contemporary with and sharing many characteristics with the oralist movement) that in the late nineteenth century "growing social diversity and shrinking social space threatened many Americans' sense of national identity."[41] Nativism, never far from the surface of American life, resurged with calls for immigration restriction, limits on the employment of foreigners, and the proscription of languages other than English in the schools. To say that sign language made deaf people appear foreign was to make a telling point for these educators. That foreignness should be avoided at all costs was expressed as a self-evident truth.

"Foreignness" had two related meanings. As with the manualists' metaphor of darkness, this was a metaphor with two centers. Looking from the outside in, the metaphor suggested a space within American society that was mysterious to outsiders, into which hearing Americans could see only obscurely if at all. As such it posed vague threats of deviance from the majority culture. Looking from the inside out—that is, empathizing with what the oralists imagined to be the experience of deaf people—it seemed a place in which deaf people became trapped, from which they could not escape without assistance. "Foreignness" was both a threat and a plight. The deaf community, as one of a host of insular and alien-appearing communities, was seen as harmful to both the well-being of the nation and to its own members.

For many hearing people, what they saw looking in from the outside was troubling. Journals and magazines such as the *Silent World* and the *Deaf-Mute Journal,* written and printed by deaf people for a deaf audience, were thriving in every state. Deaf adults across the country were actively involved in local clubs, school alumni associations, and state and national organizations. They attended churches together where sign language was used. The great majority found both their friends and their spouses within the deaf community. According to the research of Alexander Graham Bell, the rate of intermarriage was at least 80 percent, a fact that caused him great alarm.[42]

The two chief interests of Bell's life, eugenics and deaf education, came together over this issue. In a paper published by the National Academy of Sciences in 1884, Bell warned that a "great calamity" for the nation was imminent due to the high rate of intermarriage among the deaf: the "formation of a deaf variety of the human race." The proliferation of deaf clubs, associations, and periodicals, with their tendency to "foster class-feeling among the deaf," were ominous developments. Already, he warned, "a special language adapted for the use of such a race" was in existence, "a language as different from English as French or German or Russian."[43]

Bell also warned that deaf people had proposed at various times plans to form communities based not just on shared culture and language but on geography as well. He had discovered that Laurent Clerc had once suggested that the American Asylum might donate land it owned for a community of deaf people to settle. Further, a group of American Asylum students had "before their graduation formed an agreement to emigrate to the West and settle in a common place." He reported on a scheme advanced in 1856 in the pages of the *American Annals of the Deaf* by J.J. Flournoy, a wealthy deaf man from South Carolina, to establish a separate state exclusively for deaf people. Bell noted that none of these plans had come to fruition, and he knew of no other such discussion since Flournoy's in 1856, but he warned nevertheless that "such a scheme is still favored by individual deaf mutes, and may therefore be revived in organized shape at any time."[44]

While other oralists would call for legislation to "prevent the marriage of persons who are liable to transmit defects to their offspring," Bell believed such legislation would be difficult to enforce.[45] His prescription for furthering, in light of increasing immigration, the "evolution of a higher and nobler type of man in America" and preventing the "deterioration of the nation" was that the federal government take steps to determine the "foreign elements which are beneficial to our people and those which are harmful"; the process of evolution could then be "controlled by suitable immigration laws tending to eliminate undesirable ethnical elements."[46] With regard specifically to the deaf, his solution was this: "*(1) Determine the causes that promote intermarriages among the deaf and dumb; and (2) remove them*" [emphasis his]. The causes were these: "segregation for the purposes of education, and the use, as a means of communication, of a language which is different from that of the people." Indeed, he wrote, "if we desired to create a deaf variety of the race . . . we could not invent more complete or more efficient methods than those."[47]

Bell's fears were unfounded. His findings, published in the year of Gregor Mendel's death and before the latter's research on genetic transmission had become known, were based upon a faulty understanding of genetics. Others soon countered his empirical evidence as well; most deafness was not heritable, and marriages between deaf people produced on average no greater number of deaf offspring than mixed marriages of deaf and hearing partners.[48] But the image of an insular, inbred, and proliferating deaf culture became a potent weapon for the oralist cause. Bell was to become one of the most prominent and effective crusaders against both residential schools and sign language.[49] He traveled the country delivering speeches on the dangers of deaf interbreeding, such as the one he gave to the Chicago Board of Education in which he warned that deaf people, "by their constant association with each other, form a class of society and marry without regard to the laws of heredity." The result of this "lamentable fact," as he put it, was that the "born deaf are increasing at a remarkable rate, at a greater rate, in fact, than the hearing part of the population."[50] Bell's fears would be widely repeated in newspapers, magazines, and speeches for years to come.[51]

Oralists more often tried to emphasize the empathetic side of their metaphor, however. They insisted that their intent was to rescue deaf people from their confinement not to attack them. Deaf adults consistently defended the space from which they were urged to escape and from which deaf children were supposed to be rescued. But just as deaf people resisted the oralist conception of their needs, oralists likewise resisted the portrayal of themselves by deaf leaders as "enemies of the true welfare of the deaf."[52] Like the advocates of Indian and immigrant assimilation, they spoke of themselves as the "friends of the deaf." They tried to project themselves into that mysterious space they saw deaf people inhabiting and to empathize with the experience of deafness.

They were especially concerned that "because a child is deaf he is . . . considered peculiar, with all the unpleasant significance attached to the word."[53] The great failure of deaf education, in their view, was that "in many cases, this opinion is justified by deaf children who are growing up without being helped . . . to acquire any use of language."[54] (This use of "language" to mean *spoken English* was common. Another oralist wrote that the signing deaf person was a "foreigner to all language and to all people," universalizing *spoken language* and *hearing people* into *all language* and *all people*.)[55] Peculiarity was considered part of the curse of foreignness, and "to go through life as one of a peculiar class . . . is the sum of human misery. No other human misfortune is comparable to this."[56]

This peculiarity of deaf people was not unavoidable, but "solely the result of shutting up deaf children to be educated in sign schools, whence they emerge . . . aliens in their own country!" Mary Garrett informed the Congress of Women at the 1893 Chicago World Exposition that it was the "cruel system of training the deaf differently from the hearing" that was responsible for making deaf people "peculiarly unlike those around them." Cease to educate deaf people with sign language, oralists believed, and they will "cease to be mysterious beings."[57]

Oralists believed sign language was to blame for making deaf people seem foreign, peculiar, and isolated from the nation; oralists also claimed it was an inferior language that impoverished the minds of its users. This language of "beauty and grace," in the words of Gallaudet, now was called a "wretched makeshift of a language."[58] It was "immeasurably inferior to English"; any "culture dependent upon it must be proportionately inferior."[59] The implication of foreignness, barbarism, was not left unspoken. As one opponent of sign language phrased it, "if speech is better for hearing people than barbaric signs, it is better for the deaf."[60]

Like their contemporaries in other fields of reform, oralists worried that the lives of people were diminished by being a part of such communities as the deaf community; they would not, it was feared, fully share in the life of the nation. The deaf community, like ethnic communities, narrowed the minds and outlooks of its members. "The individual must be one with the race," one wrote in words reminiscent of many other Progressive reformers "or he is virtually annihilated"; the chief curse of deafness was "apartness from the life of the world," and it was just this that oralism was designed to remedy.[61] *Apartness* was the *darkness* of the manualists redefined for a new world.

Clearly the "real calamity of the deaf-mute" had been redefined. In their annual report of 1819 the teachers of the American Asylum at Hartford did not ask if most Americans could understand signs but "Does God understand signs?"[62] To this they answered yes and were satisfied. At mid-century, the calamity of deafness still was "not that his ear is closed to the cheerful tones of the human voice" but that the deaf person might be denied "the light of divine truth."[63] When the manualist generation had spoken of deaf people being "restored to society" and to "human brotherhood," membership in the Christian community was the measure of that restoration.[64] Sign language had made it possible. The isolation of deaf people was a problem that had been solved.

By the turn of the century, however, the problem had apparently returned. Once again educators of the deaf spoke of rescuing the deaf from their "state of almost total isolation from society," of "restoring" them to "their proper and rightful place in society."[65] Once again deaf people lived "outside." They were again seen as outsiders because "inside" had been redefined. Whereas manualists had believed that to teach their students "the gospel of Christ, and by it to save their souls, is our great duty," it was now the "grand aim of every teacher of the deaf . . . to put his pupils in possession of the spoken language of their country."[66] The relevant community was no longer the Christian community but a national community defined in large part by language.

Both manualists and oralists understood deafness in the context of movements for national unity, and their metaphors came from those movements. Evangelical Protestantism brought together a nation no longer unified by the common experience of the Revolution, unsettled by rapid social and economic change, and worried about the effects of the opening of the West upon both the morality and the unity of the nation. In crafting that unity, by creating a common set of experiences for understanding the world, evangelicalism emphasized above any other kind of cultural or linguistic homogeneity a common spiritual understanding. When evangelicals saw dangers in the immigration of the time, it was not foreignness *per se* that principally concerned them but Catholicism.[67] That definition of unity was not necessarily more tolerant of difference in general, but it did mean that sign language and the deaf community were not seen as inimical to unity.

The movement for national unity at the time of the rise of oralism had a different source. This time it was the multiplicity of immigrant communities crowded into burgeoning industrial cities that seemed to threaten the bonds of nationhood. Two streams converged to make sign language repugnant to many hearing Americans: at the same time that deaf people were creating a deaf community with its own clubs, associations, and periodicals, American ethnic communities were doing the same to an extent alarming to the majority culture. At the same time that deaf children were attending separate schools in which deaf teachers taught them with both English and sign language, immigrant children were attending parochial schools in which immigrant teachers taught them in both English and their native languages.[68] The convergence was merely fortuitous, but it was not difficult to transfer anxieties from one to the other.

If the fragmentation of American society into distinct and unconnected groups was the fear that drove the oralists, the coalescence of a homogeneous society of equal individuals was the vision that drew them. For the oralists, as for their contemporaries in other fields of reform—the assimilation of the Indian, the uplifting of the working class, the Americanization of the immigrant—equality was synonymous with sameness. The ideal was achieved when one could "walk into . . . our hearing schools and find the deaf boys working right along with their hearing brothers . . . [where] no difference is felt by the teacher."[69] Just as manualism arose within a larger evangelical revival, so did oralism partake of the late-nineteenth-century quest for national unity through assimilation.[70]

People use metaphor and verbal imagery to understand things of which they have no direct experience.[71] For those who are not deaf, then, the use of metaphor to understand deafness is inevitable; they can approach it no other way. The problem is that hearing people are in positions to make, on the basis of their metaphors—usually unaware that they *are* metaphors—decisions that have profound and lasting effects upon the lives of deaf people. The most persistent images of deafness among hearing people have been ones of isolation and exclusion, images that are consistently rejected by deaf people who see themselves as part of a deaf community and culture. Feelings of isolation may even be less common for members of this tightly knit community than among the general population.[72] The metaphors used to explain deafness—of isolation and foreignness, darkness and silence—were projections that reflected the needs and standards of the dominant culture rather than the experiences of most deaf people.

The implication of this construction is that there is a quintessential, "mainstream" American community, and then there are those who are outside of it and ought not to be there. "Insider" and "outsider," of course, are relative terms masquerading as absolute ones. What is inside and outside depends upon one's perspective. Within the deaf community, hearing people are the *outsiders*. One of the ways that hearing people have claimed authority over deaf people, however, is precisely by portraying them as outsiders in an absolute sense, a portrayal that justifies reform efforts to rescue them from their supposed isolation. The rhetoric of inside and outside has accompanied every reform movement within deaf education (the current effort at what is termed "mainstreaming" being the latest instance).

While the concept of inclusion in the national community was important to oralists, it was not the only issue that fueled the movement. If the learning of English had been the sole point, alternatives other than pure oralism were available. Some manualists advocated the use of a system of "methodical signs," a method of representing English manually. (This system, however, much like the signed English systems that modern-day schools have been experimenting with since the 1970s, was itself controversial, for reasons that I explore in chapter 5.) Others argued for the exclusive use of fingerspelling in the schools.[73] The use of English was not, however, all that concerned oralists. Manual communication itself—whether in the form of a distinct language or as a code for English—was objectionable to them. To discover why oralists opposed all forms of manual communication, we need to move beyond the debate over what makes an American to a deeper and knottier question all cultures ask themselves and answer in various ways: what makes a human being?

TWO

Savages and Deaf Mutes:
Species and Race

At the 1899 convention of the American Association to Promote the Teaching of Speech to the Deaf, the president of Amherst College, John M. Tyler, gave the keynote address. America would "never have a scientific system of education," Tyler insisted to his audience of oralist teachers and supporters, "until we have one based on the history of man's development, on the grand foundation of biological history." Therefore, the "search for the . . . goal of education compels us to study man's origin and development," he contended, and he then outlined for his listeners the two major theories of that origin and development. The first was the creationist theory, the belief that "man was immediately created in his present form, only much better morally, and probably physically, than he now is. Man went down hill, he fell from that pristine condition." The second was the theory of evolution. Tyler felt confident that he could "take for granted" the truth of the theory of evolution and that most of his listeners had "already accepted it."[1]

Here was a crucial cultural change that separated those first generations of teachers who used sign language from the later generations who attempted to do away with sign language. Most of the former came of age before the publication of Charles Darwin's *Origin of Species* in 1859, and had constructed their understanding of the world around the theory of immediate creation. Most of those opposed to the use of sign language belonged to a younger generation whose worldview was built upon an evolutionary understanding of the world.

While natural selection, the mechanism Darwin advanced in 1859 to explain how evolution worked, was not widely accepted in the United States until after the turn of the century, the general idea of evolution itself quickly found widespread acceptance.[2] Evolutionary thinking pervaded American culture in the years that oralism became dominant in deaf education; evolutionary analogies, explanations, and ways of thinking were ubiquitous. Psychologists theorized mental illness as evolutionary reversion; criminologists defined the "criminal type" as a throwback; social policies were defended or attacked on the basis of their ostensible likelihood to further or stunt evolution; and even sin came to be described as "a falling back into the animal condition."[3] Evolutionary theory set the terms of debate in deaf education as well. It was no coincidence that oralist theory began to transform deaf education in the United States during the same period that evolutionary theory was radically changing how Americans defined themselves and their world. The most important aspect of that change for deaf people and their education occurred in attitudes toward language—specifically, the relative status and worth of spoken and gesture languages.

Tyler continued his address by admonishing his audience of teachers that the recent discovery of the laws of evolution gave them important new responsibilities. For while humanity was "surely progressing toward something higher and better," there was no guarantee that it would continue to do so. Echoing a neo-Lamarckian interpretation of evolutionary theory common at the time, one that was especially popular in the United States, Tyler explained that continued human evolutionary progress would require active effort.[4] The human race would continue its "onward and upward" course only if certain "bequests from our brute and human ancestors" were consciously eliminated. Quoting from an unidentified poem, he exhorted his listeners to "Move upward, working out the beast, / And let the ape and tiger die."[5]

Just as the adult must put away childish things, Tyler explained, so must the human "slough off" that which is "brutish." By studying the characteristics that separated the higher animals from the lower and tracing "how Nature has been training man's ancestors at each stage of their progress," teachers could find vital "hints as to

how we are to train the child today." If, in short, they could "find
what habits, tendencies, and powers Nature has fostered, and what
she has sternly repressed," then they would know what they ought
"to encourage, and what to repress." It was crucial, Tyler insisted,
to "make our own lives and actions, and those of our fellows, conform to and advance" what had been the upward "tendency of human development in all its past history"—else their "lives will be
thrown away."[6]

Tyler's speech would have held no surprises for his listeners. His
ideas were the common coin of both educated and popular discourse
by 1899, and nothing he said would have seemed the slightest bit
radical or unusual to his audience of oralist teachers. Indeed, it would
have confirmed beliefs already firmly held and, to their eyes, explicitly associated with their work—an association that concerned the
relationship, for their generation, between speech and gesture, on
the one hand, and humanity and lower evolutionary forms on the
other.

A common speculation throughout the nineteenth century was
that humans had relied upon some form of sign language before they
had turned to spoken language.[7] The idea seems to have originated
with the French philosopher Etienne Bonnot de Condillac in the mid
eighteenth century. When Condillac historicized Locke's empiricist
epistemology, taking Locke's explanation of the psychological development of the individual and projecting it onto the history of the
human species, he naturally directed his attention to the question of
the origin and development of language. In the section of his *Essay
on the Origin of Human Knowledge* (1746) titled "Of the Origin and
Progress of Language," Condillac began with the conventional affirmation that reason and speech were gifts from the Creator to "our
first parents." Having satisfied orthodoxy, Condillac then went on
to speculate on how language *might* have been invented by people if
by some chance it had been necessary to do so—say, if two untutored
children had survived the great flood alone and had had to create a
new language between them. Suggesting this hypothetical circum-
stance allowed Condillac to theorize, on the basis of sensualist philosophy, that such children would first be limited to inarticulate cries,
facial expressions, and natural gestures in their communication with
each other.[8]

In the 1746 work, he supposed that gestures—or what he termed the "language of action"—would be confined to the early stages of linguistic and intellectual development, and because of its inferiority would gradually be superseded by speech. As the German historian Renate Fischer has recently pointed out, however, Condillac revised this view markedly in his *Grammar* of 1775, after having visited the Institution for Deaf Mutes in Paris and conversing with its founder, the Abbé de l'Epée. He had now come to believe that the "language of action" was not necessarily inferior to speech in what it could communicate, and could be "extended sufficiently to render all the ideas of the human mind." What Fischer called "this revolutionary view about the independence of language efficiency from its medium" was also the view of most nineteenth-century American manualists, with this important exception: unlike Condillac, manualist assertions that language was originally a gift from God were not mere formalities but a matter of fundamental belief.[9]

By the nineteenth century, the question of the origin of language had become an important topic of philosophical discussion, and Condillac's theory on the primacy of gesture had found a great many adherents. Manualist teachers, most of them college-educated men, were well aware of the discussion. As experts on sign language, they were naturally interested in the possibility that gestures preceded speech, and frequently alluded to the theory in their professional journals and conferences. They were pleased by and took pride in the idea that "sign or gesture language is of great antiquity," that "many philologists think that it was the original language of mankind," and that sign language might have been, "in the designs of Providence, the necessary forerunner of speech."[10]

As evangelical Protestants, manualists interpreted the theory in terms of biblical history. According to their creationist understanding, humanity had come into the world in essentially its present form. They disagreed on finer points—the precise nature of the first humans, for example. Some held to the literal story in Genesis and argued that God had created Adam and Eve with a complete language ready for use; others sought to adapt the biblical account to recent intellectual trends and treated it more loosely, suggesting that God had originally given humans the capacity for language and had left them to develop that capacity themselves over time. Of those who believed that language developed over time, many argued that some form of gesture or sign language must have been used before spoken language.[11] But even though humans were thought to have perhaps developed in some ways since the Creation, such as in language, it was widely held that humans had remained the same morally and intellectually—or had actually degenerated.[12] So the idea that sign language preceded speech would not imply inferiority within the framework of their Protestant beliefs. Indeed, it was a mark of honor.

Oralist educators of the late nineteenth century, however, would show an even greater interest in the idea, and give a very different interpretation to its significance. To the manualist generation, "original language" meant "closer to the Creation." It would hold quite different connotations for post-Darwin oralists, for whom it meant, instead, closer to the apes. Humanity had risen rather than fallen, according to the theory of evolution, and was the end product of history rather than its beginning. In an evolutionary age, language was no longer an attribute inherent in the human soul, one of an indivisible cluster of abilities that included reason, imagination, and the conscience, conferred by God at the Creation. It was, instead, a distinct ability achieved through a process of evolution from animal ancestors. Sign language came to be seen as a language low in the scale of evolutionary progress, preceding in history even the most "savage" of spoken languages and supposedly forming a link between the animal and the human. The "creature from which man developed in one direction, and the apes in another" probably used rudimentary forms of both gesture and speech, as one writer in *Science* speculated. While in humans the "gesture-language was developed at first," speech later supplanted it. On the other hand, "in the apes the gesture-language alone was developed."[13]

Linguists of the late nineteenth century commonly applied to language theory what has been called "linguistic Darwinism": inferior languages died out, they argued, and were replaced by superior languages in the "struggle for existence."[14] Gestural communication seemed to have been an early loser. The American philologist William Dwight Whitney, for example, believed that human communication once consisted of "an inferior system of . . . tone, gesture, and grimace"; it was through the "process of natural selection and survival of the fittest that the voice has gained the upper hand."[15]

The languages of early humans could not be directly studied, of course; no fossils are left recording speech, gesture, or expressions of the face. Anthropologists, however, began in the latter decades of the nineteenth century to see the so-called "savage races" as examples of earlier stages of evolution. Assuming a model of linear evolutionary progress, they depicted them—Africans, American Indians, Australian aborigines, and others—as "living fossils" left behind by the more rapidly progressing cultures.[16] This provided an ostensible means to study "early" human cultures and languages.

The eminent British anthropologist Edward B. Tylor, for example, noted in his *Researches into the Early History of Mankind* that "savage and half-civilized races accompany their talk with expressive pantomime much more than nations of higher culture," indicating to him that "in the early stages of the development of language . . . gesture had an importance as an element of expression, which in conditions of highly-organized language it has lost." While Tylor took a great interest in gestural language, was apparently familiar with British Sign Language, and had friends who were deaf, he held to the prevailing evolutionary assumption that sign language was a primitive and therefore inferior form of communication.[17]

Garrick Mallery, a retired Army colonel who studied American Indian cultures for the Bureau of Ethnology in the Smithsonian Institution, was probably the foremost expert in the nation on Indian sign languages, and his articles and lectures were sometimes reprinted in the *American Annals of the Deaf.* Along with other anthropologists, he believed that while early humans had probably not used gestures to the complete exclusion of speech, it was likely that "oral speech remained rudimentary long after gesture had become an art." While Mallery associated sign language use with a lower stage of evolution, he nevertheless had a genuine fascination and respect for sign languages. He defended aboriginal users of sign language against charges that they employed gestures only because their spoken languages were deficient. The common traveler's story, that some aboriginal spoken languages were not sufficient by themselves to permit conversations after dark, was not true, he insisted. He argued that the use of sign language was largely a function of the number of disparate languages spoken within a region—"as the number of dialects in any district decreases so will the gestures"—since, he believed, the primary use of sign language was intertribal communication. Still, Mallery viewed the transition to speech as a clear indication of human progress. For example, the invention of writing influenced people to "talk as they write," he believed, and therefore to gesture less. He speculated that gesture signs were most common among people who hunted—"the main occupation of all savages"—because of the need for stealth and were then used in other contexts simply by force of habit. It was undeniable to Mallery that the use of gestures existed in "inverse proportion to the general culture." He concluded that the "most notable criterion" for distinguishing between "civilized" and "savage" peoples was to be found in the "copiousness and precision of oral language, and in the unequal survival of the communication by gesture signs which, it is believed, once universally prevailed."[18]

Mallery did not believe, however, that sign languages were *inherently* inferior or primitive—indeed, he argued that they could potentially express any idea that spoken languages could. Nearly one hundred years before modern linguists rediscovered sign languages and began to take them seriously as authentic languages, Mallery spoke confidently of "conclusive proof that signs constitute a real language." His argument, rather, was that sign languages were *historically* inferior—that is, they were relatively undeveloped because less used in recent times than spoken languages.[19]

This distinction between inherent and historical inferiority, however, was not often observed by popular writers or the critics of sign language in deaf education. For most it was simply the inferior language of inferior peoples. The language used by deaf people became increasingly linked in the public mind with the languages of "savages." References, such as Edward Tylor's, to "the gesture-signs of savages and deaf-mutes" became commonplace in both popular and scholarly publications.[20] Darwin himself wrote of gestures as a form of communication "used by the deaf and dumb and by savages."[21] After noting that sign languages were "universally prevalent in the savage stages of social evolution," Mallery suggested that it was likely that "troglodyte" humans communicated "precisely as Indians or deaf-mutes" do today.[22] A contributor to *Science* commented that sign languages were used by "the less cultured tribes, while the spoken language is seen in its highest phase among the more civilized," and then added that sign language was also used "in the training of the deaf and dumb." He concluded that "the gesture language is a rudimentary one, which is now on the decline."[23] A reporter for the New York *Evening Post,* in an article on the prolific gestures of Italian immigrants, noted that "philosophers have argued that because among most savages the language of gesture is extensive," the use of gesticulation with or in lieu of speech is a "sign of feeble intellectual power, and that civilization must needs leave it behind." He pointed out that deaf people as well as American Indians also used gestures to communicate.[24]

One might expect the literature of deaf education to deal in more concrete terms with issues related to the actual lives of deaf people. But here too the association of sign language with peoples considered inferior colored all discussion, with oralist teachers fretting that sign language was "characteristic of tribes low in the scale of development." Gardiner G. Hubbard, president of the Clarke Institution for Deaf-Mutes, one of the first oral schools, complained that the sign language of deaf people "resembles the languages of the North American Indian and the Hottentot of South Africa." J. D. Kirkhuff of the Pennsylvania Institution asserted that as "man emerged from savagery he discarded gestures for the expression of his ideas"—it followed that deaf people ought to discard them as well and fell upon teachers to "emancipate the deaf from their dependence upon gesture language." A leading oralist in England, Susanna E. Hull, wrote in the *American Annals of the Deaf* that since spoken language was the "crown of history," to use sign language with deaf children was to "push them back in the world's history to the infancy of our race." Since it was the language of "American Indians and other savage tribes," she asked, "shall sons and daughters of this nineteenth century be content with this?"[25]

The theory that speech supplanted sign language in an evolutionary competition was so common that the oralist Emma Garrett could make an elliptical reference to it as early as 1883 and assume her readers would understand the allusion: "If speech is better for hearing people than barbaric signs," she wrote, "it is better for the deaf; being the 'fittest, it has survived.'"[26]

Manualists had been well aware, of course, that American Indians used sign language. In fact, delegations of Indians were occasional visitors to schools for the deaf, where they conversed with deaf students and teachers in pantomimic signs. On one such occasion, in 1873 at the Pennsylvania Institution, "it was remarked," as Mallery explained it, "that the signs of the deaf-mutes were much more readily understood by the Indians than were theirs by the deaf-mutes, and that the latter greatly excelled in pantomimic effect." Mallery thought this was not surprising "when it is considered that what is to the Indian a mere adjunct . . . is to the deaf-mute the natural mode of utterance."[27]

But while manualists often compared the sign language of deaf people to that of American Indians, in the same paragraph they were apt to compare it to the high art of pantomime cultivated by the ancient Romans or to note the syntactical features it shared with ancient Latin, Greek, Hebrew, or Chinese (see chapter 4).[28] None of these comparisons were thought to demean sign language. Rather, they were merely evidence that gestural communication was an ability "which nature furnishes to man wherever he is found, whether barbarous or civilized."[29]

If sign language appeared to have been used more in the past than in the present, this did not imply inferiority to them in the same way it would for the oralist generation. When the manualists thought of progress, it was social progress, an accumulation of knowledge, of accomplishment, not an improvement in the actual physical and intellectual capacities of human beings. As Harvey Peet affirmed for his colleagues in 1855, "we find in our philosophy no reason to reject the Scriptural doctrine, that the first man was the type of the highest perfection, mental and physical, of his descendants. Races of men sometimes improve, but, in other circumstances, they as notoriously degenerate. It is at least full as philosophical to suppose the inferior races of men to have been degenerate descendants from the superior races, as to suppose the converse."[30]

One theory of history for their generation was that civilizations rose and fell rather than climbed continuously; languages and peoples did not ascend ever higher over the course of history but rather had "their birth, growth, and culmination, like the language of the Hebrews for instance, or the splendid tongues of Greece and Rome."[31] Languages could not perpetually progress, for the "tendency of every language is toward change, decay, and ultimate extinction as a living organism." The examples of Sanskrit, Hebrew, Greek, and Latin were evidence that all languages changed over time and finally "passed into that doom of death and silence which awaits alike the speaker and the speech."[32] Languages changed, but they could as well decline as improve; there was no reason to assume that present languages were better than past ones.

Americans who came of age in the late nineteenth century looked to a different past than this. Because sign language was supposed to have been superseded long ago by speech, it was to their way of thinking necessarily inferior. As such, it deserved extinction. An oralist in 1897, pointing out that manualists had often commented upon the similarities between the sign languages of American Indians and deaf people, suggested that he would not "question the truth of this observation, nor deny that it is worth noting." He would attribute to the observation, however, a very different significance than had his predecessors. While "savage races have a code of signs by which they can communicate with each other," he wrote, surely "we have reached a stage in the world's history when we can lay aside the tools of savagery." Because of "progress in enlightenment," schools were "fortunately able now to give our deaf children a better means of communication with men than that employed by the American Indian or the African savage." And just as sign language had been supplanted by speech in the advance of civilization, so too was the use of sign language in deaf education—"like all the ideas of a cruder and less advanced age"—being rendered unnecessary by progress.[33]

If oralists associated sign language with Africans, what did they do when they encountered African-American deaf students? Information specifically on the education of black deaf children is difficult to come by; the subject was rarely raised at conferences or addressed in school reports and educational literature. At least in the south, however, where schools for the deaf, like schools for the hearing, were typically segregated, oral education was clearly not extended to blacks on the same basis as whites.

At the 1882 convention of American Instructors of the Deaf, for example, after the superintendent of the North Carolina Institution for the Deaf and Dumb and the Blind had given a report on the new oral program established in his school, he was asked, "has any experiment been made in the institution to teach colored children?" The superintendent answered that "in a separate building, one mile from the main institution, there are thirty colored children . . . with a separate teacher in charge. No instruction has been given in articulation, and none will be given at present."[34]

Five southern schools for black deaf students were listed in the *American Annals of the Deaf* annual directory in 1920—North Carolina, Texas, Maryland, Virginia, and Oklahoma.[35] Two of those, the Virginia State School for Colored Deaf and Blind Children and the Oklahoma Industrial Institution for the Deaf, Blind, and Orphans of the Colored Race, were the only two schools in the United States that still described themselves as "manual"—by this time all others schools for the deaf described themselves as "oral" or "combined." The white schools in both of these states were listed as "combined," with the majority of their students being taught orally. North Carolina did teach slightly over half of its black students orally—but four out of five of its white students were so taught. Maryland used oral methods with two of the twenty-four black deaf students it had in school, and with 110 of its 129 white students. The Texas Deaf, Dumb, and Blind Institute for Colored Youths had converted from "manual" to "combined" about ten years earlier; nevertheless, by 1920 it was still teaching fewer than a third of its students by oral methods, while at the Texas school for white deaf students, nearly three-fourths were taught orally. In addition, the school reported that only one of its twelve teachers was an oral teacher and that the oral class consisted of thirty pupils, a size that would effectively preclude, in the view of oral teachers both then and today, successful teaching by oral methods. By contrast, the Texas school for white students had an average of ten pupils in their oral classes, the typical size in other state schools for oral classes.[36]

Overcrowded classes were apparently a problem generally at black schools in the south. A black deaf teacher from the North Carolina school, Thomas Flowers, expressed to the 1914 convention of teachers his hope that soon "certain discouraging features will be lifted from the teachers of the colored deaf" so that "the work will then give results." Among these discouraging features were poor facilities, low pay for teachers, and the "large and miscellaneous classes."[37]

A survey of black schools for the deaf finally appeared in the 1940 *American Annals of the Deaf,* much later than the period under consideration here. That survey reported that of sixteen segregated schools or departments for black deaf children, eleven were *still* entirely manual. While other schools throughout the south joined northern schools in pushing deaf people to rise, as they saw it, to full humanity by abjuring sign language, this was apparently not considered as significant a need for deaf people of African descent.[38]

This provision of oral or manual education according to race may not have prevailed to the same degree in the North, but since there were no separate schools for blacks, the evidence is harder to find and more circumstantial. Thomas Flowers had been a student in the oral program at the Pennsylvania Institution from 1886 to 1895 where, as he later wrote, the teachers "saw beyond this dusky skin of mine, into my very soul." Since in 1908 he wrote that he had been the first black student to graduate from the Pennsylvania school and the first deaf student to graduate from Howard University, he would not, however, appear to have been a typical case.[39] When, at the 1914 convention, the above-mentioned superintendent from North Carolina averred that "North Carolina was the first state in establishing institutions for the colored race, although other states are falling into line," Philip G. Gillett, superintendent of the Illinois school, immediately rose to protest that "Illinois has had an institution for colored deaf-mutes for over thirty years." With heavy sarcasm he added that this institution was in fact the same one that white students attended. Black students, he was proud to say, "have always attended on precisely the same basis and have the same advantages that the whites have had." Unfortunately, Gillett quickly added that "it is unnecessary to discuss that question here," and he and the convention moved on to other topics.[40]

On the other hand, the Clarke Institution in Northampton, Massachusetts, the preeminent oral school in the country, makes no mention in its annual reports of accepting black pupils or training black teachers during this period, and in 1908 it appears to have affirmed a policy of excluding blacks. In that year an African-American woman made inquiries about entering the Clarke Institution training program for teachers. The principal of the school, Caroline Yale, wrote to Mabel Bell, who had apparently inquired on the young woman's behalf, to express doubts about accepting the student. The Clarke Institution had "never had an application for a colored student in our Normal Department" before, she wrote, and she doubted "whether with the large number of southern teachers which we have this could be done." She was "certain that some of our southern girls would violently object" and worried that "we should very likely lose some or all of them." The records do not reveal the outcome of this issue, but in her letter Yale thought it unlikely that the student could be accepted.[41]

This limited and circumstantial evidence is far from conclusive. In any case, before the great migration of African-Americans to the north after the First World War, there were relatively few blacks living in the northern states. Given the low incidence of deafness as a percentage of population, few black children would have attended northern schools for the deaf.[42]

Race was not the only issue involved in this hierarchical construction of evolutionary progress. As a linguistic atavism, sign language was portrayed not only as a throwback to "savagery" and "barbarism" but, worse yet, as a return to the world of the beast. One of the effects of evolutionary theory, after all, was to change the way that people answered the question, "What is it that separates us from the animals?" Animals have always been the ultimate "other" for human beings, and throughout history people have defined themselves in relation to them. Every culture has kept available a large stock of answers to the question of what makes humans unique—for example, that humans possess reason, histories, and cultures, that they can feel pain and suffer, that they have self-consciousness and consciences, that they use tools and alter their environment. One could compile a very long list of such attempts—intriguingly persistent attempts—to definitively distinguish humanity from every other species of creature.[43]

"What separates us from the animals?" is a question of rich potential for the student of human culture. Much of how a people define themselves, their sense of individual and cultural identity, can be found in their answers to this most basic of questions—what Thomas H. Huxley called the "question of questions for mankind."[44] For the manualists of the early to mid nineteenth century, the possession of an immortal soul was the preeminent characteristic that distinguished humans from all other species. Contained within the concept of the soul were other, *subsidiary* signs of human uniqueness, faculties such as language, morality, and reason, which humans had and animals did not. These, however, were secondary to, existing merely as a result of, the human soul.

The manualist teacher Luzerne Rae, for example, in 1853 described "thoughts and feelings" as the "spiritual children of the spirit," meaning that they were manifestations of spirit and therefore spiritual themselves. Language, on the other hand, was the "sensible form" of the spiritual—that is, it made the spiritual accessible to the senses—and was the material expression of the higher, nonmaterial realm. Language, then, whether in its aural or visual form, did not take place within spirit but was merely the outward means of communication between spiritual beings who existed perforce in a physical state. It was only the "embodiment" of thoughts and feelings into language that could "enable them to pass through the senses." Language was physical—Rae called it "the body of thought"—and therefore secondary and derivative. Spirit was primary and original.[45]

Language, therefore, while an important characteristic of humanity, did not define humanity. It was merely the visible expression of the invisible essence within. In 1850 the manualist Harvey Peet allowed that "language is one of the surest tests of humanity" but hastened to add that "language" was by no means the equivalent of "speech." Deaf education had been rarely attempted in the past, he explained, because until recently "the power of speech seemed the only difference between reasoning beings and animals devoid of reason."[46] While spoken and gestural languages were undeniably different "in material, in structure, in the sense which they address, and in the mode of internal consciousness," nevertheless, the "man whose language is a language of gestures . . . is still, not less than his brother who possesses speech, undeniably a man." Furthermore, while language was of great importance, it remained secondary: "Another prerogative that distinguishes man from the most sagacious of the mere animal creation . . . yet higher than language . . . is religion." And "religion" for him consisted preeminently in the knowledge of a Creator and of the immortal soul within.[47]

The foremost task of the Reverend Collins Stone, a manualist teacher at the Hartford school, was "imparting to the deaf and dumb a knowledge of the soul." He accomplished this, he explained, by calling the attention of his students to the ways in which they differed from the things and creatures around them: "there is something in the child which they do not find in trees, animals, or anything else." This "wonderful 'something' is not his body, or any part of it." Within this "something" resided intelligence, imagination, the ability to use language, and the moral sense. It conferred immortality. Once the pupils understood that it is "this that 'thinks and feels,' and makes us differ from the animals and things about us," they are then "prepared to be told that the power that manifests itself in these different ways is called the soul." Without that knowledge, the uninstructed deaf person was reduced "to the level of mere animal life," capable only of "mere animal enjoyment."[48]

This definition of education was shared widely by the teachers of Stone's generation. Lucius Woodruff lamented that without education the deaf person was "looked upon, by many, as well-nigh a soulless being, having nothing in common with humanity but his physical organization, and even that imperfect."[49] With an education made possible by the use of sign language, Henry Camp wrote, deaf people could be "raised from their degraded condition—a condition but little superior to that of the brute creation—and restored to human brotherhood."[50] For J. A. Ayres the "right development of moral and religious character is the most important part of all education"; with the use of sign language "the deaf-mute is restored to his position in the human family, from which his great loss had well nigh excluded him, and is enabled to hold communion with man and with God."[51] Coming to know God was the greatest aim of education, and one could not know God without first knowing about the soul. If deaf people were not "led to conceive of a thinking agent within them, distinct from their corporeal existence," then they could "form no correct conception of God, who is spirit."[52]

The historian Paul Boller, among many others, has written of the "shattering effect" that evolutionary theory had on "traditional religious thought about . . . the uniqueness of man."[53] While traditional religious beliefs about the place and nature of humankind were certainly challenged and altered, however, the belief in the uniqueness of the human continued unabated. Explanations for that uniqueness were adjusted to meet new realities, and by the late nineteenth century the most common explanation for why humans were fundamentally different from other animals was no longer that they possessed a soul but that they possessed articulate speech (or alternatively, intelligence, of which speech was both the crowning achievement and necessary concomitant). As Thomas H. Huxley, the great defender of Darwin's theory, wrote, "reverence for the nobility of manhood will not be lessened by the knowledge, that Man is . . . one with the brutes, for he alone possesses the marvellous endowment of intelligible and rational speech."[54]

The belief that speech is the crucial attribute that separates humans from the animals is by no means associated exclusively with evolutionary thought. The idea was hardly new—it goes back at least to ancient Greece and can be found throughout the nineteenth century in European and American literature. However, during the first half of the nineteenth century in America, the possession of a soul became the predominant expression of fundamental difference between human and animals; during the latter half of the century the emphasis shifted to the possession of speech. Part of the reason for this shift was the argument, made by Darwin in *The Descent of Man,* that the faculties that earlier had been placed under the higher and unifying concept of the soul, which were explained by the existence of the soul and had appeared to clearly separate humans from the animal kingdom, were in fact present in less developed form in other animals. Abilities that had been previously regarded as unambiguously human were instead explained as more highly evolved forms of abilities that had first appeared at earlier stages of evolution. The idea of a soul, Darwin and others argued, was no longer necessary to explain them.[55]

The soul was not, at any rate, easily adapted to an evolutionary explanation of the human past. To speak of the possession of a soul as the characteristic that separated the human from the animal, and at the same time to speak of humans developing from animals, was problematic at best. At what precise point did humans acquire souls? Did immortal souls evolve like other attributes, or had they been specially created at some point and infused into creatures previously not human? The concept of a soul certainly can be and has been by many religious thinkers reconciled with evolutionary theory. However, in the same way that the "argument from design" (that is, the theory that the adaptation of living things to their environment was evidence of a designing intelligence) was rendered unnecessary and marginalized by evolutionary theory, though of course it could not be "disproved," so was the soul made unnecessary as an explanation for human capabilities. In addition, evolutionary theory was but one aspect of a general movement toward scientific naturalism in public discourse; in both scientific and public discourse, the soul as an explanation for human nature diminished rapidly in importance. As nineteenth-century American Christians had been used to speaking of the term, the soul was neither convenient to think of as a product of evolution nor amenable to scientific description.[56] Speech, on the other hand, was both.

Thomas H. Huxley, for example, wrote that an important part of the explanation for the "intellectual chasm between the Ape and the Man" involved the senses and muscles necessary for the "prehension and production of articulate speech." The "possession of articulate speech is the grand distinctive character of man," and a "man born dumb," he continued, "would be capable of few higher intellectual manifestations than an Orang or a Chimpanzee, if he were confined to the society of dumb associates."[57] Sociologists such as Charles Horton Cooley agreed that the "achievement of speech is commonly and properly regarded as the distinctive trait of man, as the gate by which he emerged from his pre-human state."[58] School books for children echoed the point: "animals have a variety of natural cries. Speech belongs to man alone."[59]

Educators of the deaf also began to allude to this reformulation of human uniqueness. An oral teacher at the Pennsylvania Institution entered into her monthly report that despite the difficulties of oral training, speech was "one of the distinguishing characteristics between man and the lower order of animals—we think it is worth the labor it costs."[60] Mary McCowen, founder of Chicago's McCowen Oral School for Young Deaf Children, thought that learning to speak was "the highest act of human evolution" and wrote about the lack of speech as a condition from which deaf children could "gradually rise."[61] Lewis Dudley, one of the founders in 1867 of the Clarke Institution, wrote that "the faculty of speech more than the faculty of reason, puts mankind at a distance from the lower animals."[62] He elsewhere suggested that deaf people who used sign language felt themselves to be less than human. When he visited a school in which sign language was used, the children looked at him, he wrote, "with a downcast pensive look which seemed to say, 'Oh, you have come to see the unfortunate; you have come to see young creatures human in shape, but only half human in attributes; you have come here much as you would go to a menagerie to see something peculiar and strange.'" He contrasted the demeanor of these children with that of a young girl he had met who had recently learned to speak: "the radiant face and the beaming eye showed a consciousness of elevation in the scale of being. It was a real elevation."[63]

Not only was speech the mark of the human, but sign language was increasingly the mark of the brute. Benjamin D. Pettingill, a teacher at the Pennsylvania Institution, in 1873 found it necessary to defend sign language against charges that it was nothing more than "a set of monkey-like grimaces and antics." A manualist teacher at the Kendall School for the Deaf in Washington, D.C., Sarah Porter, complained in 1893 that the common charge against the use of sign language—"You look like monkeys when you make signs"—would be "hardly worth noticing except for its . . . incessant repetition." A teacher from Scotland wrote to the *American Annals of the Deaf* in 1899 that it was wrong to "impress [deaf people] with the thought that it is apish to talk on the fingers." And an oralist educator concluded in 1897 that "these signs can no more be called a language than the different movements of a dog's tail and ears which indicate his feelings."[64]

Sign language as deaf people use it employs not just the hands but the face, and this too would be interpreted differently by the manualist and oralist generations. Before evolutionary theory became widely accepted, it was commonly believed that only humans could *consciously* use facial expression. For example, the work of Sir Charles Bell, author of *The Anatomy and Philosophy of Expression* (1806) and foremost authority of his time on the physical expression of emotions, rested on the premise that humans had been created with specific muscles intended for the sole purpose of expressing emotional states. The ability to reveal the emotions through expression, he believed, was a gift from the Creator, a natural channel for human souls to communicate with one another unimpeded by artificial convention. It was, as Thomas H. Gallaudet phrased the idea, "the transparent beaming forth of the soul."[65]

In 1848 the manualist educator Charles P. Turner could claim that "the aspect of the brute may be wild and ferocious . . . or mild and peaceful . . . but neither in the fury of the one, nor the docility of the other, do we see anything more than natural instinct, modified by external circumstances." His readers would not have been perplexed or surprised by his belief that "man alone possesses the distinctive faculty of *expression*." Only the human being possessed a soul, and facial expressions were "the purposes of the soul . . . impressed upon the countenance." His observation, therefore, that facial expression was "an indispensable concomitant" to sign language, and that sign language owed "its main force and beauty to the accompanying power of expression," was intended, and would be understood, as high praise.[66] Thomas H. Gallaudet agreed, marveling that "the Creator furnished us [with] an eye and countenance, as variable in their expressions as are all the internal workings of the soul."[67] The expressions of the face, as a means of communicating feelings and thoughts, were seen as both distinctly human and wonderfully eloquent. Instructors of this generation, for example, delighted in telling of sign masters who could recount biblical tales using facial expression alone so skillfully that their deaf audiences could identify the stories.[68]

Charles Darwin's *The Expression of the Emotions in Man and Animals,* however, signaled that an important change in attitudes toward facial expression was under way. Expression, for Darwin, was not a God-given gift nor a mark of humanity nor the outward expression of the unique workings of the human soul. Darwin criticized previous works on the subject, arguing that those who, like Bell, tried to "draw as broad a distinction between man and the lower animals" as possible by claiming that emotional expression was unique to humanity, did so out of the mistaken assumption that humans "came into existence in their present condition." Instead, humans shared many expressions in common with animals, he argued, and the origins of human expression were to be found in their animal ancestors. Indeed, the similarities between humans and other animals in this regard was itself additional evidence that humans "once existed in a much lower and animal-like condition."[69] In short, facial expression was no longer distinctly human, but, like gesture, a mere vestige of our animal past.

It was not long before popular writers were commenting on the "special facility" that apes have for "the more lowly forms of making one's self understood"—that is, the use of "gesture-language" and "facial muscles as a means of expression."[70] Teachers of the deaf expressed the change in attitude as well. An anonymous letter to the *American Annals of the Deaf,* signed "A Disgusted Pedagogue," criticized the use of sign language in the schools because it caused teachers to "grimace and gesticulate and jump."[71] A manualist teacher complained of oralists who ridiculed signers for their "monkey-like grimaces."[72] Facial expression and gestures both were spoken of as the "rudimentary and lower parts of language," as opposed to speech, the "higher and finer part."[73] Deaf people were advised to avoid "indulging in the horrible grimaces some of them do," lest they be accused of "making a monkey" of themselves.[74] A writer in *Science* used a somewhat different metaphor, writing of students at a school for the deaf as "inmates making faces, throwing their hands and arms up and down. . . . The effect is as if a sane man were suddenly put amidst a crowd of lunatics."[75] Given the theory of the time that insanity was a kind of reversion to an earlier stage of evolution, the metaphor may well be related to the comparisons with animals.[76]

The belief that gestures preceded speech in human history, then, took on radically different meanings once evolution became the dominant way of understanding the past. For the manualists, the ability to use sign language had been, no less than the power of speech, an ability contained within the soul. It was a gift that the "God of Nature and of Providence has kindly furnished" so that deaf people might come to know that they possessed a soul and were thereby human.[77] Hearing people benefited from the use of gesture as well. Why did the Creator grant to humans the wonderful ability to communicate with face and gesture, Thomas H. Gallaudet asked, if not "to supply the deficiencies of our oral intercourse, and to perfect the communion of one soul with another?"[78]

For the oralist generation, however, sign language came to be in itself a subhuman characteristic. What had been the solution to the problem of deafness became the problem. By the turn of the century, it was "the grand aim of every teacher of the deaf to put his pupils in possession of the spoken language of their country."[79] Speech had become the "greatest of all objects," as Alexander Graham Bell expressed it; to "ask the value of speech," he believed, "is like asking the value of life."[80] The value of speech was, for the oralists, akin to the value of being human. To be human was to speak. To sign was to step downward in the scale of being.

In that formulation, an unfortunate by-product of evolutionary theory, lies much of the reason for the decline of manualism and the rise of oralism. Other social categories and hierarchies were at work, however. Teaching with sign language, as it happened, was primarily men's work while oral teaching was seen as women's work. Why this was so, what effect it had on the fight over sign language, and what it tells us about the construction of gender at the turn of the century are the subjects of the following chapter.

THREE

Without Voices: Gender

In 1980 Myra Strober and David Tyack noted that historians of education were "turning a familiar fact into a historical puzzle."[1] The familiar fact was the nineteenth-century transformation of teaching from a predominantly male to a predominantly female profession, and the puzzle was why it occurred. Those who study the history of deaf education confront the same puzzle but with an added wrinkle: the entry of women into the schools for the deaf as teachers coincided with the movement to eliminate the use of sign language from those schools.

Teaching in the common schools came to be a predominantly female occupation for both economic and cultural reasons. The rapid expansion and multiplication of schools created a demand for large numbers of teachers, while school boards were unwilling or unable to pay salaries that could attract and retain male teachers. Young women teachers could generally be hired for half the salary of men. At the same time, the greater access to education that young women were achieving was increasing the supply of women with formal educations. Additionally, production that had been performed domestically by women was being increasingly moved from the home to the factory, encouraging young middle-class women to seek some measure of financial independence outside the home as teachers.[2]

As Strober and Tyack observed, however, if supply and demand were all that mattered, women would have entered many diverse occupations throughout American history that they have not in fact entered. Cultural values made it possible to see this particular form of paid work, outside of the home, as appropriate to "women's sphere." Advocates argued not only that female teachers would be more economical, which would not have been a sufficient argument, but that they would make superior guides for young children. What were seen as women's natural attributes—their patience, gentleness, capacity for self-sacrifice—made them ideal for the role. Conversely, teaching would be beneficial for women as preparation for motherhood.[3] Catherine Beecher, for example, wrote in 1843 that the "great purpose in a woman's life—the happy superintendence of a family—is accomplished all the better and easier by preliminary teaching in school. All the power she may develop here will come in use there."[4]

Women moved into the teaching profession in large numbers in the schools for the deaf later than they did in the common schools—not until the 1860s, as opposed to the 1830s and 1840s in the common schools (see table 3.1). The rise of the female teacher in schools for the deaf paralleled the rise of oralism. Furthermore, oral teaching was assumed from the start to be women's work. The early speech teachers hired by the state residential schools were invariably women. In 1869, when the board of directors of the Pennsylvania Institution decided the school should offer lessons in speech, it directed a committee to nominate a "suitable female." When in 1881 the same school established a separate branch for oral instruction—in order to prevent the oral pupils from being exposed to the signing of the older students—it was staffed entirely by female instructors.[5] And when in 1868 the principal of the Illinois Institution sent a teacher to the Clarke Institution at Northampton, Massachusetts—one of the first and the most famous of the "pure oral" schools—to study oral methods in order to establish a class in speech at Illinois, he chose one of his few female teachers to make the trip.[6]

By the turn of the century, schools for the deaf—especially the purely oral schools and the oral departments of schools with both oral and manual departments—had become predominantly female spaces. Every one of the teachers at the Clarke Institution, from its founding in 1868 through 1904, were women. Clarke also functioned as a training school for teachers of the deaf, and of the seventy-seven teachers it trained during that period, all but two were women. Emma and Mary Garrett's "Home for Training in Speech of Deaf

Table 3.1

Female Teachers in the Common Schools and the Schools for the
Deaf, 1850–1910

	Percentage of female teachers in common schools	Percentage of female teachers in schools for the deaf
1850	38	4[a]
1858	na[b]	12
1870	59	33
1880	62	53
1890	66	60
1900	71	65
1910	79	73

Sources: "Tabular Statement of American Schools for the Deaf," *American Annals of the Deaf,* January issues, 1850–1910; Harris Taylor, "The Ichthyosaurus, the Cave Bear, and the Male Teacher," *Association Review* 2 (October 1900): 363; Edward Clarke, "An Analysis of the Schools and Instructors of the Deaf in the United States," *American Annals of the Deaf* 45 (April 1900): 231; Thomas Woody, *A History of Women's Education in the United States* (1929; New York, 1974), 499; Myra H. Strober and Audri Gordon Lanford, "The Feminization of Public School Teaching: Cross-sectional Analysis, 1850–1880," *Signs: Journal of Women in Culture and Society* 11 (Winter 1986): 222–24.
[a]1851.
[b]not available.

Children Before They Are of School Age" in Philadelphia also trained teachers, and from its founding in 1892 until at least 1900, neither employed nor trained any men. The teaching staff of the Pennsylvania Institution, one of the strongest advocates of oral teaching among the state residential schools, was 85 percent female by 1904.[7] At the turn of the century, forty-two of the forty-five exclusively oral public schools in the United States were headed by female principals; thirty-four employed no male instructors. The teaching staffs of all oral schools combined included 184 female teachers and twenty male; that is, they were 90 percent female when deaf schools as a whole were still only 65 percent female.[8] As a Gallaudet College professor observed in 1904, in the day schools (which were typically oral), "the teachers are, almost to a woman, women."[9]

Women were clearly associated with oralism, but the causal relationship is less clear. Did the growth of oralism promote the hiring of women? Conversely, did the hiring of women promote the cause of oralism? The answer, I think, is yes to both questions. Women were sought out and hired by the schools for the deaf at least in part as a result of the rise of oralism; women, in turn, were active advocates of oralism and contributed to its progress as a movement. The contest of the oral and manual methods was a gendered issue.

The hiring of women by the schools for the deaf accelerated during the Civil War because, as one teacher of the deaf phrased it, the war "thinned the ranks of our speaking [that is, nondeaf] professors." This happened not only because of the war's toll on the nation's young men but also because a decline in teachers' salaries relative to prices during the inflation of the war years made attracting male teachers more difficult.[10] Schools for the deaf hired women in part, then, for economic reasons; in most cases women did not have better opportunities for paid employment, and, as in the common schools, they could be hired for roughly half what male teachers were paid.[11]

The introduction of orally taught classes, however, made inexpensive female labor even more attractive. Oralism increased the cost of educating deaf children at the same time that school enrollments were going up. (Large numbers of children were deafened by an epidemic of cerebro-spinal meningitis, commonly known at the time as spotted fever, during the 1860s.)[12] While a teacher could lecture to a large class in sign language or to a slightly smaller one with finger-spelling, in an orally conducted class the students needed to sit close enough for lip-reading. Lessons in speech, moreover, required individual instruction.[13] The president of the New York Institution estimated in 1868 that with oral methods "more than double the number of teachers will be required."[14]

Just as Catherine Beecher and others advocated the hiring of female teachers in the common schools by emphasizing that they would work for less money, supporters of oralism advocated the hiring of women at low wages as a way to offset the costs of the smaller classes.[15] Gardiner G. Hubbard, for example, told a Massachusetts Senate committee in 1867 (convened to hear arguments for and against the establishment of an oral school in Massachusetts) that while oral teaching required smaller classes, oral teaching "does not require any particular art or skill in the teacher;" therefore "the teaching can be carried on principally by females." For this reason, oral instruction need not be more expensive after all, he explained.[16] The employment of women would help to subsidize the higher cost associated with oral education.

Table 3.2

Female Teachers and Deaf Teachers in Schools for the Deaf,
1852–1920

	Percentage of female teachers in the schools for the deaf	Percentage of deaf teachers in the schools for the deaf
1852	5	38
1858	12	41
1870	33	41
1880	53	29
1890	60	26
1900	66	17
1910	73	17
1920	77	15

Source: "Tabular Statement of American Schools for the Deaf," *American Annals of the Deaf,* January issues, 1852–1920.

An additional expense associated with the oral method was that it meant the loss of a source of inexpensive labor the schools had previously relied upon: deaf people themselves. Deaf teachers had long been employed at the schools—by the 1850s they accounted for more than 40 percent of all teachers—and their salaries had typically been much lower than those of hearing teachers.[17] In oral schools, however, deaf teachers could no longer fulfill this function of reducing costs. Most deaf adults were strong opponents of oralism. Deaf people could not teach speech nor, in most cases, communicate orally. Even if they could, oralists did not believe that deaf people should constitute a social group. To hire deaf teachers would imply otherwise, that deaf people had something to teach each other, that there was in fact a significant group experience.[18] Among oralists it was the "general opinion that the deaf should never teach the deaf"; as one teacher wrote, "to make the deaf teach the deaf is but to undo our work."[19]

The increase in the percentage of women teachers during these years was paralleled, then, by a corresponding decrease in the percentage of deaf teachers (see table 3.2). One reason, perhaps, that the entry of women into the schools for the deaf took place later than in the common schools was that deaf teachers had provided the same benefit that women teachers had in the public schools, lower costs. There is of course some overlap in the table's figures, since some teachers were both deaf and female. However, since schools cut back on the hiring of deaf teachers soon after they began to hire women in large numbers, and since women were more commonly hired for the younger classes where oral instruction became the rule, there were never large numbers of deaf women as teachers. Note also that the number of deaf teachers initially held steady during the 1860s, while the number of female teachers rapidly increased—*both* were in demand as a result of the Civil War. After the war, and with the rise of oralism, inexpensive female labor replaced inexpensive deaf labor.

The low salaries of deaf teachers appeared to have attracted more controversy than those of female teachers. At the conventions of teachers of the deaf, debates occasionally erupted over the pay differential between deaf and hearing teachers. At the 1890 convention, for example, one teacher rose to condemn as "a blot upon the fair name of our profession" the fact that deaf teachers received "little more than half the salary paid their hearing associates." A female deaf teacher next rose to ask why it was that deaf people and hearing people were paid equally by other employers but not by schools for the deaf. Curiously, she did not mention the wage inequality based on sex; even if deaf teachers were paid the same as hearing teachers, she would still, as a woman, earn far less than her male colleagues. Two male teachers then spoke in turn and at length to deplore the lower salaries of deaf instructors, declaring that teachers "should be paid according to ability." A fifth speaker finally mentioned women's pay as well, but only to make the point that wage inequalities were inevitable: of course the schools pay different groups of people differently, he argued—women also, like deaf teachers, are paid less, and both instances merely reflect the inexorable workings of supply and demand.[20] The example of women was raised to *justify* pay inequalities between deaf and hearing teachers, to suggest that there were natural laws involved that ought not to be tampered with; comparing deaf teachers to women was meant to reinforce the natural inequality of deaf people, since it was even more self-evident that women ought to be paid less than it was for deaf teachers. A final speaker, however, claimed that at his school there were no distinctions in salary made between deaf and hearing teachers: "It is not said to candidates for employment or promotion: 'Can you hear? or, Are you deaf?' but 'How well can you do the work.'" To emphasize the systematic fairness and absence of prejudice in his school, he blithely added that each "department has its own grades in salaries, one set of grades for male teachers and another for female teachers." Apparently no one present saw any irony in this.[21]

This is not to say that women never objected to their salaries. Emma Garrett, first principal of the oral branch of the Pennsylvania Institution, repeatedly protested the low wages offered to both herself and the female teachers under her charge. She complained in 1882 that as *principal* of the oral branch, her salary was "several hundred dollars less than the aggregate salary of some [male] *teachers*" at the main branch. She also protested to the board of directors on behalf of a new teacher that "$500 is not a sufficient salary for an intelligent and capable woman to receive" and urged an immediate increase. And she wrote to the board in support of her sister, Mary, a teacher at the school, who had requested that the board raise her salary from $500 to $700—an amount, she pointedly reminded them, that would still be "much less than the salaries paid by Pa. Institution to their male teachers."[22]

One important objection to the hiring of women had been, in the past, their supposed inability to control or discipline the older boys. It was argued, as one female teacher of the deaf recounted it, that in the common schools it was "the larger and older boys who always instigated and executed a successful rebellion, defied the authority of the teacher, and drove him from the door of the schoolhouse in mortification and dishonor."[23] The usual minimum admission age for the manualist schools had been ten to twelve; earlier than that was said to be "too young wisely to be divorced from a mother's care" by being placed into a boarding school and too young to undertake the rigors of the classroom.[24] Since many students started school at an even later age and remained into their twenties, female teachers were generally thought unequal to the task of maintaining order.

Oralism, however, was associated with the lowering of the age at which deaf children began school, and advocates of oralism were invariably also advocates of lowering the admission age.[25] A variety of arguments were advanced for this change. Since many children lost their hearing from childhood diseases, teachers of speech were anxious to begin work with such children before they lost whatever speech skills they had developed before becoming deaf. Younger children were furthermore thought to learn speech and lip-reading skills more readily than older children. Since oral training added another skill the child had to learn while in school—and a highly difficult one at that—teachers maintained that extra years of schooling were required. Finally, oral teachers worried that deaf children left alone would be prone to communicate by gesture; if they were to be prevented from falling into this habit, they had to be caught young and the "speech habit" instilled early.[26]

Many male teachers objected, however, to their schools being "made nurseries for infants." The argument over the admission age is instructive, for it reveals that manualists and oralists conceived of the nature of education and their roles as teachers quite differently. Manualists, usually men, argued that pupils who entered school younger than ten or twelve were unable to cope with the kind of knowledge they thought important (and interesting) to teach. Education meant laying up "stores of historical, geographical, and scientific knowledge." Lowering the age meant that children would begin school "too young to grapple with this work successfully, because their minds lack the necessary degree of strength and power of application."[27]

There were two goals of education, both of which required maturity. First, there were academic subjects to be mastered, and "considerable maturity of mind is necessary to success in so high a range of subjects" such as were offered at the schools, "much greater than is ordinarily possessed by children commencing younger than ten." Second, there were the moral and religious aspects of education, of no less importance than the intellectual. Deaf children often came to school "ignorant of the simplest religious truth," living in "pagan darkness." After they left school, they may well not have religious instruction available to them. It was therefore

> of the highest importance that they should enjoy these means of grace at an age when . . . their minds have become sufficiently expanded to comprehend the great subject of religion in its various bearings and relations; when their judgment has so matured as to enable them to appreciate motives and results; when their hearts are most likely to be abidingly impressed by the truth and the Spirit of God. Can any portion of human life be selected so favorable to these great ends as that between ten and eighteen?[28]

When manualists considered extending the years of schooling for deaf students, they were more inclined to advocate adding an extra year or two of instruction for exceptional senior students, not for younger students. The schools at Hartford and New York in 1852 created high classes within their institutions for their more advanced students to continue their studies, and other schools soon followed, long before primary education for young children was added. The establishment of Gallaudet College in 1864, for that matter, preceded the lowering of admission ages below the age of ten at most schools. And when they did discuss providing education for younger pupils, the age of eight was as young as most manualists were willing to consider. They were trying to reach the intellect, to appeal to the moral nature, and for this their students "must have arrived at years of discretion, possessing considerable maturity of mind."[29] Such were the tasks that these teachers found both agreeable and suitable to their status as professors, as ministers in many cases, and as men.

Oralists, on the other hand, spoke chiefly of instilling habits. The habit they were particularly concerned with, communicating by speech, was not one that came naturally to deaf children. If they were not caught young, sign language—what the manualists had always called the "natural language of the deaf"—would become their first language. As one of the founders and trustees of the Clarke Institution, Lewis Dudley, said, what was crucial "for these unfortunates is, to take them young, and to make the English language their vernacular." For support Dudley invoked Samuel Johnson, who "used to say that 'a good deal could be made of a Scotchman if he were caught young.'" So it was for deaf children.[30] The goal of the teacher was to see "their habits of speech well formed, and their habits of lip-reading well fixed."[31] Habits, as opposed to abstract and worldly knowledge, would ordinarily be the province of the child's mother, but, they believed, most mothers were unfortunately ill equipped to cope with the special conditions created by deafness. What oralist teachers sought to prevent was the natural impulse of a mother, upon finding that her child was deaf, to "substitute signs for speech"; when this occurred, "soon the fatal habit of silence is formed and the pernicious practice of pantomime is confirmed."[32] The proper habits that mothers were ordinarily expected to instill in their children would have to come from elsewhere.

The most extreme expression of this concern with early influences and habit formation was what was called the "home school" or "infant school." Here the age of admission was as low as two years of age.[33] The imperative to implant proper habits coupled with the fear that children would resort to signs outside of the controlled atmosphere of the school overrode for the home-school supporters their uneasiness with taking deaf children out of their homes and congregating them in schools. Once children were admitted to Emma and Mary Garrett's Home School in Philadelphia, for example, they were not allowed to visit home nor to take vacations of any kind outside of the school—not even at Christmas—during their entire "six or seven years residence." The Garretts thought it "vital that there should be no interruption by vacation of the children's training" and that pupils remain at the school "until the habit of speech is fixed."[34] They feared that family and friends would lack the stern self-control necessary to abstain from gesturing when oral communication failed. Too many lapses of this sort could disrupt the formation of the proper habits and spoil all the careful work of the school. Vacations were also not taken at the Sarah Fuller Home School for Little Deaf Children in Boston nor at the McCowen Oral School for Young Deaf Children in Chicago, while at the Albany Home School for the Oral Instruction of the Deaf, the annual vacation consisted of the third week of September.[35]

The ultimate goal of these home schools, however, accorded with the oralist emphasis on promoting the integration of deaf people among the hearing and maintaining the bond between them and their families. Once the speech habit had become firmly established, they believed, the children could be safely returned to the home. Moreover, early proponents even argued that the students would then be able to use their speech and lip-reading skills to attend their local public schools as if they were not deaf at all. Thus, even though they advocated taking the child away from the home for a few years early in life, it was in the service of a goal even more radical than that of the typical oralist: through this early training, deaf children would learn to function virtually identically to hearing children. Their integration would be total. Their deafness would become, for all practical purposes, irrelevant.[36]

In most cases, the age of admittance at the new oral schools was set at five or six, and the older, established schools followed suit as they instituted oral training.[37] The effect of lowering admission ages was to further expand the already growing number of deaf children entering the schools, and this increased the financial incentive for

schools to hire women as less expensive alternatives to male teachers.[38] However, the new emphasis on early education made women
more attractive to the schools not only for reasons of economy but
also because of widely accepted beliefs about feminine nature and the
proper role of women. The care and teaching of young children was
a part of woman's "sphere." As one female teacher argued, "ladies
are incomparably better teachers for young children than males" because they are "endowed by nature with stronger parental impulses";
they also possessed "purer morals, on which account they are more
fit to be the exemplars and guides of young children than males."[39]
The lowering of the admission age, then, made women teachers seem
more appropriate than they had seemed previously, because young
children were thought to need the care and nurturing of women.
Teachers would act not just as teachers but as surrogate mothers as
well. A female faculty made the boarding schools appropriate places
for children, and at the same time young children made the schools
appropriate places for women; by eliminating the objection concerning the discipline of older boys and filling the schools with children
of an age thought to require the care of a mother, teaching the deaf
was brought within the sphere claimed by and reserved for women.[40]

Aside from the home schools for very young children, oralists
generally sought to replace boarding schools with day schools. The
concerns most commonly expressed were that boarding schools fostered a sense of solidarity and commonality among deaf people and
encouraged the use of sign language, which could be prohibited in
the classroom but which proved devilishly hard to stamp out beyond
the classroom doors.[41] This was only one aspect of the rhetoric used
by day school advocates, however. Another important criticism of
boarding schools was that they took children out of the home, away
from the family, and, especially, away from their mothers. Manualist
boarding schools were attacked for taking children out of home to
live with people with whom they communicated using a language
that their *parents did not understand.* Oralists lamented not only that
signing deaf people were "aliens in their own country" but also that
children who signed became "life-long foreigners in their own families."[42] During vacations from boarding schools the children would
go home to people who could not understand them and who would
yearly become less significant and less close to them than the usurpers
of the "real" family, their schoolmates and teachers.

Raising children outside of the home required strong justification. In the 1840s Catherine Beecher had criticized boarding schools, convents, communes, and other such communities as inferior to the family home, which she described as the "true Protestant system . . . based not on the conventual, nor on the Fourierite, nor the boarding-school systems, but on the Heaven-devised plan of the family state."[43] "By the middle of the nineteenth century," as the historian Margaret Marsh has noted, the "home had become the source of spiritual renewal for middle-class white Americans," and the spiritual center of the home was the wife and mother.[44] Of decreasing importance as a site of production or commerce as the century progressed, the home came to possess chiefly a *sentimental* importance, in the sense that Ann Douglas has used the term. For Douglas, sentimentalism "asserts that the values a society's activity denies are precisely the ones it cherishes; it attempts to deal with the phenomenon of cultural bifurcation by this manipulation of nostalgia."[45] During the time that the home, along with the family and the domestic wife and mother, were actually becoming increasingly marginalized in the social and economic life of the nation, their marginalization was denied by sentimental idolization. Precisely because of this denial, then, home, family, and motherhood—all that went into the nineteenth-century cult of domesticity—could be fashioned into a very powerful rhetoric.

Day schools and oralism were both promoted as ways of preserving the family, of keeping children at home with their mothers, where they were said by nature to belong. The use of sign language, this "strange vernacular of signs and gesture in place of the satisfying, comforting language of kith and kin," was condemned as "making institutional life a pleasant part of existence and obliterating the joy, the comfort and the stimulus of home life."[46] In a speech advocating day schools before the Chicago Board of Education, Alexander Graham Bell charged that "the policy has been to isolate [deaf] children from people who can hear and break them from home ties."[47] Samuel Gridley Howe likewise warned in 1867 that when deaf children were sent to residential schools, a "link is stricken out of the chain of associations which binds them to home; they lose the influence of home discipline, of the affections of home," and they become more attached to school than to home and neighborhood. "Wise people," he concluded, "are exceedingly reluctant to send their children away from home to be herded together in large boarding-schools."[48]

Day schools, numerous by the turn of the century, experienced

Table 3.3

Growth of Day Schools and the Oral Method in Day Schools,
1900–1920

	Total day schools	Oral-method day schools	Total day-school pupils	Day-school pupils taught by oral method
1900	44	36	708	604
1905	55	54	953	912
1910	64	63	1,394	1,324
1915	70	68	1,907	1,891
1920	72	69	2,014	1,961

Source: "Tabular Statement of American Schools for the Deaf," *American Annals of the Deaf*, vols. 46, 51, 56, 61, 66 (January issues for 1901, 1906, 1911, 1916, 1921).
Note: Day schools were first reported separately from residential schools in 1898 for the 1897 school year; only 22 day schools were reported, with a total of 438 pupils; since it seems highly unlikely that the number of day schools doubled in three years, the figures in that first year were probably incomplete.

continued growth between 1900 and 1920 (see table 3.3). Just as the hiring of women teachers was considerably advanced by the parsimony of boards of directors, so was the attraction of the day school enhanced by the practical matter of reduced cost. Day-school advocates faced a practical problem, however, in that deaf children were not nearly numerous enough to support day schools in any but the larger cities. Deaf children in most towns and rural areas would still have to attend centralized schools if they were to get an education. Some reformers, such as the home-school supporters, advocated sending children to the regular public schools after special intensive training in oral skills, but this option was never practicable for the majority. Boarding schools continued to receive the majority of students.

If the boarding school could not be done away with immediately and all deaf children therefore could not remain at home, the alternative was to make the boarding school more like a family home. The cottage plan, an arrangement in which children would live in small groups with house-mothers rather than in dormitories, began to be adopted by many schools. These groups were supposed to replicate family life and, in the parlance of the institutions, were often called "families." The Pennsylvania Institution, for example, recommended in 1890 the "segregate or family plan," because it "renders a public

Institution more like a home with its domestic comforts." In their advertisements and literature, schools began to emphasize their home-like atmosphere and family organization.[49]

Women were seen as being more suited to this newly defined role of the teacher. This was women's work, as women's work was constructed at the time. Men were not competent at it, as men's competence was construed at the time. Men felt neither competent nor comfortable with the task. It was not just that teaching became *seen* as women's work but that the work had itself been transformed; the pupils were younger, the goals and methods of teaching had changed, and the model teacher no longer conformed to the image of the model male but rather to the model female. Sylvia Chapin Balis, a deaf teacher who taught her classes with sign language, wrote disapprovingly of the new attitudes. In 1900, when women accounted for 65 percent of the profession, she wrote that she did not believe that "this disparity of sex in our profession is to be accounted for altogether by the matter of wages" but rather that "stalwart young men evade and avoid the sentimental methods that are becoming a part of the profession."[50]

The historians Myra H. Strober and Audri Gordon Lanford believe that grading in the common schools was designed to accommodate female teachers, since the younger children could then be given to the women and the older to the men.[51] In the schools for the deaf, the so-called combined system operated in a similar fashion, and again it reinforced the association of oral teaching with women. "Combined system" meant different things to different people; when it originated in the 1860s and 1870s, it usually meant that all forms of communication were made available to all children, including oral communication with those who seemed capable of communicating in this way. By the turn of the century, however, the combined system in most cases had come to mean that all children would begin school in oral classrooms; those who failed to make progress after some specified period of time (which could range from two to five years or more) would be transferred to manual classes (which increasingly came to mean finger-spelling alone, without sign language). The orally taught primary grades were nearly always taught by women. Thus the system reinforced the association of women with oral methods.

In the older grades, however, while men taught the manual

classes, women still taught the oral ones. The association of men with manual classes was not only because they avoided teaching young children but because they also tended to resist teaching by oral methods, regardless of the age level.[52] The belief, then, that teaching in oral classes was women's work was not based entirely upon the ostensible affinity of women and young children for one another. It was also because of the way the work was defined: the "teaching of the oral method," it was commonly said, "is one of infinite patience and repetition."[53] As more and more schools adopted oral methods, references to the tedious nature of the work of teaching the deaf became increasingly common. Women were said to be better suited for it because of their superior patience and capacity for selfless labor. The work of the oral teacher was described by a male director of a school—and this was meant as *praise*—as the "daily repetition of a simple task, which women, far more than men, supply for our work."[54] A male teacher commented on the remarkable "amount of patience displayed by the [oral] teacher. I have seen her go over and over the same kind of work day after day, and appear happy and contented when I could see little improvement."[55] The male president of the Clarke Institution at Northampton described the work this way [emphases added]:

> The gentlemen . . . who manage the pecuniary affairs of this Institution are only too glad to commit the management of these children and the *incessant task* of their education to the *patient* hands, the *active tongues,* and the *conscientious fidelity* of women. . . . If the *detail* and daily *routine* of this school seem to be made up of *trifles*—of *small matters again and again repeated* . . . let us be grateful for that *self-denying spirit,* that *patience* and *perseverance* which have wrought these trifles and this *drudgery* of instruction into such a pure and perfect work.[56]

Deaf education was not described this way before oralism supplanted sign language and women supplanted men. Male teachers in the deaf schools had always regarded themselves as researchers and philosophers in addition to being teachers. Their work was typically described in the romantic and distinctly masculine terms of exploration and discovery. Teaching the deaf was considered a great opportunity for the "student of rare psychological phenomena," possessing "great interest to every inquirer into the structure of the human mind." Instructors wrote learned articles speculating upon what could be learned about human nature from the mind of the uneducated deaf person, who was often described as a kind of noble savage in the midst of civilization and a fascinating subject for philosophical study. "To the philosophical mind," the learning processes of deaf children were "matters of deep interest and instruction." The "phenomenon presented by the mind in such circumstances . . . furnish an *experimentum crucis* to test the merits of any given theory on certain important points in mental and moral philosophy."[57] Manualist teachers investigated the nature of sign language and its relation to spoken language in the belief that it shed light on the nature of thought.[58] They were apt to speak of their work as an adventure among a people so different from the hearing that to live among them was to explore a rich and profoundly mysterious world. Teaching deaf students was akin to "*missionary* work among unenlightened nations." It was, in short, a "high and momentous undertaking."[59] This kind of description of teaching at schools for the deaf disappeared, however, as the image of both deaf people and the occupation of teaching deaf people was domesticated—in both senses of the word. The virtues of the intrepid explorer and rescuer of lost souls gave way to the homely and passive virtues of patience and fidelity.

Oralism, then, was an important factor in encouraging the hiring of women in the schools for the deaf. But women were not just passive beneficiaries of the preference for female oralist teachers. They were ardent advocates as well. While male activists in the oralist movement were often more visible—they were more likely to speak at conventions, head organizations, and write for journals— nevertheless the great majority of oralist teachers and heads of oralist schools were women. This fact was often alluded to at the time, as when, at a convention of instructors of the deaf in 1878, a male instructor addressed "the ladies here who represent the system of instructing the deaf and dumb by means of articulation."[60] A contemporary observer and supporter of the oralist movement noted in 1905 that the oralist movement was "essentially 'a woman's movement,'" in which "women instructors have played the leading part, and borne the brunt of the fight."[61]

Why would women have been more prone to support oralism than men? Professional self-interest could have been part of the reason—oral teaching had become their specialty. Perhaps of greater importance, however, were the experiences women drew upon from their own lives. Women were themselves struggling to find a voice in nineteenth-century America. The position of deaf people who did not speak would have resonated with their own experience of being unable to speak on their own behalf.

Women had been fighting against the proscription of female public speech for most of the century, and many prominent women—such as Sarah and Angelina Grimke, Frances Wright, Sojourner Truth, Lucy Stone, Elizabeth Cady Stanton, and Lucretia Mott—had been since the 1820s and 1830s openly and successfully challenging the taboo. But for most women public speaking was still a risky undertaking. When Cornelia Trask of the Illinois Institution urged, in 1868, the hiring of more women as teachers, one of the arguments she had to confront was that "ladies are not available for exhibition"—that is, they could not present deaf pupils to the public at the exhibitions periodically held to generate support for the schools. Trask did not directly challenge the argument but rather sidestepped it, suggesting that, after all, "it should be the scholars who are brought forward in exhibitions, *not* the teacher."[62]

At the exhibitions of the traditional manual schools, deaf children would perform recitations and answer questions from the audience in sign language while their male teachers interpreted what they said into spoken English. The process of speaking through a third party may well have struck some women as not unlike the process by which they were still often heard in public—if they had something to say, they usually had to find a man to say it for them, to be, in effect, their interpreter to the public world. Women teachers were in this way "muted" when they attended the conventions of American Instructors of the Deaf, for example. At the 1870 meeting, the first since the outbreak of the Civil War and the first at which considerable numbers of women were present (of ninety-four delegates present, twenty-two were women), women apparently sat through the official proceedings in silence. Not one woman delivered a paper. No woman was recorded as having participated in discussions. No woman was among the eight nominees to be officers of the convention, and none was appointed to committees. The protest of a deaf delegate, that the committees so far appointed were made up entirely of hearing members, led to the observation by a male hearing member that women were also excluded. He suggested that "inasmuch as the circular of invitation embraced the members of the different institutions, both male and female, it might not be improper to put some ladies on the committees." Another male instructor pointed out that although the "custom has been not to appoint either lady members or deaf-mute members upon committees," he believed it was time to change that custom. A motion that women be appointed (deaf members seem to have been left out of the motion, but this is not clear in the record) was accepted. The victory seems to have been for the sake of principle only, however, for no women subsequently were appointed to committees.[63]

Again at the 1874 convention, women were not recorded as participating in any way.[64] At the 1878 meeting, women were not *entirely* silent, but nearly so: of 219 "Addresses and Remarks" listed in the index, two came from women. This in spite of the fact that thirty-three of the ninety-three delegates present were women.[65] At the start of this convention, the newly elected president suggested that the female members participate in the voting and that they do so with "uplifted hand"—apparently to spare them the unseemly participation in a voice vote.[66] If anyone noticed the irony of the oralist teachers being unable to use their voices and having to communicate with hand signs instead, it was not noted in the printed record.

Deaf members had also always voted by show of hands, while the hearing men usually voted by voice.[67] The women teachers could hardly have overlooked this parallel between their own position and that of deaf people. While the hearing male teachers were shouting out aye and nay, the deaf and female members were together silently raising their hands. (This use of voice as a hierarchical marker, incidentally, is not by any means confined to Western society. Disappearing Mist, an Iroquois chief, reported to Garrick Mallery, the nineteenth-century expert on American Indian sign languages, that Iroquois women and children had always in the past used sign language when in the presence of warriors and elders; to use their voices was considered disrespectful. The practice had declined in recent years because of—in Mallery's words—"modern impudent youth and the dusky claimants of woman's rights.")[68]

This 1878 convention was the first, however, to hear a paper written by a woman, Laura Sheridan, a teacher at the Illinois school. But she did not read it herself. Although she was present, a male colleague read it for her. Laura Sheridan was deaf—or rather she was what at the time was referred to as "semi-mute." That is, she had lost her hearing after having learned to speak and was able to speak quite well. Whether she did not read her own paper because of her deafness or because of her sex is unclear; there were no other instances of women writing papers and having them read by men. Until Sheridan, female members of the organization did not submit conference papers. Male deaf teachers had delivered their own papers in the past, but not many. At the next meeting, in 1882, Sheridan again had a paper to present, and this time she stood before the convention and read it herself. She was the first woman to do so.[69]

At the same convention, Emma Garrett became the second. The atmosphere does not appear to have become any more conducive to female participation in general, however. Of the 152 "Remarks and Addresses" listed in the index, two were from women. One was a two-sentence answer to a request for information, the other a brief announcement by Garrett that she would be reading her paper in the afternoon.[70] Although women increasingly presented papers at subsequent conventions, the men continued to dominate the give-and-take of discussion and debate on the convention floor. In 1886, while more than 40 percent of the delegates were women, a mere 3 percent of the "Remarks and Addresses" came from women.[71] Four years later, by which time 60 percent of teachers of the deaf were women, women still offered no motions and seldom participated in discussions. While eighty-eight men spoke 532 times, seventeen women spoke a total of twenty-three times. Men were apt to engage in debate, speaking repeatedly in the course of a discussion; women rarely spoke more than once and their comments were brief and sporadic.[72] Sylvia Chapin Balis, a teacher at the Ontario Institution for the Deaf, later remarked that the common assertion "that women are constant talkers" was puzzling—her observations at teacher conventions inclined her to believe "the ability of men in that line appears far more highly developed."[73]

Even when not outnumbered by men, women still found it difficult to speak publicly. At the convention of Articulation Teachers of the Deaf in 1884, where women outnumbered men nearly two to one, a male delegate moved that a "question box" be created and that "the ladies present be invited to write questions upon subjects relating to the teaching of articulation and lip-reading" and to place them into the box. In this way, women could have their questions answered without having to ask them orally. The motion passed after the chairman, Alexander Graham Bell, spoke in favor of it, asserting that "we have been very glad to hear from those ladies who have ventured to ask questions and make remarks, and we are glad to have more come forward." When oralists lamented that deaf people were unable to communicate with the hearing, deaf people countered that this was not so, that they got along quite well with pencil and paper. This did not satisfy oralists, however, who said that writing notes was too unwieldy and inefficient a means of communication. But it was how women asked questions at the convention of Articulation Instructors in 1884. (The box netted six questions, by the way, with five directed to male delegates. Presumably the more than one hundred female delegates present were using some other method of acquiring and exchanging information, possibly preferring means not under the control of the male chair.)[74]

If deaf people lacked voices literally, women lacked them figuratively. Female oralist teachers were perhaps acting out of empathy, an unarticulated sense that their own lives and those of deaf people shared something crucial in common. When teacher Sylvia Balis protested that given "the large number of women employed in educating the deaf," they should "have more voice than at present" in the running of their schools and professional organizations, and when Emma Garrett declared that she must unite her "voice with those who claim that these deaf-born but not dumb-born children can be taught to use their voices," they were calling upon a metaphor of great power and relevance for women of their time.[75] Thus, the populist and suffragist Mary Clyens Lease objected to "laws she had no voice in making" that women must "obey in dumb silence."[76] Elizabeth Cady Stanton used the metaphor frequently, demanding "for woman a voice in the government under which she lives . . . a voice in choosing those who make and administer the law." Stanton told a Senate committee in 1892 how "Shakespeare's play of *Titus Andronicus* contains a terrible satire on woman's position in the nineteenth century—'Rude men seized the king's daughter, cut out her tongue, cut off her hands, and then bade her to call for water and wash her hands.' What a picture of woman's position!"[77] And what a vivid picture, we might say, of how Stanton and other women of her time conceived of their oppression.

This is not to say that voice was a novel metaphor for power, but for women of the middle to late nineteenth century it was an especially pervasive and potent metaphor. Barbara Bardes and Suzanne Gossett have noted that "the power of the female voice" was a common theme in fiction throughout the nineteenth century: "vocal women" were regularly depicted as powerful women. In their view, women were aware that the ownership of a public voice, "even more important than a demand for voting rights," was a way of "claiming her place as subject rather than as object, as self rather than as other."[78]

This after all was what oralists claimed to seek for deaf people, a voice with which to speak to the "larger world" of the hearing (analogous to the "public world" of men), as opposed to the cramped and hidden (or "private") world of the deaf. The unfortunate irony was that this perception was not shared by the objects of their concern. Most deaf adults experienced sign language not as limitation but as liberation. They argued that because of the inherent and unavoidable difficulties of speech and lip-reading, the prohibition of sign language "closes both hearing and deaf society to the orally taught. . . . There is absolutely no social side to pure oralism for the average deaf person." Deaf adults usually agreed that teaching oral communication to children who were capable of it was a good thing but objected that these communication skills could be taught without depriving them of sign language and the community of signers. They argued that while speech and lip-reading, for a minority of deaf people, might sometimes suffice for individual conversations, sign language offered the *only* means "by which the deaf may understand sermons and lectures, participate in debate and discussion, and enjoy mental recreation and culture." They lacked voices, access to the world around them, and the power of free expression, they said, precisely when they were deprived of the use of sign language. When they were among fluent signers, they possessed the capacity to express themselves and to understand the expressions of others effortlessly and fluently. This they could not do when *confined* to speech and lip-reading.[79]

Oralists, however, appear to have paid very little heed to deaf adults. Deaf people, in fact, repeatedly called attention to the virtual absence of deaf adults willing to endorse the oralist endeavor. Amos Draper, a professor at Gallaudet College who was himself deaf, pointed this out in 1895: "No fact is more observable with regard to the adult deaf than that they are unitedly opposed to this theory of teaching. . . . Not only former pupils of schools not pure oral, but also those of pure oral schools themselves join in this opposition. In a word, it is practically the universal attitude of the adult deaf."[80]

Successive presidents of the National Association of the Deaf, such as Olof Hanson in 1912, argued strenuously that their membership, while not opposed to oral instruction per se, were adamantly and nearly unanimously "opposed to the exclusive use of the oral method for all the deaf, and . . . particularly opposed to the abolition of the sign language." Hanson claimed that "fully 90 per cent of the deaf entertain these views, and among them are many educated by the oral method."[81] At the annual meeting of the American Association to Promote the Teaching of Speech to the Deaf, the superintendent of the Oregon School for Deaf-Mutes rose to challenge an oralist speaker: "how interesting it would be," he suggested, "to have a deaf man stand upon this platform . . . and defend the oral method orally. . . . We do not see such a deaf man here." In fact, he observed with no little irony, "We see a very notable absence of deaf people. They take no great interest in this convention except to criticize it; they show no enthusiasm about the work of this convention." How could the assembled delegates take seriously their own educational philosophy when "the deaf themselves reject what we are having to say" and when it "leaves the vast majority of its subjects embittered, more or less dissatisfied, unappreciative, disloyal . . . to the method by which they were educated, indifferent, if not hostile, to its progress." There must be something "radically wrong" with oralism, he continued, if it "cannot turn out deaf graduates who appreciate the value of the methods by which they were instructed." Since, he concluded, "practically all organizations of deaf people, great and small . . . from one side of the world to the other [are] hammering against the pure oral method, it seems to me an adequate explanation should be forthcoming from its friends."[82]

The capacity of the oralists to ignore the opinion and advice of those who were the products of their schools is striking. Again and again, organizations of deaf people issued condemnations of the oral method. Again and again, opponents of the oral method urged oralists to listen to the opinion of their own graduates. It "cannot be an inspiring thought," the aforementioned Gallaudet professor wrote, "to any honest teacher to feel that his pupils will condemn his method as soon as they reach years of discretion and experience in life."[83] How was it that this astonishing fact was so rarely acknowledged by oralists?

At least part of the explanation is that most oralists identified deafness solely with childhood; deaf adults seem hardly to have existed in their thought-world, just as they were rarely a part of their social world or workplace. The deaf adult was excluded from both the theory and practice of most oralist deaf education. At the 1910 joint meeting of the National Association of the Deaf and the World Congress of the Deaf, an American member asked rhetorically of the oral method, "What becomes of its graduates? Where are its Hansons? Its MacGregors? Its Tildens? Its Job Turners?" He knew of no orally trained deaf adults whose lives could compare with these successful and illustrious graduates of sign-using schools.[84] But if successful oral deaf adults were hard to find in the outside world, they were even harder to find in oralist rhetoric. Not only was the average age of the deaf pupils in the schools lowered, but the way that teachers thought of the subjects of their work changed accordingly. One of the hallmarks of the oralist cause was its constantly reiterated use of the image of the child. The object of manualist interest and study was *the deaf,* while for the oralists that object was (in the most commonly used phrase) the *little deaf child.* When they spoke in praise of deaf people, it was not for the successes and achievements of adults but for a kind of passive courage attributed to deaf children for the mere act of existing as deaf children, for daring to be "poor unfortunates," for being victims.

The use of the child as symbol served to both diminish the sense of difference between the deaf and the hearing and to defuse the cultural conflicts at the core of the oralist/manualist debate. Mary Ryan has shown how female iconography began to be incorporated into traditionally male parades for a similar purpose after the Civil War:

> Their status as the quintessential "other" within a male-defined universe made [women] perfect vehicles for representing the remote notions of national unity and local harmony. Similarly, as nonvoters they could evoke the ideal of a nation or a city freed of partisan divisions. As supposedly domestic creatures,

they could stand above the class conflicts generated in the work-place. Defined by their roles as wives and mothers, women provided excellent symbols for ethnic solidarity: through marriage and childbirth they knit the bonds of ethnic communities. Finally, when the Civil War magnified the power of the state, the female allegory of the Goddess of Liberty evoked the soothing, humanizing imagery of maternity and nurturance. [T]hese symbols . . . washed out the actual social differences within the polity.[85]

If women in the nineteenth century occupied, in Ryan's words, a "depoliticized cultural field," children occupied one even more radically depoliticized; the very real cultural conflicts that were embodied in the oralism/manualism debate were effectively masked by the superimposed image of the child. One reason oralists were so successful with parents and legislators was because they were able to position themselves as working simply and selflessly for the best interests of the child (which was implicitly or explicitly defined as the adoption of oral methods) while appealing to manualists to end the divisive "war over methods" and join them in helping the children. The oralists were able to shift the debate to a discussion of what was "best for the child," on which terrain oralists had a distinct advantage—they could make their appeal in a predominantly female voice. Not only was that voice perceived to be above cultural and political conflict—in common with children—but it was one that spoke with cultural authority on the subject of what was best for the child. Deaf adults who signed, on the other hand, were defined by oralist discourse as failures and therefore hardly worthy of authority or emulation.

The deaf person was consistently represented by oralists as simply an unfortunate child with a special burden, an object of pity, with needs not essentially different from those of any sick or suffering child. When they argued that sign language made deaf children "peculiar," "aliens in their own land," and put them on the level of "savage tribes," they were arguing against the manualist belief that deaf people were fundamentally different from hearing people. They were arguing that any differences that existed were the result, not the cause, of sign language use, and that deaf people could become and should become virtually the same as hearing people. This belief was challenged by the opposition to oralism by deaf adults and their insistence on framing the debate in political terms. Oralists refused to acknowledge deaf adults because they saw in them the embodiment of the conflict and divisiveness that they wished to efface; they focused, instead, on the figure of the child, who hovered, pure and pitiable, above the debate.

When the focus was not on the child, it was on the parents, especially the mother, of a deaf child. Here also the appeal of oralism was "founded on sentiment and sustained by sentiment," as a deaf leader charged, its attraction based not upon demonstrable success but upon sentimental appeals to parents. Against protests that many orally trained deaf children could not make themselves understood outside the home and the school, that "ninety percent of the orally taught deaf drop their acquired speech, except with near relatives, and resort to writing," that oral training took too much time away from other learning and was not worth the time and labor it cost, oralists were likely to counter that the sound of a child's voice to its mother was worth any price.[86] "As I recall an instance of a mother for the first time hearing her little one say 'love mamma,'" wrote one teacher, "the amount of work sunk into insignificance in comparison to the happiness of that mother."[87] One of the most common themes of oralist writings concerned the feelings of the mother when she discovered her child's deafness:

How discouraged when from those lips no sound of "mamma" comes. A day, a month, a year, and still no word of love. . . . Mamma, mamma, love, baby, are repeated over and over again, and upon some uttered sounds . . . hangs the tireless mother's hope of ultimate success. . . . His education becomes a matter of serious thought, but knowing the great influence which children have upon each other, the mother, not without good reason, hesitates to place her little boy among those who would alienate him from her by giving him a language different than her own.[88]

The tragedy of deafness was that the child who signed might "look upon the English language *of its mother* as an unknown" [emphasis added].[89] The focus of the oralist rhetoric was primarily on the child and the effect of its deafness on its mother, secondarily on the joy that the teacher felt when her long patient efforts were rewarded by hearing the child speak, and far less frequently on the life of the deaf adult.[90]

This is not to say that the manualists had not also been guilty of romanticizing and sentimentalism. Manualists had a wide streak of paternalism, and deaf people were by no means treated as equals in their world. But the successful deaf adult was present there, not merely in their rhetoric but physically in their schools, at their conventions, in their circles of friends, and in the pages of the profession's journal. While their work was primarily among children and young adults, their mission as described was to an entire people. The deaf adult, a strong presence in both their literature and their work, was an integral part of the world they inhabited.

If oralists rarely in their writings lifted their eyes from the child, they also rarely had to lift them to a deaf adult in the everyday course of their work. At manual schools, not only had deaf adults comprised 40 percent of the teaching staffs on average, they had also been present as teachers' assistants and dormitory supervisors, bakers and cooks, gardeners, seamstresses, janitors, and maintenance workers. In a few schools deaf people were principals and head teachers. Their presence was important not only because they were exemplars for deaf pupils, but because they were examples for hearing teachers of what their students would one day become; they served as sources of information and as reminders for the hearing teachers of what was important, what was needed, what was possible. Oralism did away with or severely limited this fruitful contact between hearing teachers and deaf adults. Most oral schools had policies against employing deaf adults: they could not teach speech; they might be tempted to use sign language and therefore be a source of contagion; and finally, if the primary purpose of oralism was to integrate deaf people into the world of hearing people, then to hire deaf teachers to teach deaf children would defeat that purpose from the start.[91] This exclusion meant that an important way for hearing teachers to check theory against reality, to know firsthand the outcomes of their work, was lost—the deaf adult need not even figure into their talk about their work. It meant that oralism, like deaf children, could exist forever in a land of potential, where progress was always being made and final reckonings were never necessary. Oralism was itself always a child, always promising great things to come in some future time.

The shift to oralism, combined with the Victorian ideology of woman's sphere, helps to explain the shift to women teachers in the schools for the deaf. Oral teaching, in part because of the younger age of the pupils and in part because of the different teaching techniques, was seen as women's work. Schools that used oral methods of instruction employed nearly all female teachers. In the schools that used both oral and manual methods, there was a gendered job specialization, with women teaching the oral classes and men the manual. Oral teaching became associated with women, and manual teaching with men; as the number of students educated orally increased, so did the number of women teachers.

Conversely, the shift to a female teaching force served to promote oralism. The feminization of the teaching profession by no means "caused" the ascendance of oralism. Oralism has faded today without a corresponding shift to male teachers, and oralism has found favor in other countries at times when their teaching corps were entirely male. The connection is neither intrinsic nor inevitable. In this particular time and place, however, women teachers were, for culturally specific reasons, far more likely to be advocates of the oral method than were men.

 Had there not been gendered job segregation and an ideology of essential gender differences, what most deaf people see as a tragic period in the history of deaf education might well have taken a less extreme form. While the schools for the deaf probably still would have moved in the direction of oralism, they might have retained a more balanced approach, basing methods of education on the predilections and circumstances of individuals. Schools whose philosophies were not based upon an essentialist and monolithic ideology of gender might have found less appealing the similarly monolithic ideology of oralism.

Plate 1. "Miss Dillingham Rendering the Marseillaise Hymn in the Sign Language," at the 1879 graduation ceremony of the New York Institution for the Instruction of the Deaf and Dumb. The fascination with sign language among the nineteenth-century public meant that events such as these that featured deaf students giving speeches and recitations in sign language often attracted diverse audiences and newspaper coverage. From *Frank Leslie's Illustrated Newspaper*, 12 July 1879. (Courtesy of Gallaudet University Archives.)

Plate 2. First convention of the National Association of the Deaf, 1880, in Cincinnati. The NAD, an organization run entirely by and for deaf Americans, was founded as an umbrella organization for the state associations. It became the primary vehicle by which deaf Americans fought oralism. (Courtesy of Gallaudet University Archives.)

Plate 3. Students at the Michigan School for the Deaf in Flint (*top*) and the Washington School for the Deaf in Vancouver (*bottom*) perform the hymn "Nearer My God to Thee" in sign language. Public sign language performances, typically involving popular and traditional songs with religious or patriotic themes, were frequent events at manualist schools for the deaf. *Top:* from *Silent Worker* 18, no. 8 (May 1906); *bottom:* from *Silent Worker* 23, no. 9 (June 1911). (Courtesy of Gallaudet University Archives.)

Plate 4. Students on the steps of Chapel Hall, National Deaf-Mute College, Washington, D.C., about 1890. Established in 1864 by act of Congress, the college (renamed Gallaudet College in 1894 and then in 1986 Gallaudet University) has long been an institution of great cultural significance to the American deaf community. The women at the right of the photograph were among the earliest female students at the college, which began admitting women in 1886. (Courtesy of Gallaudet University Archives.)

Plate 5. First meeting of the Alumni Association of the National Deaf-Mute College, 1889. Alumni associations such as this, and others connected to the state residential schools, were criticized by oralists who wished to discourage deaf people from forming social ties and lifelong associations with other deaf people. (Courtesy of Gallaudet University Archives.)

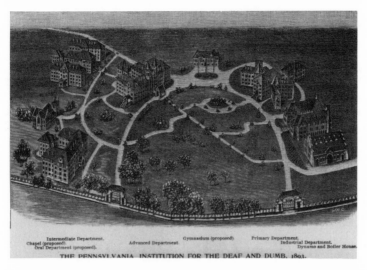

Plate 6. Sketch made in 1893 of the new campus of the Pennsylvania Institution for the Deaf and Dumb, opened in 1892, on the outskirts of Philadelphia. Founded in 1820 with a few dozen pupils, by 1893 the school had grown to be one of the largest in the country, with nearly five hundred pupils. Note the as-yet-unfinished "Oral Department" building; with its own dormitories, dining room, classrooms, assembly hall, and playground, its purpose was to keep oral students separate from the other students. Separate buildings would soon be unnecessary, however, since by the turn of the century nearly all the school's students were taught exclusively by oral means. From H. Van Allen, "The Pennsylvania Institution," in *Histories of American Schools for the Deaf, 1817–1893,* ed. Edward Allen Fay (Washington, D.C.: Volta Bureau, 1893).

Plate 7. The five hundred pupils of the Illinois Institution for the Education of the Deaf and Dumb attending chapel, 1893. All the state residential schools held weekly services in sign language. Manualists argued that because the difficulty of reading lips at a distance made such assemblies impractical, strict oralism would impair the religious life of deaf students. From Philip G. Gillett, "The Illinois Institution," in *Histories of American Schools for the Deaf, 1817–1893,* ed. Edward Allen Fay (Washington, D.C.: Volta Bureau, 1893).

Plate 8. Dining room of the Kansas Institution for the Education of the Deaf and Dumb, 1893. In images such as this, oralists saw an unregulated, semiautonomous deaf world created in the residential schools for the deaf. From S. Tefft Walker, "The Kansas Institution," in *Histories of American Schools for the Deaf, 1817–1893,* ed. Edward Allen Fay (Washington, D.C.: Volta Bureau, 1893).

Plate 9. Dining room of the McCowen Oral School for Young Deaf Children in Chicago, 1893. Many oral schools tried to recreate the atmosphere of a family home. They favored smaller schools or, where that was not possible, organized dorms on the "cottage plan" and dining rooms into small groups with faculty at each table. This allowed closer supervision by hearing adults, an essential element where sign language was forbidden. As Mary McCowen explained in the text accompanying the photograph, the "advantage of this constant presence of the teacher is that the child struggling to express a thought is given at once the proper word, and thus unconsciously forms the habit of trying to express himself in words rather than in motions, which he must otherwise inevitably do." From Mary McCowen, "The McCowen Oral School for Young Deaf Children," in *Histories of American Schools for the Deaf, 1817–1893,* ed. Edward Allen Fay (Washington, D.C.: Volta Bureau, 1893).

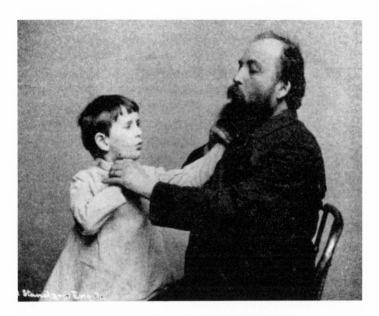

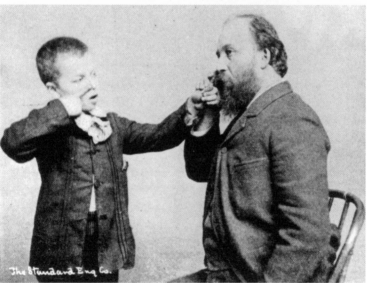

Plate 10. A speech lesson. By the turn of the century most deaf students, except those in the segregated schools for African Americans in the South, were devoting an ever-increasing portion of the day to lessons in speech and lip-reading. Deaf adults frequently complained that so many hours were spent in the arduous and often fruitless task of learning oral communication that insufficient time remained for academic and vocational instruction. From D. Greene, "The New York Institution for the Improved instruction of Deaf-Mutes," in *Histories of American Schools for the Deaf, 1817–1893,* ed. Edward Allen Fay (Washington, D.C.: Volta Bureau, 1893).

Plate 11. Speech classes were by necessity small, since they required much individual attention. In the absence of hearing, the senses of sight and touch must take its place in learning to reproduce sound. Here students peer into their mouths with mirrors, attempting to duplicate the mouth and tongue movements their teacher demonstrates, while the girl at the right in the top photograph uses her fingers to try to find the proper tongue placement. *Top:* from Philip G. Gillet, "The Illinois Institution," in *Histories of American Schools for the Deaf, 1817–1893,* ed. Edward Allen Fay (Washington, D.C.: Volta Bureau, 1893); *bottom:* from Louise E. Drew, "The Passing of the Dumb," *Harpers Weekly,* 3 June 1911.

Plate 12. Students receiving "auricular training" to improve their ability to make use of any residual hearing they possess, in the parlor of the McCowen Oral School in Chicago. Note the boy at the back and left—his teacher has him turned away from her so that he has to rely solely on what he hears through the speaking tube. From Mary McCowen, "The McCowen Oral School for Young Deaf Children," in *Histories of American Schools for the Deaf, 1817–1893,* ed. Edward Allen Fay (Washington, D.C.: Volta Bureau, 1893).

THE CLASS HEARING, WITH THEIR TEETH, A VOCAL AND INSTRUMENTAL CONCERT.

Plate 13. *Top:* "A Young Lady Hearing Conversation for the First Time."
Bottom: "The Class Hearing, with Their Teeth, a Vocal and Instrumental
Concert." As the emphasis shifted from the use of sign language to oral
communication, new devices that promised to conquer deafness were regu-
larly touted in the press. Both from *Frank Leslie's Illustrated Newspaper,* 13
December 1879.

Plate 14. Fearing that American Sign Language would deteriorate as a result of the efforts to ban it in the schools, the National Association of the Deaf from 1910 to 1920 produced a series of more than a dozen films to preserve for posterity speeches, sermons, stories, and poetry by people they considered masters of the language. Plates 14 to 17 are taken from that film series. Here George Veditz, president of the NAD from 1907 to 1910 and originator of the project, is pictured presenting a speech titled "The Preservation of the Sign Language." (National Association of the Deaf, 1913; courtesy of Gallaudet University Archives.)

Plate 15. Robert P. McGregor, "A Lay Sermon: The Universal Brotherhood of Man and Fatherhood of God." McGregor was the first president of the National Association of the Deaf, from 1880 to 1883. (National Association of the Deaf, 1913; courtesy of Gallaudet University Archives.)

Plate 16. Amos G. Draper, "The Signing of the Charter of Gallaudet College." Draper became the second deaf professor at Gallaudet College when he was hired in 1879 as professor of Latin and mathematics. (National Association of the Deaf, 1913; courtesy of Gallaudet University Archives.)

Plate 17. Edward M. Gallaudet, "The Lorna Doone County of Devonshire, England." Gallaudet, youngest son of Thomas H. Gallaudet, was the first president of the National Deaf-Mute College (Gallaudet College) from 1864 to 1910. Gallaudet was hearing, but because his mother, Sophia Fowler Gallaudet, was deaf, he grew up fluent in sign language. (National Association of the Deaf, 1913; courtesy of Gallaudet University Archives.)

FOUR

From Refinement to
Efficiency: Culture

In 1892 Edward Miner Gallaudet surveyed the state of his profession with alarm. According to Gallaudet, during the fourteen years from 1817 to 1831 that his father had been principal of the American Asylum for the Deaf, every one of its hearing teachers had been a college graduate. Among them were such luminaries as the geographer William C. Woodbridge and Frederick A. P. Barnard, later president of Columbia College in New York. Moreover, the American Asylum had maintained a majority of college graduates on their teaching staff, during most years, until 1873. Recently, however, the number of teachers with college degrees had been rapidly declining. Citing the case of what he said was a typical school (which he left unnamed), where the proportion of college educated teachers had plummeted from 50 percent in 1865 to a mere 17 percent in 1875, Gallaudet called for measures to aid in the recruitment of better educated teachers.[1] Gallaudet's figures were confirmed by a survey taken the following year, which found that the percentage of college educated teachers in the profession as a whole had dropped to 16 percent.[2]

The Reverend Benjamin Talbot, looking back in 1895 upon his forty years as a manualist teacher of the deaf, described his early colleagues as "college graduates of high standing, fitted by natural endowments and by acquired attainments for the highest ranks in the learned professions." When he first arrived at the Ohio Institution for the Education of the Deaf and Dumb in 1854, the teaching staff consisted of "five speaking gentlemen, all graduates of colleges of *83* the first rank, and three deaf-mutes, two educated at Hartford and one in Columbus" (a college education was generally not available to deaf people until the founding of the National Deaf-Mute College, later Gallaudet College, in 1864). "This proportion," he added, "held good continuously till the writer left, in 1863, and for two or three years later." In the years after the Civil War, however, it had become increasingly difficult to retain "liberally educated speaking gentlemen." Schools were forced to fill out their ranks with men and women of lower attainments and lesser permanency.[3] Other teachers of the older generation joined Gallaudet and Talbot in criticizing what they saw as the "greater proportion of mediocre teachers" and called for more active recruitment of those who possessed "culture, refinement, and literary taste."[4]

Some of the concern expressed by older teachers may have been disguised criticism of the increasing number of women in the field—since few female teachers had been to college, the two issues overlapped. Cornelia Trask of the Illinois Institution saw a connection between the two in 1868, when she complained that women were often deemed unqualified to teach at the schools for the deaf simply because they lacked classical training—a qualification she found ludicrous.[5]

Resistance to female teachers among men does not, however, account entirely for the concern over changing standards in the field; the decline in college-educated teachers and principals was not solely a result of the increasing numbers of women entering the profession. Like their female colleagues, men in the profession were far less likely to have attended college than their counterparts before the war.[6] Differences other than those of gender separated the new generation of teachers from the old. The complaints about declining standards were also expressions of a larger conflict within American society—what Max Weber called "the struggle of the 'specialist type of man' against the older type of 'cultivated man.'"[7] They were symptoms of a clash between a generation that prized classical learning and refined sensibility and one that held business values and practical skills in higher regard. Disagreement over the use of sign language was one expression of those different values, and it became a focal point for conflict between the two generations of teachers.

Teachers of the manualist generation proudly maintained that "in no other country is the culture of the deaf mute carried to so high a point as here," and they credited this triumph to the "class of men" who made teaching the deaf their career—"cultivated men," "gentlemen of liberal education," possessed of "talents that would adorn any profession in life."[8] Those who became teachers of the deaf in the manualist generation had not been specially trained for that profession in college—or for any other profession, for that matter, except perhaps the clergy. They were educated to be educated men— that is, to do well in whatever gentlemanly pursuit they chose. Most colleges of the time built their curricula around a core of classical studies. At Yale College, for example, admission examinations in 1828 required knowledge of Latin and Greek grammar as well as familiarity with canonical authors in both languages. Students continued their study of ancient languages and literature in each of their four years of college. Other required courses, such as rhetoric and oratory, involved substantial measures of classical study as well.[9]

Yale College, as it happened, was *alma mater* to a great many teachers of the deaf. According to E. M. Gallaudet in 1879, Yale had over the years "furnished, from its graduates, a much larger number of instructors of deaf-mutes than any other [college]." In fact, all six of the principals of the American Asylum at Hartford, since its founding in 1817—including his father, Thomas Hopkins Gallaudet—and every one of the principals of the largest school in the country, the New York Institution, since its founding in 1818 had been Yale alumnae.[10] A teacher at the New York Institution, acknowledging in 1900 the "falling off in the number of Yale graduates who have entered the profession," proudly claimed that five out of eight of the male teachers at his school since 1818 had been college educated, and one-third of them at Yale.[11]

The teachers who came from Yale and other colleges had been, throughout their educations, immersed not only in the study of Greek and Latin but in a worldview that held up ancient Greece and Rome as pinnacles of cultural achievement. The ancient languages were deemed superior to modern languages, the ancient arts unrivaled by anything since.[12] The intellectual world of the manualists was deeply rooted in their study of the classics; when they wished to support an argument, the examples that sprung to mind were from the ancient world. When they quoted authority, they quoted Cicero. When they reached for the illustrative or edifying story, what came to them was something they had read in Horace or Livy. When they referred to sign language as the "noble language of signs"—which they did at every opportunity—they were not indulging in mere hyperbole. In the minds of the manualists, sign language was indeed a refined language of distinction; this was so because, oddly enough, sign language was linked in their minds with the ancient world in several ways.

The manualists did not think of sign language as people do today, nor did they speak of it in quite the same terms as they would of English or Latin or French. It *was* a language to them and they explicitly defended it as such.[13] In the next breath, however, they spoke of it as an art. They used interchangeably the terms "language of signs" and "language of pantomime"; in contrast to later oralists (and to linguists today), they made no clear distinction between the two. Instead of a difference in kind, what they saw was merely a difference in degree: the language that deaf people and their teachers used was a more highly developed and complex version of the basic pantomime of which anyone was capable. Becoming fluent in sign language was for them a matter not only of learning a vocabulary and a grammar—a language—but the perfecting of an artistic skill. Students of sign language did not merely gain fluency in the language, they "cultivated the art."

As it happens, pantomime was a highly developed and well-respected art form among the ancient Romans, a fact that fascinated the manualists. They believed that what the Romans performed on the stage was not significantly different from what teachers and pupils in the schools for the deaf performed in the classroom every day. Harvey Peet, principal of the New York Institution, treated the two as equivalent: "Of the extent to which this *language of signs* has been cultivated in ancient times," he wrote, "we may judge by the testimony of Cicero, that the *pantomime* of Roscius rivaled his own polished sentences in clearness and variety of expression" [emphases added].[14] The Reverend Collins Stone, of the American Asylum at Hartford, explained that in the "golden days of Grecian and Roman refinement, the art of expressing ideas by pantomime was much cultivated, and was carried to a high degree of perfection." He told the story of how "Cicero, the eloquent Roman orator," and "Roscius, the great comedian," competed to see "which could express a thought most forcibly, the one by his gestures, the other by his words." That such a contest could even be conceived was proof, he said, of the advanced state of the art. Considering the attention they had given to pantomime, Stone found it puzzling that the Romans had not discovered the art of instructing the deaf.[15]

So too did Harvey Peet. Not only could sign language be "traced to periods of high antiquity," Peet also believed it was "certain that the ancient Greeks and Romans had their modes of spelling words on the fingers" and that the knowledge of finger-spelling was "generally diffused among men of letters." Even though the Romans did not apparently use pantomime for the education of the deaf, Peet ventured that Pedro Ponce de Leon, the sixteenth-century Benedictine monk who was thought to be the first instructor of the deaf in Europe, may have been "led to the discovery of the art of teaching the deaf and dumb" by his awareness of the "perfection to which the language of pantomime was cultivated on the Roman stage." Thus did Peet make those he called "the learned and wise men of antiquity" by a circuitous route the true fathers of deaf education.[16]

To manualists, then, the sign language that deaf people spontaneously turned to and which their hearing teachers consciously studied for use in the classroom was an art that had once graced the ancient world, only to fall into disuse after the decline of Western civilization into the "dark ages" that had followed. The use and cultivation of sign language in the present was to them the revival of a high Roman art form. It was not merely a practical pedagogical technique nor just the most effective means of communication with deaf people but a way of entering into a world of the past, of sharing in what the ancients had themselves cultivated and revered.

This ancient and newly revived art of pantomime was, they believed, "a worthy companion, and rival of the sister arts, poetry and painting."[17] Sign language was similar to painting, according to the teacher J. M. Francis, for it "pictures for the eye, for the moment, that which finds a more enduring representation on the canvas of the artist." The analogy with painting, Francis thought, was suggestive of the "rank to which the sign language is entitled, as an art"; indeed, he believed that "it may be properly ranked among the highest arts" and that the difficulty of becoming a "master" was comparable.[18]

Manualists did not intend the label "art" as deprecatory in any way. Belonging to a time prior to the intellectual separation of the arts and sciences, they did not habitually or automatically rank one more highly than the other. Indeed, on occasion they found it equally appropriate to refer to the "noble science" of signs or to give impartial endorsement to both "its claims as an art, and a science." Harvey Peet thought it was significant that a deaf man, Quintus Pedius, became, according to Pliny, one of "the most eminent painters of Rome," since "eminence in the art of painting, we need not say, implies a very considerable intellectual development" and an equally considerable "moral development." This impressive cultivation of the deaf artist's intellectual and moral attributes, he believed, had been "undoubtedly derived through the language of pantomime, probably in part by frequenting the pantomime of the Roman stage."[19] As an art comparable to painting, mastery of sign language implied intellectual and moral achievement, while at the same time its use fostered intellectual and moral growth.

Manualists admired the art of sign language especially for its beauty, one of the highest ideals of ancient philosophy. They avowed that "for beauty and effective expression it is not surpassed by any language ever yet spoken or used."[20] Sign language was as often referred to as the "beautiful language of signs" as it was the "noble language of signs"; both were stock phrases in the manualist rhetoric, and they signified similar values. "The heart is the noblest part of human nature," affirmed Lucius Woodruff as he praised the "power over the hearts of our pupils which this beautiful language gives us."[21] In the more utilitarian years of the later nineteenth century, beauty would be found lacking in practical value, and would slip from its place as a peer and counterpart to truth. In the manualists' world, however, beauty mattered. When they spoke of sign language as a "singularly beautiful and impressive language," and claimed that it possessed "a beauty and charm not surpassed by the painted landscape or the scenery of the stage," they were paying the highest compliments they knew how to bestow.[22] If a choice had to be made between them, the Reverend Henry B. Camp wondered "whether the language of *signs* or of the *articulate voice* would, in itself, be preferable, so graphic and beautiful is the former in comparison with the latter."[23]

Manualists attributed to the beauty of sign language its efficacy with young deaf pupils. They described the minds of uneducated deaf children as "dormant"; what was needed was a form of stimulation to "awaken" them. The effect of the beauty of sign language was that "dormant faculties are aroused, and traces of mind are sometimes discovered and developed where all seemed dark and hopeless." They claimed they never failed to encounter "a ready and graceful response from the minds of Deaf Mutes to the beautiful language of signs" and that "the attention of even the dullest is arrested by a masterly display of the beautiful language of signs."[24] Thomas H. Gallaudet believed sign language to be so precious in this way that no one should ever teach deaf children "if he does not cherish and cultivate it to the highest degree of force, beauty and grace which it is possible for him to reach."[25]

Manualists, when they disputed with oralists, appealed to their sense of the beautiful. It was simply wrong, they insisted, to deprive the deaf child of "the pleasure and aid of his own beautiful and graphic language."[26] Conversely, some manualists argued against teaching speech to those profoundly deaf from an early age because their speech could never be considered beautiful. Most such deaf people spoke "harshly" in tones that were "unnatural and distasteful," while producing "contortions of the countenance most unpleasant to behold." Deaf people "of refined taste" would naturally shrink from using their voices once they became aware of the reactions they provoked.[27] The Reverend John R. Keep was typical, if less delicate than most, when he observed that "the filing of a saw, and the shriek of a steam whistle combined, could not produce a more disagreeable sound than that which is made in some of these artificial attempts at speech by the deaf and dumb."[28] Similarly, lip-reading was faulted for being incapable of conveying the beauty of language. "Through the language of signs alone," manualists argued, could deaf people "enjoy the charms of eloquence, and so much as they can ever know of poetry, or follow a gifted leader in prayer or praise, to the higher regions of devotion." Lip-reading could never provide more than a "cold and imperfect appreciation" of what hearing people heard and deaf people saw in the richness of their respective languages.[29] The appreciation for beauty was fundamental to the self-conception of the nineteenth-century cultivated gentleman and provided an ostensible link with the philosophers of the ancient world. For manualist teachers it stood for a set of values they thought essential to education. The "beautiful language of signs" became deeply implicated in their vision of themselves and their work.

Manualists also enthusiastically pointed to what they believed were significant resemblances between sign language and the ancient languages—not Roman pantomime but Latin and Greek. At a Massachusetts Senate committee hearing convened in 1867 to decide whether to establish an oral school in Massachusetts, an advocate of oralism criticized sign language as being "unarranged." The Reverend William Turner, a long-time teacher at the American Asylum and a Yale graduate, countered by giving an example of a sign language sentence and informed the Senate committee that it was "just the way the ancient classical languages would arrange the idea." Indeed, he told them, "all the ancient and classical languages of the world are arranged exactly in the order of the deaf and dumb language." Turner argued for the superiority of sign language on the basis of it being "more classical, more in accordance with the languages of those ancient nations which have made the greatest attainments in literature—the Greeks, the Hebrew, the Latins—than our own language is." This was a crucial point for Turner, and it led him to a conclusion that would dumbfound and perplex his younger oralist opponents: the syntax of sign language was the correct one—"It is our language that is misarranged."[30]

Other manualists made similar arguments. For example, in the course of an article criticizing oralism, Harvey P. Peet thought it worthwhile to point out the resemblances between sign language and Latin, noting that "if we should express in signs, the question 'Who is a good man?', the order of signs would correspond to the Latin of Horace, *Vir bonus est quis?*"[31] Edward Miner Gallaudet may have been making a subtle connection between sign language and classical languages when he titled his protest of the passing of sign language in deaf education "Must the Sign-Language Go?" echoing Andrew West's famous 1884 essay "Must the Classics Go?" a protest of the decline of classical study in college education. In that essay, West made the case for the study of ancient languages by arguing, in part, that the grammar of classical languages was "immeasurably superior to modern languages. . . . What does English, French, or German grammar amount to? Simply *debris* of the classical languages, mixed with barbaric elements."[32]

Manualists saw sign language as a refined and beautiful language only when it was properly used, however. The practice of language criticism as a means of distinguishing between the vulgar and the refined has a long history, dating back in the West at least to Cicero. The historian Kenneth Cmiel has described the outpouring of criticism of popular English usage from refined elites in nineteenth-century America. Defenders of an older neoclassical tradition of public speech fought against the new "middling" styles of popular rhetoric; defenders of the neoclassical "grand" style associated it with the social authority invested in the liberally educated gentleman. Those who advocated middling styles were constructing a new hierarchy of authority that favored professionals and businessmen.[33]

Nineteenth-century manualists were language critics as well, guarding the condition of sign language and criticizing its misuse as zealously as any guardian of English purity. Since sign languages change like all languages, some of the criticism resulted from the unease that seems always to accompany linguistic change. Laurent Clerc, for example, was reported to have complained in 1867 that "the graceful signs" of earlier years were being "degenerated or changed into other ugly signs."[34] As we shall see in the next chapter, criticism also often focused on keeping sign language "natural" and preventing what were seen as arbitrary elements from creeping into it.

Much of the rhetoric of sign-language criticism and the kinds of concerns manualists raised over usage, however, mirrored the rhetoric and concerns of the guardians of tasteful and refined English usage. Lewis Weld, for example, cautioned his colleagues in 1851 that the average deaf person did not possess "the best taste in the use of his vernacular, any more than uneducated persons who hear have those ideas of grace, beauty, and propriety of expression that belong to enlightened minds." Sign usage therefore had to be strictly guided by teachers "who possess good taste, judgment, and discrimination."[35]

Lucius Woodruff in 1849 raised issues of taste and refinement to address the question of proper facial expression when signing. Woodruff worried that deaf people were too often guilty of "violating good taste" as a result of their tendency to "grimace." This was in part, he thought, a result of early habits formed in the home when deaf children used exaggerated gestures and facial expressions to communicate their needs, but it was also in part the consequence of the "want of refinement which, of course, is natural to uncultivated mutes." With hearing children "great pains are taken to cultivate the manners, and impart correctness, propriety and even elegance of speech," and the signing habits of deaf children required no less attention. For just as the "uncomely manners and language" of hearing children "betoken ill-breeding," so also do the "uncouth looks and actions of the mute evince that he has been the subject of similar neglect." Deaf children should look to previous graduates of their schools, among whom were many "examples of a high degree of polished manners and graceful expression." Since young instructors usually learned much of their sign language from their students, Woodruff feared they too often fell into the same unpleasant habits as well. If teachers attended to "the cultivation of what is graceful and pleasing," then their students would follow their example. Facial expression was of course an integral facet of sign language, but only careful instruction from refined teachers could "lead to the cultivation of what is graceful and pleasing, rather than uncomely and disagreeable."[36]

The importance of cultivating *decorum*—a value applied by the ancient Romans, nineteenth-century advocates of refined English usage, and manualist teachers to the appropriate choice and use of gestures and expressions—resided in the intimate connection all made between outer behavior and inner character. The connection was reciprocal: physical comportment in all its aspects reflected the inner self and was therefore a window for others onto a person's character; it also helped to create that character—the manner in which deaf people signed had an "influence on the minds of deaf-mutes themselves," and could "produce that refinement of the feelings and sentiments which is so important to the character."[37]

Sign language, properly understood and properly employed, could be used to educate and to elevate deaf people, they believed. The potential benefits of a highly cultivated sign language, however, extended beyond its salutary effects on deaf people. As in ancient Rome, oratory was considered to be at the heart of education in early- and mid-nineteenth-century schools and colleges. The power to move audiences was seen as outward evidence of inner virtue. In ancient Rome, an elaborate system of gesticulation was an essential part of oratorical theory and practice; the training of the orator included detailed prescriptions for matching the appropriate gestures with particular ideas and emotions. Quintilian believed that the mastery of *gestus* was indispensable to effective oration.[38] Manualist teachers thought that mid-nineteenth century American oratory was impoverished by the increasing lack of this component of classical oratory and could be much improved through a wider knowledge of sign language. "How much greater power their eloquence would have," Thomas H. Gallaudet suggested in 1848, if only orators would "*act out* thoughts as well as speak them." It was "greatly to be regretted," he believed, "that much more of this visual language does not accompany the oral . . . in all our social intercourse."[39] In 1850 J. Addison Cary of the New York Institution declared that Gallaudet's wish was already coming to pass—sign language was becoming more and more familiar to the public through "its exhibition in the classroom and on public occasions"—and he contended the "art of public speaking has been and will be still further improved by the cultivation of the language of signs." Such improvement would inevitably follow upon the increasingly widespread familiarity with sign language, since "the public speaker, ashamed of his insignificant gesticulation, cannot fail to see in those natural elements an aid to speech worthy of his most careful study."[40]

Some argued that a wider knowledge of sign language would have benefits even more profound and far-reaching than the enrichment of American oratory. If sign language were "vastly more cultivated than it is, and employed in the early training of children and youth in our families, schools, and other seminaries of learning," Thomas H. Gallaudet wrote, "we should find its happy results in all the processes of education, on all occasions where the persuasions of eloquence are employed, and in the higher zest which would be given to the enjoyments of social life."[41] Others urged that sign language be added to the college curriculum as well, where it would enhance the education of the gentleman. "I believe the day will come," J. M. Francis confidently predicted in 1859, "when it will be regarded worthy of a place among the studies of everyone who claims a liberal culture."[42] J. C. Covell, in an 1870 address (the title of which—"The Nobility, Dignity, and Antiquity of the Sign Language"—illustrates the manualist regard for the language of deaf people), foretold that "the time is not far distant, when the language of signs will be taught as a language in conjunction with philology, in most of the seminaries of learning in our land."[43]

When manualists argued against oralism, they argued in the terms that made sense to themselves, confident that if they could make the oralists see sign language as they did, make them understand the true nature of sign language—which the oralists had obviously, they thought, misconstrued—they could turn them into fellow admirers of the language. They praised the "beauty and grace" of sign language; they insisted there was "a play, a naturalness, a lifelike expressiveness about the language of signs, that makes it superior to any other language"; they spoke portentously of "pantomime, which that prince among orators, Cicero, not only admired, but also desired to learn—pantomime, which made Roscius a power among the ancient Romans"; and they were baffled when such paeans did not persuade.[44]

The teachers who embraced oralism after the Civil War were preoccupied by more modern concerns and were the products of a different kind of education. They had not, for the most part, attended college. Those few teachers of the deaf who did attend encountered curricula far different from those experienced by previous generations of college students. American colleges were undergoing a metamorphosis in the years after the Civil War. The traditional liberal arts course of study that all students had shared in common was becoming a thing of the past. Schools such as Harvard were creating a more flexible curriculum by instituting the elective system. Classical study was surrendering its favored place to modern languages and sciences, and oratory and rhetoric were in decline. In the antebellum years, the traditional course of study had been thought vital to the development of mental discipline, morality, and strength of character, but Americans were increasingly of the opinion expressed by Andrew Carnegie in 1902, that students of the classics "waste energies upon obtaining a knowledge of such languages as Greek and Latin, which are of no more practical use to them than Choctaw."[45]

More likely than a college education for young teachers of the deaf was a course of study at a "normal school"—that is, a teacher training school—typically for one year. Instead of a broad, liberal education, they received specialized, professional training in the techniques of teaching. This training was usually for teaching hearing children, since normal schools specifically for teachers of the deaf were slow to get started despite frequent assertions of the need for them. When such schools began to be established, prior training or experience in the education of hearing children was often required for admission, although requirements varied widely. Teachers of the deaf were increasingly seen as simply teachers, not unlike other teachers, but with a specialization in deaf education.

The first school of this kind, opened by Alexander Graham Bell in Boston in 1872, required for admission "a good English education . . . , a correct ear, a practical knowledge of teaching, and a pleasant and attractive bearing toward children." In 1881 Emma Garrett (a graduate of Bell's program) founded the Summer School of Oral Training for Teachers of the Deaf in Scranton, Pennsylvania. Her admission requirements were simply "a good English education and a love of children." In 1883 the Wisconsin Phonological Institute in Milwaukee established a normal school with a public day school for the deaf attached for practice teaching; entering students were "required to hold a Milwaukee assistant teacher's certificate, or its equivalent, or shall have completed one year of the advanced course of a State normal school." The one year course of study emphasized such classes as "anatomy and physiology of the human voice," the "science of the elements of speech," and "pedagogy for the deaf."[46]

The background and training of this new generation of instructors were reflected in the kinds of articles they published in the *American Annals of the Deaf* in the latter decades of the century. While manualists had published on a wide variety of topics, embracing philology, psychology, philosophy, history, and theology, oralists focussed their writing on educational practices—the technical aspects of teaching speech and lip-reading, classroom management, and pedagogical technique. They were specialists, and as oralism became ascendant the *Annals* was transformed into a professional journal of the modern type, more narrowly concerned with issues directly related to professional practice.

While manualists decried this change as a lowering of standards, oralists not surprisingly saw things differently. They believed that standards had in fact risen with the advent of oralism, a result of the increased expertise demanded of teachers by the new teaching methods. Not until teaching the deaf "became inspired of a new ambition," wrote one oralist, "took upon itself a new responsibility and labor," and "*broadened* to include . . . the giving of speech to the dumb and ability to read speech on the lips to the deaf," were standards necessarily changed from a general college education to specialized training. The "newer work was too difficult" and the "principles underlying it and permeating it were too obscure" for teachers to come into it without such training. Oralism, in their view, was a step forward in the progress of deaf education from simpler beginnings to a more complex, advanced, and difficult stage, and the replacement of liberal education by specialized training was a natural and integral element in that process.[47]

These changes in the teaching corps of schools for the deaf were part of larger cultural changes taking place throughout American society. Most of the manualist teachers were of a class of men who had long been looked up to in America as cultural leaders. They were being replaced in the years after the Civil War, both in the schools for the deaf and in the esteem of Americans, by professionals narrowly educated for specialized fields. This shift in cultural authority was expressed by the movement in education away from the classical values of refinement and liberal learning, and toward practical and specialized knowledge. The new cultural leader in America was neither the clergyman nor the gentleman of broad learning but the professional, the businessman, and the scientist.

Professionalization was one part of the shift in authority. Another was what one historian has called America's "saturation with business-industrial values and practices" during this period.[48] The "saturation" was evident in the answer an oralist teacher gave in 1907 to the question of what should replace the inefficient methods of training teachers of the past: "The answer may be given in a word," he answered—"the factory, the factory principle and system in everything."[49] A third rising language of authority in America, in addition to those of the professions and business, was that of science. The label "man of science" was synonymous with integrity and an unwavering commitment to objective truth. Public fascination with science was reflected by a proliferation of popular magazines that reported on developments in science and technology, a notable example being *Popular Science,* which began publication in 1872. Scientific vocabulary began to be commonly used to confer legitimacy on other, less prestigious vocations; educators, including educators of the deaf, increasingly spoke of their field as a "science" and tried to conform their own professional rhetoric as closely as they could to the rhetoric of the natural sciences.

The convergence of the vocabulary and values of professionalism, business, and science culminated after the turn of the century in the "efficiency movement," epitomized by the cultural ascendance of "scientific management." The "gospel of efficiency" permeated mainstream institutions, from businesses to schools, hospitals to prisons. Frederick Winslow Taylor, author of the 1911 treatise *The Principles of Scientific Management* and leading apostle for the efficiency movement, urged that the same principles that applied to the efficient operation of the factory be "applied with equal force to all social activities: to the management of our homes . . . our churches, our philanthropic institutions, our universities."[50] Popular magazines repeated Taylor's call for the universal application of the laws of scientific management and efficient living.[51]

The "practicality" movement in education was one expression of this climate. University presidents such as David Starr Jordan of Stanford urged a movement "toward reality and practicality" in education, and school principals discussed "getting away, to an extent, from the mere scholastic education, and developing the practical side."[52] As one educator of the deaf put it: "Some education is useful; some is merely ornamental. That education is useful which aids its possessor, in one way or another, better to fight and win the battle of life." The "battle of life" was no longer primarily a religious or moral battle, as it had been for the manualists, but a commercial one. There was, among teachers of the deaf, as elsewhere, a "growing tendency to protest and revolt against a system of education that many believe to be more ornamental than useful, more theoretical than practical." Ornamental education was seen as aristocratic; practical education was democratic, because it fitted the mass of people for everyday work.[53]

Schools for the deaf, which had always taught trades, followed the same trend as the public schools in giving greater emphasis to industrial education by increasing the number of trades taught and the amount of time dedicated to them.[54] The Convention of American Instructors of the Deaf added an "industrial section" to their organization in 1895; for the first time, industrial arts teachers were invited to attend the convention as members and to give papers. Many shared the view of the printing instructor who avowed that his work was "of equal, if not greater, importance than that of the school–rooms," for it was the industrial training classes that the deaf student would "find most practical and most valuable when he goes forth to 'fight life battles.' "[55] Such teachers argued that "every subject is susceptible of an industrial or vocational interpretation," and if one was not, it had "doubtful value in the curriculum and should be dropped."[56] Even art classes had to be defended as beneficial from a "utilitarian point of view," valuable for "economic reasons" and as "a necessity to science and society, to industry, commerce, and business," because, as one art teacher explained, "the 'beauty' and 'feeling' arguments are difficult for many to understand."[57]

In 1911 the state superintendent of schools for Wisconsin told a gathering of teachers of the deaf that they had been, and were still, ahead of the public schools on this issue, that industrial training had "first shown its practicability in the education of those who were more or less defective." He noted that the work being done in Booker T. Washington's Tuskegee Institution was "similar to that done in our schools for the deaf" and asserted that "no better thing could possibly be done for the negro boys and girls than that," in the same way that "no better thing could possibly be done for the boys and girls who are defective in hearing than to teach them to be self-supporting, self-respecting citizens." In the past, he lamented, many teachers had held the mistaken notion that "education was something up in the air, a sort of a mystical, peculiar thing that people could get, and we called it culture." In recent years, however, people were "coming to a more satisfactory definition of culture than that," one that put practical skills first. "Education should be useful for everyone, but to those suffering from a handicap it must be useful to enable them to earn a living."[58]

Emma Garrett deprecated the value of a college education for deaf people. She thought that, with the great progress being made in oral education, deaf students would soon be able to attend college with hearing students if they wished. However, she believed that in most cases they ought to "devote themselves to something that would be of more practical advantage to them." This of course was something no manualist would have ever thought to say. The idea that education in itself might not possess intrinsic value was utterly foreign to their world. Garrett's comments possibly were directed as much against Gallaudet College, where deaf college students were most likely to attend, as they were against college education in general. The existence of Gallaudet College was always an irritant to oralists, who considered it the enemy's stronghold (and were doubly galled that it was federally supported). They often advised their students not to attend, and at least one oral school, charged Edward M. Gallaudet in 1895, deliberately withheld knowledge of the college's very existence from them.[59]

The drive for practicality had the effect in deaf education of reinforcing the oralist case against sign language. Sign language was impractical, many argued, because it was not useful in the workplace, where coworkers and bosses would not understand it; a deaf worker "must be able to make his wishes known to them by means of speech or to receive information by means of speech reading, for very few employers will stop to communicate by writing."[60] Oralists were convinced that sign language was an impractical language; deaf people would enjoy the luxury of attending schools for the deaf for a relatively brief period of their lives, they explained, and "when they leave them they have to compete with hearing and speaking people in the struggle for existence." In that struggle "the language of pantomimic signs is almost valueless."[61] The deaf businessperson "would be more successful," they thought, "were he able to speak and read the lips." For the employee, the orally skilled deaf person would be supposedly "able to take his orders from the lips of his employers, and to respond or to ask for directions orally. The saving in time and trouble in this way is one that no business man will fail to estimate."[62]

The 1884 conference of Principals and Superintendents of Institutions for Deaf-Mutes devoted an entire session to a discussion of the question of "what practical value is articulation to the deaf in the prosecution of business." It featured, on the one hand, oralist teachers citing examples of students who had gone on to successful careers in business and insisting that their success was the result of their oral educations, and, on the other, deaf adults coming forward insisting that they always communicated at work by writing, regardless of their oral skills, since speech and speech-reading were too uncertain and unreliable.[63]

Even the advocates of day schools—which, being small and decentralized, had fewer resources for manual training—used vocational education arguments for their schools. Day schools could better fit industrial training to the labor markets of specific locales, they contended, since "a boy from a factory district would not choose the trade a boy from a mining, or a lumbering, or an agricultural district would choose." Furthermore, they offered more opportunities for practical learning because "the training given in school is applied at home." Girls could get valuable training for the future when they helped their mothers to "mend clothes, take care of baby, set the table, wash the dishes, take care of their room, and prepare the different dishes they have learned to cook at cooking school." Boys benefited by helping their fathers to "put up screens, storm windows, fix a broken chair."[64]

In 1908 the oralist Fred DeLand asserted that manualism was "now generally admitted unwise from an economic and educational point of view." He found it difficult to believe that in earlier years—even though an oral education would have been of "material assistance in aiding the deaf child to become a more helpful member of society"—sign language had been promoted and used by people "who then considered the salvation of the pupil's soul . . . paramount to an educational course." It was preposterous, he thought, that "the ability to comprehend religious doctrine was the goal that every pupil was supposed to strive for in 1860," especially when schools might have offered an educational course to "enable the average pupil to enter upon a useful career in commercial or industrial circles." The eventual success of the oral method, he wrote, had resulted from the efforts of "progressive educators whose first aim was to save the deaf child from being a burden on society, and who preferred to equip it with the knowledge and the methods of the people with whom it had to compete for existence and from whom it gained its sustenance."[65]

When DeLand discussed the problems of deafness, economic and industrial concerns were invariably foremost. To use sign language was to "isolate this class of human beings from general society and from many industrial occupations." He lamented the "social and industrial deprivation suffered by the deaf and 'dumb' in being shut out from all positions of profit and honor." He argued that the goal of oralism was "to unite them with the hearing in every way possible, commercially, socially, and industrially [and] enable them to compete on equal terms."[66] This point of view reflected, of course, not just an ideology but the reality that deaf people, like their hearing neighbors, were less and less likely to work independently in their own homes or on their own land. The increasing industrialization of American society meant that young people could no longer go into the trades of their parents as artisans or farmers but had to compete for jobs in a labor market. Even though the proposition that oralism made deaf people more employable was arguable—and many deaf people did argue the point—it was plausible; whatever its merits, in the prevailing cultural climate it was a compelling argument to make, and it was the oralists who made it, leaving the manualists muttering about beauty and Roman refinement, notions that had largely lost their charm.

While oralists such as Alexander Graham Bell generally conceded that deaf people may not "become perfect in manner and speech," what really mattered was that they be "able to converse readily and to carry on the ordinary business of commercial life."[67] Bell often spoke of deaf education in businesslike terms, asserting that it was "an investment that yields profitable returns in the increased productiveness of these classes." Educating deaf people made sense because their "wealth producing powers are so enormously increased by education"; there was simply "no 'charity' in the matter," he wrote—"*it pays!*"[68] Emma and Mary S. Garrett echoed this reasoning, arguing that "it is really economy to give them the advantages which will make them like normal people in their ability to communicate with their fellows and, therefore, self-supporting and useful citizens."[69] This sort of rhetoric in support of social spending has since become commonplace, but it had not been so earlier in the nineteenth century. It was not the way that manualists had spoken of their work; they were alms-givers, helpers with a Christian mission whose profits and rewards were of a less material nature. Oralists saw their task, at least in part, in business terms, and it conditioned the kinds of decisions they would make at the same time that it increased the appeal of their cause.

The use of the term "handicapped" to apply to deaf people arose in this context, a reflection of the new conception of education. It previously had been a term confined chiefly to horse racing, being derived from an English game of chance, "hand-in-cap," in which each player had an equal opportunity to win. A horse that was handicapped in a race was weighted with stones in order to make it more the equal of other, slower horses in the race. Educators in the late nineteenth century increasingly described modern industrial life as analogous to a horse race; deafness began to be described as a "serious handicap in the race for life." Alternatively, borrowing Darwin's phrase, people who were deaf were "by this defect handicapped in the struggle for existence."[70] Education was useful to deaf people only insofar as it helped them to "win the battle of life," oralists argued, and in this battle—or struggle, or race—"the language of pantomimic signs is almost valueless."[71]

To the manualist generation, deaf people had been considered "afflicted." The affliction came from God; whether it was considered a result of human sin or merely mysterious, it was nevertheless the "decree of Providence" and the "condition in which God has placed them." Deafness was a burden to be borne, not something to be overcome—not, at least, "until the time arrives when human imperfections will be done away with."[72] The oralist preference for "handicapped" reflected both the language of evolutionism and the business consciousness of late-nineteenth-century American culture, both of which emphasized competitiveness. Deafness became more an impediment to worldly success than a burden to the spirit. Oralism was intended to eliminate, so far as was possible, that impediment.

After the turn of the century, the language of practicality evolved into the language of efficiency. As a teacher of the deaf told his colleagues at a 1914 convention, "In this modern day everybody and every movement is coming to be measured by and for efficiency."[73] In the efficiency rhetoric of the time, the great enemy was *waste*. Waste was everywhere impairing national efficiency; in deaf education it came in the guise of sign language. Although by this time sign language was already banned in most classrooms, oralists were concerned that many students continued to use sign language outside of the classroom. In 1911 Frank Booth, editor of the *Volta Review* (since 1910 the name of the former *Association Review,* the journal of the American Association to Promote the Teaching of Speech to the Deaf), exhorted his colleagues to eliminate the waste represented by extracurricular signing: "in these days of scientific management and of utilization of waste products," it was unacceptable to permit this "waste attending the nonutilization of teaching and learning opportunities." Sign language, he believed, would "defeat, by process of waste by just so much as it is used" the attempt to teach oral English. The "waste from signs in our schools is extravagance—all waste is that—and if waste were a statutory offense, this waste which is so costly to helpless deaf children, not to say to the State, would be criminal."[74]

John Dutton Wright, principal of the Wright Oral School, agreed. In 1915 he wrote that it was "absurd to expect to do efficient oral work without surrounding our oral pupils with a speech atmosphere and insisting upon their passing all their waking hours" using speech and lip-reading as their sole means of communication.

A. L. E. Crouter, principal of the Pennsylvania Institution, elucidated what form this "insisting" might take. Ensuring the "future progress and efficiency in the education of deaf children," he wrote, would require more "efficient supervision" of deaf students by hearing adults, "outside of the classroom, on the playground, in the shop, everywhere." This would mean "constant daily association morning, noon, and night with the child"; only then could teachers be certain that students always used their time outside of class constructively.[75]

Another measure of the oralist preoccupation with efficiency was the support they gave to a national movement to rationalize the spelling of English words. The late-nineteenth-century spelling reform movement was advocated with claims that it would increase efficiency and facilitate the Americanization of immigrants; at both points it intersected with the oralist movement. It is not surprising, therefore, to find calls for spelling reform coming from a convention of oralists in 1884: "speed the good work of the spelling reformers," Emma Garrett exhorted her colleagues, for the benefit of "both hearing and deaf children." Alice E. Worcester of the Clarke Institution lamented the "irregularities and inconsistencies" of English spelling, and suggested that all education would benefit "if words were spelled as they are pronounced and pronounced as they are spelled." J. H. Brown reproached the English language for its "orthographic irregularities," urging that something be done about this "unsystematic manner of representing spelling." Throughout the history of English, he complained, "there does not appear to have been any attempt at a scientific representation of sounds by letters."[76]

Oralism and spelling reform also intersected in a curious episode that illustrates how highly oralists valued efficiency. Early in the nineteenth century, Alexander Melville Bell had devised a system of phonetic spelling capable of representing any sound humans were capable of articulating. He had designed it as an aid to elocution and called it "Visible Speech." His son, Alexander Graham Bell, saw potential in it for teaching speech to deaf children and introduced the system to teachers of the deaf. For several decades it enjoyed great popularity among speech teachers, nearly all of whom were familiar with its use.[77]

One aspect of Visible Speech that troubled a few oralists such as Emma Garrett, however, was that the symbols "have no currency outside the school-room." Since the oralist movement aspired to make the education of deaf children no different from the education of hearing children, this made Garrett uneasy. Using an arcane system of representation with deaf students that was not used in the world outside was too much like using sign language. On the other hand, if the symbols were to be adopted nationally as a "universal alphabet," she ventured, that would be a different matter; in that case her objections would be obviated, and it would certainly be an "improvement upon our defective alphabet."[78] This, as a matter of fact, was just what some oralists advocated.

In reply to a letter that appeared in the *Scientific American* in 1907, which had called for simplified spelling for the benefit of the "Anglo-Saxon commercial world," Mabel G. Bell, wife of Alexander Graham Bell, protested that "science already offers a perfect phonetic alphabet," the "great scientific invention" known as Visible Speech. While it was not yet widely known outside of deaf education circles, she explained, it soon would be; her husband was dedicating his father's estate to the publishing of books written in Visible Speech symbols, and to the "training of persons whose profession it shall be to teach its use in public schools."[79] Some oralist teachers even took to writing some of their correspondence in Visible Speech symbols; a deaf woman in later years recalled receiving such a letter from a teacher soon after her graduation: "the only thing contained in it of which I am certain is my own surname at the beginning, the writer's full name at the end, and the place from which it came, but that I discovered by a diligent scanning of the post-mark. I am still waiting to learn all that comes between those two names."[80] The *Association Review* began a "Visible Speech Department" in 1908 to promote the system, publishing articles on its uses and stories written with its symbols. While books were indeed published written entirely in Visible Speech symbols, their use seems to have been largely limited to oralist teachers and their classrooms. They did not apparently catch on anywhere else.[81] Likewise, the spelling reform movement—a distant cousin to oralism, to be sure, but in the same extended family of efficiency reforms—never made much headway and eventually passed quietly away.

The emphasis on practicality and efficiency, beyond its more obvious impact on the debate, had the additional and more subtle effect of undermining the persuasiveness of the traditional manualist arguments, which were of the most "impractical" nature. The beauty of sign language, its claims to refinement, and its similarity to Latin were virtues that had largely lost their appeal. Lacking visible productive worth in the economy or a constructive role in evolutionary progress, beauty lacked utilitarian value. The argument that sign language was beautiful or that the speech of deaf people was not made no sense to oralists. Emma Garrett told the Convention of American Instructors of the Deaf that "it is sometimes urged by those who are opposed to speech for the deaf, that some of them do not speak pleasantly, but I do not consider that any argument against it." Others agreed that "surely the voice of a deaf person, no matter how exact the rhythm, can never be considered musical or pleasant to the ear; but it is the utility of speech that is appreciated."[82]

Fred DeLand in 1908 recounted a story of a father who, in the early days of oral education, decided to transfer his deaf daughter from a manual school to an oral school. A manualist teacher reportedly protested, "but she will lose this beautiful language of signs." To DeLand, this was a preposterous sentiment, and he could only explain it as an expression of a "delusion that appeared to have taken possession of every educational institution in the country."[83]

"Refinement" no longer possessed the cultural value that it had earlier in the century. Even if it had, sign language had lost its claim to refinement once evolutionary thought relegated it to the world of the primitive. The ancient world had also lost status for similar reasons, and so the association of sign language with the world of ancient Rome was no longer a helpful one. An evolutionary worldview meant that it was more difficult to view past societies as the equal, let alone the superior, of those in the present; the ancient world was no longer held up as the pinnacle of Western cultural achievement, in part a result of evolutionary theory. The study of the past might be useful for understanding the "laws of development," or to satisfy the yearnings of the nostalgic, but for the majority who welcomed progress and modernity, it no longer served as the model and exemplar it once had. The way in which sign language and the ancient world would be linked in the post-evolutionary world was evident in a paper given by Garrick Mallery to the American Association of Science and reprinted in the *American Annals of the Deaf*. In it he argued that all cultures "retained marks of their rude origin," among them the use of sign language or gestures; the less advanced a culture was, the more distinct the marks would be. Pantomime and "elaborate rules for gestures in oratory" were prominent in ancient Rome, he noted, and modern Italians, as one of the less developed European peoples, continued to use many of the ancient gestures.[84]

While manualists went on extolling the glories of ancient Rome, oralists were more in tune with the current status of foreign nations in America. The nation most in favor at the time was not ancient Rome but modern Germany, the undisputed leader in both science and education. As Bruce Kimball has pointed out in his study of professionalism in America, Germany was the model for late-nineteenth-century American educators and academics, and "the attribution of American practices to Germany . . . helped to legitimate those practices."[85] It did so for the cause of oralism, since Germany was seen as the fountainhead of oral methods. Just as American scholars traveled to Germany for prestigious advanced degrees, so did oralist educators make pilgrimages to Germany to study German technique and report back to their colleagues.[86] The preeminence of Germany meant to many Americans that if Germany was practicing oralism and America was not, something was probably wrong with American practice.

Emma Garrett pointed out that "practical Germany has taught the deaf to use their voices for a hundred years" and intimated it was about time that American schools caught up.[87] Aware of the higher prestige among Americans that "practical Germany" possessed—as compared with hopelessly impractical France—oralists took to reminding their listeners at every opportunity of the respective points of origin of the two methods. In the Detroit *Tribune,* Alexander Graham Bell carefully explained that the sign method was "known as the French system while the oral method was known as the German system." In letters to newspapers he took pains to mention that "oral schools were established by Heinicke in Germany and Braidwood in Great Britain, and the sign language method originated in the school of Abbé de l'Epée in Paris, France." While manualists had always said that sign language was a natural language created by deaf people, oralists referred to it as the invention of the Abbé de l'Epée, and took to calling it "the De l'Epée sign language" in their writings. One pointed out that "this sign language was used by the French for years, and possibly suited them temperamentally." Sign language was not only a foreign invention, they implied, but the invention of a nation associated in America with effete aristocracy, romanticism, and, like sign language, glories belonging to a past age.[88]

The debate over sign language represented a clash between two cultural stances, one in decline, the other rising to dominance. Andrew West, in "Must the Classics Go?" characterized the opponents of classical education as those who "care chiefly for what prepares immediately for some specific calling," "nursed on money-worship" and "imbued with the money-making spirit of the age." In the modern world, he argued, the merely " 'effective,' the 'realistic,' the perversely vulgar . . . is too apt to crowd out the thoughtful and refined."[89] Edward M. Gallaudet's argument for sign language paralleled West's assessment. He opposed those who insisted on practicality in education, maintaining that the proper conception of education should be a more "elevated one"; that while it should include "how to make a living" and "the imparting of a knowledge of the language of the country," it should go beyond that, for its "most important aim is to raise to the highest possible point of development the moral character of each individual." He challenged educators to ask themselves: "will it add to the happiness of the deaf to take the Sign-language away from them?"[90]

Deaf people thought not. But Gallaudet misconstrued the fight over sign language. It was not a question of what deaf people wished for themselves, or what they believed might add to their happiness. Sign language and the deaf community were chiefly metaphors for other matters. The real battle was fought on a more rarefied plane, encompassing such questions as the larger purposes of education in a democratic and industrializing society, the relative values of beauty and utility, and the locus and character of cultural authority in America. Indeed, occupying a central place in the fight was a late-nineteenth-century debate over the nature of nature itself, a topic to which we now turn.

FIVE

The Natural Language
of Signs: Nature

Linguists today speak of sign language*s* in the plural—American Sign Language, British Sign Language, Danish Sign Language, and so on—which, like spoken languages, are specific to their respective linguistic communities and are mutually unintelligible.[1] They describe them as "natural languages," meaning that they evolved within these specific communities and are creatures of culture and history, as opposed to such artificial languages as Esperanto, signed English systems, or computer languages. To modern linguists, sign languages (some prefer the term *signed* languages as a better equivalent to *spoken* languages) do not differ in essence from their spoken counterparts. The assumption that there is one universal sign language, widespread among the general public, is dismissed as a popular misconception arising merely from ignorance. The demonstration that sign languages are "natural" in this sense has been central to the project of the last several decades of rehabilitating the reputation of sign languages among hearing people and demonstrating that they are worthy of equal status and respect among the languages of the world.

Nineteenth-century manualists, however, did not usually speak of "sign language," and certainly not of "American Sign Language." (The latter term originated in the 1960s.) Instead, they spoke of "*the* sign language" or "*the* language of signs" (in addition to, as we have seen, "the language of pantomime" and "the language of gesture"). *108* They believed the language of signs to be universal, in this way fundamentally unlike spoken languages—it would never have oc-curred to them to say "the language of speech." Sign language was for them a single language that had spontaneously appeared among diverse peoples throughout the world and throughout history. The sign language of American deaf people was a variant of the sign languages of Britain, Russia, and every other country of the world, and it was the same as the language used by American Indians and Australian aborigines.[2]

From a modern perspective, it is difficult to understand why manualist teachers thought this way about sign language. The same differences between the various sign languages that exist now existed then, which to late twentieth-century eyes indicate obviously differ-ent languages. How could they fail to see that the differences between German and French signs and grammar were akin to those between German and French words and grammar, that these differences indi-cated different languages, and that sign language was therefore not singular but plural? They did not reach their conclusions as a result of ignorance—no one has studied the language of American deaf people more intensively than they, and they were quite familiar with foreign sign languages. Rather, they came to it through a way of thinking about sign language, deafness, and ultimately human nature that was fundamentally different from that which prevails in the twentieth century.

While manualists respected sign language as a *bona fide* language, it was to them a language unlike any other. If manualists could not demonstrate empirically that sign language preceded spoken language in time and was therefore closer to Creation, they could demonstrate logically, they believed, that it preceded speech in essence and was therefore closer to nature. Like modern linguists, they described sign language as "natural," but they meant something quite different by that word. Sign language as a "natural" language did not mean, for them, that it was like spoken languages. Indeed, they conceived of the naturalness of sign language in *opposition* to the artificiality of spoken language. Sign language was not a product of culture, as spoken languages were. It was instead a direct expression of nature itself.

This was by no means an idea original to them. Condillac, whom at least some manualists had read, had said much the same thing in the previous century.[3] Manualists, however, developed a nineteenth-century American interpretation of the concept, one that partook of agrarian myths, evangelical Protestantism, and American Romanticism. As long as the meaning of "nature" and "natural" for most Americans remained relatively constant, the manualist interpretation was sustained. By the late nineteenth century, however, naturalness as an ideal was being challenged and eventually was not merely defeated but *colonized* by the competing ideal of "normality." This intellectual and indeed moral shift in American culture was crucial to the reversal in attitudes toward sign language and the deaf community.

What was the manualist conception of language before the shift occurred? In 1869 the Reverend Collins Stone described spoken words as "simply the conventional and arbitrary representatives of ideas." When first encountered, words "convey no meaning whatever to the mind" in and of themselves but "must be explained by some other means, before they have any significance or power of suggestion."[4] Like most nineteenth-century scholars, manualists stressed that modern spoken languages were essentially arbitrary, in most cases possessing no necessary or natural connection to the ideas they expressed. In the distant past words may have been mimetic—a few words retained qualities of onomatopoeia—but most had long ago slipped their moorings with reality and were free floating signifiers, owing their significance merely to social agreement.

Sign language, however, was a different sort of language. Stone asserted that, unlike spoken language, sign language "needs no process of translation to make it understood." J. C. Covell noted that while "words, with few exceptions, have no natural correspondence with the things which they express," signs were "imitative in their very essence." Building fluency in sign language meant acquiring a facility at "imitating nature." For R. H. Kinney, it was "the language of nature." Thomas H. Gallaudet agreed, claiming that the "natural language of signs" was "not an arbitrary, conventional language" but rather "a picture-like and symbolical language, calling up the objects and ideas which it is designed to denote in a portraying and suggestive way, which no oral, written or printed language can do." Sign language, in short, "copies nature."[5]

Luzerne Rae illustrated how meaning was inherent in visual signs: "a straight line, whether traced on the earth or gestured in the air," is understood everywhere to signify "moral rectitude," while a crooked one stands for the opposite. "The distinction is not arbitrary," Rae argued; "it evidently has its ground and origin, *in rerum natura* [in the nature of things]." Like smiling, frowning, and other facial expressions denoting emotion, he believed such signs were instantly and universally understood.[6]

Whether or not natural signs existed prior to arbitrary language in history, Rae had no doubt that they necessarily preceded them in the life of the individual. People learned the words of arbitrary spoken languages, he contended, only through the use of natural signs: "you pronounce to me, for example, the word *aversion*. I can get no hint at all in regard to your meaning, until you add the natural sign of the word, which is, the turning away from an object with an expression of dislike upon the countenance." Even after the meanings of arbitrary words were learned, they still required the mediation of natural signs in order to function as language. When we hear a word, it "suggests some natural sign"; then "this natural sign suggests, in its turn, the particular thought or feeling which it is adapted to express, which was in your mind when you spoke to me, and which is now in mine also. *How* it does this . . . we cannot tell. It is one of the ultimate facts of nature."[7]

Natural signs occupied an intermediate space between reality and arbitrary words. "Words of themselves do not convey ideas except at second-hand," wrote Benjamin D. Pettingill, a teacher at the Pennsylvania Institution, who elaborated the distinction between artificial and natural language: "All artificial languages are destitute of any life or meaning in themselves. They are based upon a natural language, and derive their significance from it. This natural language consists chiefly of expressions of the countenance, gestures, and involuntary muscular movements; the varied intonations of the voice; the actions which accompany words spoken or written, and pictures, whether made in the air or on paper, or otherwise."[8]

Sign language was for Pettingill "a more natural, a more expressive, and, in many respects, a better language" because, as "representatives of external and internal nature," gesture signs were "self-interpreting and universally intelligible." While deaf people used gesture signs far more than hearing people, and some nationalities such as the French and Italians gestured more than others, gestures were natural and common to all of humanity—even the reserved British and Germans were apt to use gesture for emphasis and "forcible" expression, he wrote. For authority he turned to Quintilian, who observed in the first century A.D. that despite "the great diversity of tongues pervading all nations and people, the language of the hands appears to be common to all men."[9]

Now, anyone unversed in American Sign Language who has watched a conversation among American deaf people without an interpreter knows full well it is anything but transparent. Such an observer has no more chance of following the conversation than a listener with no knowledge of Russian would have following a conversation between two Muscovites. American Sign Language, as it is used today, is by no means what anyone would consider pantomime. While many of the signs of American Sign Language and other national sign languages can be traced to pantomimic or iconic origins, most are no longer perceived to be iconic by their users but rather function as arbitrary linguistic symbols just like spoken words.[10] Apparently, therefore, either the sign language in use today in the United States is far different from that used in the last century and has become considerably less transparent over the years or the manualists must have meant something different by "natural," "picture-like," and "universally intelligible" than is apparent at first glance.

It does appear that sign languages (and probably all languages) become less mimetic and more arbitrary over time. Nancy Frishberg was one of the first modern linguists to describe in detail the process by which "signs have become less transparent, pantomimic, and iconic, [and] more arbitrary, conventionalized, and symbolic." Many signs are originally created by visual description—in some ways similar to pantomime yet governed by the rules of the language—emphasizing the salient attributes of the object, action, or concept in question. When on subsequent occasions the same signers wish to describe the same object, action, or concept, a more abbreviated version of the series of gestures first employed will suffice. Eventually, a single sign, depicting one attribute from the series first used, will be all that is necessary, and that one sign may then evolve further and further away from the original pantomimic one until all iconicity is lost and its connection with the original is no longer apparent. What was at first a species of rule-governed pantomime has become an abstracted sign, no more self-interpreting than a spoken word.[11]

American Sign Language, then, probably has become less mimetic since the nineteenth century. This is not, however, a sufficient explanation for the manualists' description of sign language, nor even the better part of one. The tendency to move from iconicity to arbitrariness is probably far more rapid during the very early stages in the development of a sign language than later. Descriptions of sign language at the middle of the nineteenth century give every indication that the sign language that deaf people and teachers of the deaf used was already composed mostly of signs that we would today describe as arbitrary. These accounts make it abundantly clear that sign language required years to learn, that it was not transparent to those who had not learned it, and that it was a highly complex and sophisticated language. Why, then, did manualists use such terms as "natural," "universally intelligible," and "self-interpreting" to describe it?

Manualists would have answered that all people possess an innate capacity to use and understand sign language but not everyone cultivates equally the art of using it. The distinction they made between the complex sign language found in their schools and the gestures and simple pantomime of which any uninstructed person was capable was a difference of degree not of kind. "Based as it is upon imitation and not upon any fixed and arbitrary standard," explained J. A. Ayres, "its precision depends in a great degree upon the skill of him who uses it."[12] The unskilled used "simple, uncultivated signs" while those adept in the art used "cultivated signs." The latter were more complex and less transparent than their uncultivated counterparts, yet they were still natural *so long as they had been originally derived from simple pantomimic signs*. Manualists saw cultivated signs as improved natural signs that retained their essential naturalness. Lewis Weld, for example, emphasized that the class of signs he termed "strictly natural" included "not those signs merely which are natural to an infant, or to a very ignorant mind, but to the most enlightened also, and applicable to the most elevated subjects of thought as well as the simplest."[13]

While the "natural language of signs," according to Thomas H. Gallaudet, was "spontaneously employed by the deaf-mute," with practice it was "gradually enlarged and rendered more and more accurately descriptive." Upon arrival at a school for the deaf, the deaf child "finds himself, as it were, among his countrymen." The teachers and other students there "use his native language; more copious, indeed, and elevated than that to which he had been accustomed, but yet virtually the same." The deaf child recognized the principles of this cultivated sign language as "the same which constituted the basis of those very signs which he and others around him have already invented and used" at home; because this cultivated language "retains its original features," deaf children learned it rapidly.[14]

Pettingill explained how it was that the uninstructed were unable to understand this "universal" language. While no "purely artificial and arbitrary signs are used in any of our institutions" and while "all of our signs have some intrinsic significance," it was nevertheless the case that "for the sake of dispatch we often abridge our signs in conversing with adepts in the sign-language." This abridgement, "of course, diminishes their intelligibility and expressiveness to outside observers who are not familiar with the sign-language."[15] In the manualist conception, then, the signs commonly used among fluent signers were, in a sense, *compressed* versions of ordinary pantomimic gestures rather than fundamental alterations of them. So long as the signer could trace the etymology of the cultivated sign to its iconic origins, it remained in essence a natural sign. Thus, even if the uninitiated could not understand sign language as used by adepts, it remained natural because it always had the potential to be *decompressed* or expanded back to its original, more highly elaborated form. It was in this way that sign language was "self-interpreting."

Thus, for example, a deaf person trying for the first time to communicate a request for milk might first pantomime a cow, and then a person milking it with alternating up and down hand motions while squeezing the fists. Presumably the modern sign for milk— simply a couple of quick squeezes of one fist, without the up and down motion and usually with an altered hand orientation—comes from such origins. It is not a sign decipherable by one who does not know its meaning, and it probably most often is learned by children as an arbitrary sign rather than as an iconic representation. Yet, according to the manualist definition, it is natural because it is derived from pantomime and, if necessary, can be expanded back to its original pantomimic form.

This conception of sign language explains many accounts by manualists of conversations in "the sign language" with American Indians or with deaf people from foreign lands.[16] It explains the story of Thomas H. Gallaudet's meeting in 1839 with the *Amistad* rebels, the Africans who, after overpowering the crew of the Cuban slave ship *Amistad* and bringing the ship to the United States, were captured and imprisoned at Hartford to await trial before the District Court. Gallaudet visited them there and reportedly "carried on a conversation of considerable length" through "natural signs," eliciting from them "information respecting the families they had left in Africa, besides some particulars of their own recent history."[17] Such conversations occurred not in sign language per se or, as the manualists would have it, in cultivated signs, but by using the expanded or elaborated form of the signs—that is, through the practiced and skillful use of pantomime. The manualist description of sign language as natural arose, then, not out of the presence of actual iconicity in the language as typically used, but from a belief that most signs, unlike words, retained essential ties with their iconic origins.[18]

This conception of the natural was rooted in Romantic-era assumptions about the interconnectedness of human activity—cultivation, that is to say—with nature. While American Romantics celebrated nature, they were ambivalent about *untouched* nature. Wilderness might be inspirational, but it also represented a failure to satisfy the biblical commandment that humans till the earth and make it fruitful. They were inclined to prefer nature that was cultivated yet not despoiled—"improved" land, in the parlance of the age. A landscape tamed and improved by human toil still deserved to be called natural so long as it was thought to be in harmony with nature—unlike the city, which was distrusted and seen as antithetical to nature. Alongside paeans to forested mountains, Romantic writers juxtaposed equally fervent praise for bucolic scenes of farms and pastures, while nature artists depicted farmhouses, country villages, and fields of crops as integral aspects of the natural landscape.[19]

The image of America as a vast garden, the "Garden of the World," became one of the central symbols of antebellum America. Most Americans of the time imagined nature in the beginning not as wilderness, of course, but as a garden, and America was commonly depicted as a new Eden, a place where innocence was regained, and where humanity might toil in harmony with nature and the divine will.[20] In the same way that their contemporaries saw no necessary contradiction in considering cultivated land "natural," manualists saw no contradiction when they spoke of "cultivating the natural language of signs." Nature and culture were not necessarily divided one against the other. The cultivation of sign language was not incompatible with calling it a natural language so long as nature's laws were obeyed and the language remained *in harmony* with nature.

Just as Eden was a garden and not a wilderness, so was the *language* used by Adam and Eve, whether spoken or signed, undoubtedly a cultivated one, according to the manualists; it would have been "copious and precise," capable of expressing the full range of human thought and emotion. Uncultivated signs aroused the same ambivalence as untouched forests—perhaps direct expressions of God's handiwork, untouched and unsullied by human sin yet incomplete until humankind had fulfilled its mission to till the earth and to subdue it. As we saw in the first chapter, uneducated deaf people were themselves depicted ambivalently as inhabiting a place of untouched potential, of both innocence and ignorance. Like deaf people, and like the uncut forest or the uncleared field, sign language left in its natural state was incomplete. Also like them, it could be cultivated and made fruitful.

While the individual signs of sign language might be, within definite limits, significantly altered and yet still retain their ties to nature, manualists claimed not only that individual signs were essentially natural but that their arrangement in sentences was as well, and here alterations were a trickier question: they believed sign language to have, strictly speaking, no grammar at all (which would come as a surprise to modern linguists who have devoted much time and energy in recent years to elucidating the grammars of the world's sign languages). Grammar was a characteristic of "artificial communication," of modern spoken languages.[21] The language of signs, on the other hand, was ordered not by artificial rules of grammar but by nature itself. Any alteration of syntactical structure was to impose a grammar where none, in nature, existed.

The difficulty the average deaf person had in learning English, the Reverend Stone explained, occurred in large part because when deaf people used sign language, they expressed themselves in the natural order of thought not "in the inverted and arbitrary forms of written language." Rather than "the subject coming first, and the action, quality and object following," as in artificial languages, when the deaf person sought to express something, "the object first attracts his attention, then its qualities, and afterward the other circumstances connected with it." Consequently, when a deaf person attempted to write English, "unless great care is exercised, his sentences are constantly running in the order of his thoughts."[22] Benjamin Talbot, superintendent of the Iowa school, agreed that this "order of signs of which we have been speaking is really not the order of *language,* but the order of thought." A simple example often given was that in sign language, unlike English, the adjective commonly followed the noun. Can anyone, Talbot asked, "think of such a thing as *a black?*" Before thinking of a quality one must first conceive of the object it describes, he insisted. "You can readily think of a black horse, a black table, or a black hat; but the idea of that something, whatever it is, necessarily comes first. The order of thought is *something thought of,* before you attempt to *clothe* it."[23]

The Reverend John R. Keep contended that hearing people had become "so familiar with artificial language, that they cannot be persuaded that the inversions which appear in signs are really in the *thoughts,* as well as in the signs." Sign language followed the order of thought, which in turn followed the order of nature: "Suppose, for example, that I strike a board. I do not strike the vacant air, seeing nothing, and having no idea of anything before me, until after I have struck, when, suddenly, a board rises up to receive the blow. I first see the board, I intend to strike it, and, with it before my sight, I strike. In exact conformity with this necessary order of nature and of fact, in describing this in signs, I say, *I a board strike.*" Keep concluded that it was "against artificial language, then, that the charge of inversion properly rests."[24]

Naturalness did not inhere in gestural communication per se, however, nor artificiality in the spoken. Manualists believed that the original language of Adam and Eve, whether it was spoken or signed, was doubtless a perfectly natural language.[25] Likewise, the ancient spoken languages were more natural than modern languages, since they were closer to the Creation and had had less time to degenerate from the primeval form. This explained, they thought, why sign language apparently resembled ancient languages more than modern ones. The syntactic forms of sign language, according to J. Addison Cary, were common "in those languages where the expressions are the most simple, primitive, natural and spontaneous," such as ancient Greek, Latin, Hebrew, Chinese, and Saxon.[26] Like the languages of the ancient world, sign language was uncorrupted by modern life; unlike spoken languages, it retained its innocence.

Agreeing that naturalness was good and artificiality bad was one thing; agreeing on where to draw the line between them was quite another. All proponents of "following nature" (and there were a great many in nineteenth-century America) confronted the same difficulty. If all could agree, for example, that a small farm was natural and a big city artificial, far less agreement would greet the question of where to place the line that divided them. To what extent could ground be cultivated and landscape altered before they crossed the boundaries of the natural? Similarly, if the gestures of the untutored deaf child were natural, how much and what kind of cultivation could those signs undergo before they verged on the artificial?

Naturalness was not necessarily intrinsic to gestural communication, and just as cities were thought to spoil nature, the wrong kind of human intervention could spoil the naturalness of sign language. If care were not taken, sign language could be made into nothing more than a manual version of artificial spoken language. The ambivalence the manualist generation felt concerning improvements on nature was expressed periodically in controversies over various attempts to improve or otherwise tinker with sign language. One such controversy concerned what were known as "methodical signs."

Methodical signs were first developed in the late eighteenth century by the Abbé de l'Epée, founder of the Institution for Deaf Mutes in Paris, by taking the sign language already in use among deaf Parisians—a "natural" sign language in the terms of both manualists and modern linguists—and extensively modifying it to represent, as a kind of visual code, the French language. He did this by inventing signs to stand for those French words that had no exact equivalents in Parisian sign language, inventing sign affixes to represent gender, parts of speech, and French prefixes and suffixes, and then using the signs in spoken French word order. It was a complicated and cumbersome system designed not for the facile communication of ideas but to precisely represent a spoken language manually. Thus, as Harlan Lane describes it, the word "gives" required five discrete signs to represent "verb, present tense, third person, singular, and 'give.' "[27]

Laurent Clerc brought this system with him from the school in Paris—he had learned it as a student there from Epée's successor, the Abbé Sicard—to the American School at Hartford, where Clerc, Gallaudet, and their colleagues adapted Epée's system to English. Methodical signs were widely used for classroom instruction (in addition to "natural" sign language, finger-spelling, and writing) until the 1830s, when teachers began to seriously question their usefulness. The idea had an inherent attraction since the learning of English was a formidable task for deaf children unable to absorb it from daily exposure in the same way that hearing children did.[28] According to critics, however, methodical signs were too unwieldy, slow, confusing, and difficult to remember for teachers and students alike. By mid-century most teachers used methodical signs sparingly or not at all.[29]

Other than their cumbersomeness (a complaint still made about the various invented systems of signed English used in classrooms today), the principal argument leveled against methodical signs was that they were contrary to nature, abandoning both the natural basis of individual signs and the natural order of thought. A few teachers believed that a simpler methodical sign system might be fashioned in such as way as to retain an essential naturalness. Lewis Weld suggested that natural signs could be altered to represent English words and yet retain their natural quality; so long as "methodical signs are founded on the natural," Weld maintained, "and become properly established and methodized under the culture of those who possess good taste, judgment, and discrimination," he saw no reason to reject them. While J. A. Ayres had occasionally spoken in opposition to methodical signs, he also thought that it might be "possible to use pure signs where the signs were not arbitrary" within a methodical sign system.[30] Most, however, agreed with Harvey Peet, principal of the New York school, who thought that while they were occasionally useful for dictation exercises designed to teach English grammar, "the signs called methodical cannot become colloquial." Sign language "syntax is not accidental," he insisted, but rather "part of the very essence of the language" and could not be altered without destroying the language. "Signs used methodically, as it is termed, tend toward degeneration," charged the Reverend Thomas Gallaudet (eldest son of Thomas H.); "let us keep our noble sign-language free from all the fetters and shackles of the arbitrary rules" that afflict spoken languages.[31]

While the question of methodical signs per se faded after the 1850s, a near-continuous discussion persisted for several decades more on the extent to which sign language might be cultivated, improved, or tampered with. They conceded the difficulty of concisely expressing abstract concepts and categories in signs that could be considered, by their definition, purely natural, and debated the extent to which arbitrary signs, to supplement those provided by nature, were acceptable. At the 1858 convention of American Instructors of the Deaf, a committee was appointed to devise a number of arbitrary signs to be discussed at the next convention. Unfortunately, the committee never made its report—the Civil War intervened and the organization did not meet again until 1868—but it was nevertheless clear that at least some manualists believed the use of arbitrary signs to be justified in the service of greater precision. Still, many insisted that "they must be as few as possible"; others suggested that "slightly arbitrary signs" would be preferable to those entirely so. In fact, before the meeting adjourned, the committee came up with a preliminary list of twelve invented signs; although this was not included in their charge, every one of the signs, as it turned out, was "significant of the root, or element, or sense of the idea." For example, the committee devised a sign to express the concept of "animal." Now, particular animals were represented in natural signs by portraying particular features—a cow its horns, a horse its ears, a tiger its stripes—but the abstract concept of "animal" was more cumbersome to express naturally. Such class nouns were usually denoted by listing three members of the class—in this case, perhaps cow, horse, cat—with an inflection that showed that the class as a whole, not the three individual members, was indicated (ASL signers today still represent certain class nouns in this way). The committee intended to replace this method with an arbitrary sign, but the sign they came up with was a compound that literally signified "a breathing body." Every other sign they devised also bore either some natural significance or was a compound of naturally significant signs. Even when giving themselves permission to depart from nature, manualists instinctively hewed as closely to it as they could.[32]

Another way that teachers sometimes made signs "slightly arbitrary" was by incorporating finger-spelling handshapes into natural signs in order to represent specific English words. While today such "initialized signs" are common, they presented a serious challenge to the manualist conception of sign language as natural. A younger member of the teaching profession, Isaac Lewis Peet, in 1868 proposed a lengthy list of such signs. A few of his proposals—for instance, that the sign translated as *law* be initialized to stand for the words *rule* and *principle*—are in common use today. Most of them, such as initializing the sign for *stay* to indicate *continue, dwell, reside,* and *abide,* either never caught on or have long since passed out of use. Such signs were viewed suspiciously or rejected outright by many manualists, especially the older generation. "This method is entirely arbitrary," J. M. Francis argued, "and opposed to the genius of the language." The "preservation of our art as a natural language," he warned, depended upon preventing the "substitution of arbitrary for natural signs." Another teacher noted that when choosing among synonymous signs, he would always "select the one I thought most natural."[33] Others were less certain of their position. Lewis Weld suggested that "conventional or arbitrary" signs might be used "for convenience sake and to save time," but only in informal circumstances. They might, for example, be "employed in jesting, but rarely in elevated discourse."[34]

As for syntax, few advocated using sign language in English word order (with some notable exceptions, among them Edward M. Gallaudet).[35] The argument in favor was that this method of signing would help deaf students better learn English while avoiding the cumbersome grammatical contrivances of methodical signs. Most, however, agreed with Robert Patterson of the Ohio school: "Artificial in its character as it is, it wants the life, the fire, and the strength requisite to reach and stir 'the mystic deeps' of the mute's mind" (a mind that differed in essence from the mind of a hearing person, a subject to which we will return).[36] Horace Gillet of the Indiana school argued that signing in the order of English was just as unnatural as depriving deaf people of sign language altogether; it would "darken and often hide the meaning to the pupil, for he does not think in that order." Sign language was a "natural language, to be used according to the peculiar genius of that language," he insisted, while English was a system of "conventional symbols, to be used according to the laws of English syntax"; the two ought not to be mixed. Ordinary laws of syntax were made by human beings and therefore varied among spoken languages; not so sign language, which answered to higher laws. When asked about the rules for the use of this language, John Keep answered, "we have one simple rule, viz: to follow nature."[37]

The ambivalence and uncertainty these teachers experienced when they pondered the naturalness of sign language, their contradictory urges to diligently improve sign language and simultaneously to preserve its naturalness, their struggle to find the ideal proportion of nature and cultivation, paralleled the conflicts other Americans were experiencing trying to reconcile the twin ideals of nature and progress. Manualists sought the improved but unspoiled "middle landscape" in sign language just as other Americans sought it in their land, manners, art, and poetry. This was one reason teachers engaged in such earnest and impassioned debates over sign language—it stood for much outside itself. The controversy was one manifestation of the tension inherent in holding onto the image of America as Eden while at the same time endorsing commercial growth and technological innovation. Sign language was both nature and art, God-given but improved by humankind, highly cultivated but essentially unspoiled. Sign language was one means of reconciling conflicting ideals and making them whole.

Ralph Waldo Emerson had expressed similar concerns in his 1836 essay *Nature*. He too thought that language in past times was "more picturesque" and more rooted in natural imagery than it had of late become. The words of honest and simple people still kept close to nature, however: "It is this which gives that piquancy to the conversation of a strong-natured farmer or back-woodsman, which all men relish." A person's ability to speak in images from nature depended on "the simplicity of his character, that is, upon his love of truth." Speech not grounded in nature was akin to "a paper currency . . . when there is no bullion in the vaults." In the end, "imagery ceases to be created," "old words are perverted to stand for things which are not," and "words lose all power to stimulate the understanding or the affections." Emerson, like many of his contemporaries, feared that "the corruption of man is followed by the corruption of language" and that both were occurring in the "artificial and curtailed life of cities," where thoughts and words were divorced from nature, the wellspring of both truth and eloquence.[38]

Indeed, civilizations were commonly thought to decline because of an *excess* of the very civilized attributes that had been responsible for their rise. (This view was especially common among those with classical educations, such as most manualist teachers, for whom the rise and fall of Rome served as the central model for historical explanation.) Too much civilization led to sterile artificiality and thence to decadence. The five-painting sequence of the popular American landscape painter Thomas Cole, *The Course of Empire* (1836), depicting the five stages of civilization—*Savage State, Pastoral State, Consummation, Destruction,* and *Desolation*—typified this vision. In *Consummation* the seeds of destruction are already present: a landscape dominated by human architecture, monuments to humanity's greatness and conceit.[39] This was the significance that underlay manualist attacks on arbitrary signs. Decadence and decline were always present in their debates. Signs stood for more than their immediate denotation—they represented also the possibilities of health or decline, virtue or decadence, purity or pollution.

For Emerson, as for the manualists, language, money, or anything else was valuable only insofar as it possessed *essential* value. Civilization could not, unaided, create it. Artifice could not produce it. A thing had essential value only if it stood on something solid and eternal, something that transcended human invention. Nature alone, and behind nature the Creator of nature, gave value to things. Manualist teachers did not share Emerson's optimistic faith that honest and well-intentioned people could still ground a robust spoken language in nature, but they shared his valuation of the ideal and instead vested their faith in the natural language of gesture.

The manualists' use of the potent symbolism of nature was not limited to sanctifying the natural roots and uncontrived syntax of sign language. While these features made sign language natural to all of humanity, manualists also claimed it as "the natural language of the deaf." The "natural, spontaneous facility" of the deaf child to communicate "by the expressions of his countenance and appropriate signs and gestures," Thomas H. Gallaudet maintained, demonstrated this fact.[40] Sign language was for the deaf person "an outgrowth of himself, not an appendage," according to the Reverend J. Addison Cary, "the real vernacular of the deaf and dumb"; it was so fundamental to the deaf person's mind that "the sign form is the natural mould in which it must be cast" and constituted "the matrices of his thought."[41]

Speech, conversely, was described as distinctly unnatural to deaf people. When Collins Stone wrote that sign language was "the natural language of the deaf," he added that it was wrong to compel a deaf person "to express his ideas and wants in the, to him, unnatural, distasteful and unmeaning form of words."[42] Robert Patterson of the Ohio school insisted that depriving deaf people of sign language was "unnatural, inhuman, and contrary to reason," and that even deaf children who were confined to an oral education took to "pantomime as naturally as ducks do to water" once they were "released from the unnatural restraints imposed upon them." Since deaf people were cut off from the natural elements of speech—"the modulations of the voice"—and could never acquire an understanding of the "nature of sound," oral communication by the deaf would always be "more automatic than natural."[43]

The opposition of "automatic" to "natural" should begin to suggest the significance of the phrase, "natural language of the deaf." "Automatic" was a word caught up in the nineteenth-century debate over materialism and the question of whether human life was inspired by more than mere mechanical impulse. To call the speech of deaf people automatic was to imply that it did not arise from the soul, but rather was merely the mechanistic act of an automaton. But a remark by Horace Gillet makes the point even more clear: he granted that a limited use of artificial "word signs [initialized signs] or signs in the order of words" might be occasionally justified in the classroom for the circumscribed purpose of teaching English, "as in certain exigencies the skilled physician may use unnatural means to aid nature." But it was well to remember, he reminded his fellow teachers, that "God is the author of nature" and that the "laws of nature can seldom be contravened with profit."[44]

God is the author of nature. This formulation was a commonplace of nineteenth-century natural theology: nature gave visible evidence of God's design and was the tangible expression of his will. So intimately related were "God" and "nature" that the words became virtually interchangeable.[45] One manifestation of their close connection was the popular belief that cures for every disease were available in nature, a belief that sprang from the idea that if God had put disease on the earth, as a merciful God he also would have placed remedies within reach. The advertising of nineteenth-century medicines as "natural remedies" that followed "nature's way" was based on this notion.[46]

Manualists saw sign language as nature's remedy for deafness. To say that sign language was natural to deaf people was to say that God *intended* for deaf people to use it. If deaf children of their own accord turned to gestures to communicate, apparently without being taught to do so, this was good evidence that God had designed it to be so. For T. H. Gallaudet, this "singular language which nature has taught" deaf people, "furnished by a beneficent Providence," was an example of the "great principle of *compensation*" by which "the God of nature" eased the afflictions of his creatures; "the wind has been kindly tempered," in other words, "to the shorn lamb." J. Addison Cary described sign language as a "gift of nature" to the deaf person, "to which he instinctively refers," while B. D. Pettingill insisted that "nature prompts him to [use sign language], and nature is wiser than any teacher."[47] Collins Stone wrote that "the Creator has plainly shown that he designs hearing persons to communicate by speech," but for deaf people "God has provided a language addressed to the eye. This is to the deaf-mute a natural language, and the only natural language."[48]

Luzerne Rae, commenting upon the Genesis passage rendered in the King James Bible as "the spirit of God moved upon the face of the waters," once told his colleagues that the original Hebrew actually described "God breathing upon the deep and waking its waves into motion," which makes a fine metaphor for what education was for manualists: a waking into motion, an *inspiration* that for deaf people depended upon the agency of sign language.[49] Harvey Peet, for instance, suggested that before deaf children of hearing parents went to a school for the deaf, their minds existed in a "torpid and inert state"; the "awakening of faculties is sure to take place spontaneously and rapidly," however, once the deaf child came among other deaf people who were "led by the same instincts and the same mental and physical laws" to use sign language. While the deaf pupil also needed to learn English, it was the language of signs "that penetrates the most directly to his intelligence, which clings the most naturally to his memory." The words of spoken and written languages were "comparatively cold and dead" to deaf people, Peet maintained; "signs alone are for them warm, eloquent, awakening, instinct with living thought and feeling."[50]

Awakening was often compared to the germination of a seed, a metaphor that reveals much of the manualist philosophy. The potential of human beings was contained within them just as plants were contained within seeds. The work of the teacher was to provide the conditions for growth—"the mind cannot grow of itself," wrote Henry Camp, but "requires cultivation to draw it out, as truly as the vegetable world requires the genial influence of the sunshine and the rain"—and to guide the development of character. The instructor would find, Harvey Peet admonished, that "the first tender shoots of character spring up under his eye and hand, and as he trains them, or suffers them to be warped, they will grow."[51] While teachers might give guidance and encouragement, to interfere with the child's natural growth could only do harm. Rejecting Lockean "blank slate" epistemology, manualists generally maintained that individuals came into the world with everything they could ever know already within them; to educate was "not to put things into his mind, but rather to *draw out* into consciousness what is already there." This Platonic understanding of education was, for them, a Christian concept: "The *cultivation* of the intellect is plainly impossible, unless the seeds, the germs of knowledge, have been divinely planted in the mental soil."[52] When education was described as bringing light to darkness, this was meant at times to suggest Christian enlightenment, at others, intellectual development; sometimes it called forth the image of the spring-time sun awakening the dormant seed with light and warmth. Often, all three were suggested at once—for this generation of romantic evangelicals, there could be no clear line between them.

This was the manualists' understanding of the human project on earth—to seek to understand the *nature* of the world and to see that it grew and developed into its intended state. This was progress—a process of unfolding to reach an already determined end. The same was also true of the growth of deaf education: "The spread of Institutions may be likened to the growth of a plant," wrote J. Addison Cary; "the stalk springs from the earth, and puts forth leaf after leaf, and branch following branch, until the flower appears" (which in this instance was to be a college for the deaf).[53] It was also true of individuals. Deaf people, they saw, spontaneously used their hands, faces, and bodies to communicate. They reasoned that if deaf people associated with one another and with teachers who were willing to learn their natural mode of communication, then the nature of the deaf person could unfold to reach its greatest perfection. Their task was to create an environment in which the true nature of deaf people—their inherent and instinctive ways, what today is described as comprising "Deaf culture"—could manifest itself.

Manualist teachers invested sign language with this complex system of cultural meanings revolving around the central concept of nature. The task of following nature, with its multiple layers of meaning, was no simple matter, however, and few of them tried to reconcile their varied and often incompatible uses of "natural." In some cases sign language was natural in an absolute sense, set off from the artificiality of spoken languages. In others, however, the distinction was relative—sign language was natural specifically to deaf people, as speech was to the hearing. Most manualists moved easily from one meaning of natural to the other, referring to sign language as "the natural language of signs" in one breath and as "the natural language of the deaf" in the next, without any sense of inconsistency or attempts to relate one to the other. Harvey Peet, however, was the exception. Peet attempted in a series of articles on sign language to combine both meanings in a coherent account.

Peet's understanding of sign language differed somewhat from that of most manualists, yet he managed by his own eccentric means to come to similar conclusions about its essential nature. He began one of his many articles on the nature of deaf people and their language by recounting a story, told by Herodotus, of an attempt by the ancient king Psammetichus of Egypt to ascertain the original language of humanity. The king ordered that two children be raised in strict seclusion and allowed to hear no human voice. He waited anxiously to see what their first words would be, believing that, with no models to learn from, the children would spontaneously speak to one another in the natural language of the human race. After some time, the children's attendant heard them say the word *bec,* which was Phrygian for *bread.* Disappointed, the king reluctantly conceded that Phrygian, not Egyptian, was the natural and original language of the world.[54]

Peet recounted this story because he saw in it a parallel to what he and his colleagues learned from deaf children: "in the case of each child who comes into the world without the sense of hearing, and is brought up among persons unaccustomed to communicate by gestures, the experiment of Psammetichus . . . is tried over again." For Peet, as for most of his contemporaries, to ask what was the original language of humanity was to ask what Adam and Eve spoke. Further, "original" and "natural" were so intimately related that they were practically the same thing. The first language was undeniably the most natural language possible, since it was the direct expression of God's intent, and all later languages were products of a humanity fallen from grace.

The question of the Edenic language was often debated, as was the problem of how Adam and Eve came to know that language in the first place: were they created with language inherent within them or did they have to learn it? If Adam and Eve spoke spontaneously without instruction, as Peet believed, the language they used must be inherent in the human soul. If it were inherent in the soul, it must still be accessible, for the faculties of the soul did not change over time. This was the significance of the "natural" experiment with deaf children to which the manualists considered themselves fortunate witnesses; the result of that experiment, most of them concluded, was that sign language must have been the original language. Peet did not come to this conclusion. He did, however, decide that sign language, while not in fact the original language, was nevertheless closer to it, and therefore more natural, than any spoken language in use in the modern world.[55]

Since all children vocalized from birth, Peet presumed that human beings must possess a "natural instinct to utter sounds." Even deaf infants expressed their first emotions by crying out: "in them, as well as in others, the cry of pain or of hunger precedes by months the gesture of anger or of supplication." The impulse to vocalize arose from the "natural overflow" of thought and emotion, and speech was the instinctive channel for this overflow.[56] In this sense, then, speech was more natural than sign language, and Adam and Eve must have possessed the instinct to vocalize as well. Unlike infants, however, they apparently needed no period of learning to advance from inarticulate vocalization to true language since, according to the biblical account, both spoke instantly and spontaneously. While this ran contrary to all human experience, experience was not a reliable guide in this case, Peet reasoned, since it was equally true that "according to all human experience, every oak sprung from an acorn." "There must," however, "have been a first oak." If this first oak came "from the ground at the will of the Creator," it was equally plausible to believe that Adam and Eve were created fully developed in both body and mind, with no need of instruction, "possessed of an instinctive power of speech." Peet enlisted the authority of Milton, who had Adam say (emphases added by Peet):

Straight towards Heaven my wondering eyes I turned,
And gazed awhile the ample sky, till raised

By quick *instinctive motion up I sprung,*
As thitherward endeavoring, and *upright*
Stood on my feet . . .
But who I was, or where, or from what cause,
Knew not; *to speak I tried, and forthwith spake;*
My tongue obeyed, and readily could name
Whate'er I saw.[57]

Ever since Adam's tongue obeyed his instinctive urge to name the things of the world, each succeeding generation took its language from the previous one, Peet reasoned. As language was passed down from parent to child, generation after generation, each less perfect in body and mind than the original pair, words and grammar inevitably changed and degenerated. Even apart from the confounding of tongues at Babel, languages steadily diverged from one another among the different tribes and nations. The speech of humanity became more and more distant from that pristine language spoken in Eden. Words that originally had inherent ties to their objects lost their natural significance and became increasingly arbitrary, corrupted by profane use among a fallen people.[58]

Nevertheless, Peet believed that modern speech still retained certain natural elements. While *words* were themselves nearly always arbitrary, *speech,* being more than a mere string of words, was not. Speech included "intonations, which, by their appropriateness [that is, their natural signification], seem to express even more than the word itself." This was what hearing infants at first responded to, only later learning the denotations of arbitrary words. The "melody of sound" was not ornamental but fundamental to spoken language.[59]

Deaf people, however, could never know this most natural, and therefore most potent, aspect of speech, "the grace, the impressiveness, the sense of interior life, which words derive from the tones of the living voice." The inability to hear these tones diverted thought and feeling "exclusively to the other natural channel, that of gestures and expressions of the eye and features." While speech was natural for hearing people, then, inasmuch as they understood and used its natural elements "instinctively," true speech for deaf people was impossible since it would necessarily lack those natural elements requisite to a complete language. "Artificial articulation," he argued, "however far it is carried, is not speech" but "simply a set of arbitrary signs," and therefore "useless as a medium of thought and reasoning." "It is only signs," Peet concluded, "that can in any measure replace to the deaf what speech is to the hearing."[60]

Most deaf children, however, were born into families with no knowledge of sign language. (Peet did not address the issue of deaf children of deaf parents.) As a result, the experiment of the Egyptian king and to some extent the story of Eden were reenacted every time deaf children perforce invented their own language to communicate with those around them. The deaf child, having become "accustomed to have his pantomimic efforts received with kind interest, at the first sight of an elephant or a lion, will give this new animal a fitting sign-name." Thus was every deaf child Adam, beholding the things of the world and naming them. As with Adam, for whom "the names came spontaneously to his tongue," the sign-names of the deaf child were neither arbitrary nor the products of convention; arising directly from the soul within, they were endowed with inherent meaning.[61]

This language of signs that deaf children invented to communicate with those around them was not the original language of humankind. It did, however, come out of the *same natural instinct for language given to the first humans,* for the descendants of Adam and Eve still possessed the "germ" of that ability. Furthermore, unlike modern languages, sign language was unsullied by centuries of worldly use. Even though Adam and Eve voiced the language given to them in the garden, and deaf people gestured theirs, both expressed themselves in the pure and untainted tones of a language arising directly from the uncorrupted soul. Peet thought that neither sign language nor any other language created since the Fall could ever be quite so perfect as the original language of Eden; that language had "its origin in a fuller development of faculties" than any human since could ever possess and was "a more perfect and harmonious language" than any subsequent language could possibly be. Sign language, nevertheless, was *akin* to that original language, partaking of its spirit and sharing in its pristine clarity.[62]

The twin ideas that sign language was a "natural" language and that deaf people were more "innocent" and less corrupted than hearing people meant that the deaf education became for manualists a branch of natural theology. Deaf people and their language bore explicit witness to God's design in a world in which truth was darkened and obscured by the conventions of civilization. The manualists' understanding of nature, however, and of how their work fit within its realm, was destined to be short-lived. The face of nature began to change during the second half of the nineteenth century. A new definition grew alongside the older one of the manualist era, one that would in the end overshadow if not entirely eclipse the old understanding of what constituted the natural. It was the concept of normality.

SIX

The Unnatural Language
of Signs: Normality

The manualists' discovery of nature in the language of signs and their expressions of faith in the grandeur and power of nature left oralist reformers unmoved. In the first place, as we saw in chapter 2, nature to them was what humanity was struggling to transcend through evolutionary progress. The oralist teacher Katherine Bingham, for example, told of how the explorer Sir Richard Burton had found "somewhere in the ends of the earth where no gleam of civilization had penetrated, a people of the lowest type, who could not communicate with each other in the dark, but lighted blazing fires in their huts at night, before which they exchanged such limited ideas as they possessed, using the identical 'natural' signs, no doubt, that are so eloquently extolled, and so sedulously cultivated in the great institutions of our land at the present day." This was one way of thinking of the natural, and it held little attraction for those steeped in the idea of evolution as progress. There was "a natural age for signs," she wrote, "and it is the same in the man as in the race—the age of infancy—to which signs correspond as an expression of small mental power."[1]

The generational and cultural differences between manualists and oralists were both more profound and more confounding than this, however. Oralists also insisted, contrary to manualist claims, that *speech* was the natural way for civilized humans, whether hearing or deaf, to communicate, and that the use of sign language in the mod-
132 ern world was in fact *not natural at all*. In this case they were using

"natural" to mean something quite different from what Bingham had meant in the above example, and something quite different from earlier usages common among manualists. As might be expected, when oralists and manualists argued over what was natural and what was not, as in so many other areas of their debate, their arguments did not meet head on. The confused debate that ensued over whether sign language was natural was a surface indication of deeper movements. The very idea of nature and the natural was undergoing radical change in the second half of the nineteenth century, the consequences of which persist into our own time. Inevitably, manualists and oralists argued past each other, usually unaware that they spoke the same words to express different things or that their mutual misunderstanding in the small world of deaf education was one sign of a sea change occurring in Western culture.

The common vocabulary manualists and oralists shared deceived them at every encounter. Miscommunication occurred over the most basic of questions. Did oralists, for example, teach deaf children entirely without the use of sign language as they claimed? Manualists said no. It was, in the first place, clearly impossible to do so and, moreover, they had firsthand evidence that oralists did not. After visits to schools that claimed to be exclusively oral, manualists invariably reported back to their colleagues—in the self-satisfied tones of those who have found proof of what they knew to be true all along— that sign language was indeed used and used regularly. True, they would point out, it was not used very well—the signs were simple and crude—but it was used nevertheless. Oralists retorted that this was nonsense, that they certainly did not use sign language and indeed could not do so since most of them did not even know sign language. Each side accused the other of dishonesty, hypocrisy, or willful blindness. The key to the confused debate lay in the confusion over what was "natural."

In 1873 B. D. Pettingill complained that oralists were apt to make "frequent announcements to the public that in the instruction which they give to their pupils in language the use of signs is entirely dispensed with." This was absurd on the face of it, Pettingill wrote. Since signs were intermediate between words and reality, all children, hearing and deaf, necessarily learned words through signs. For example, teachers and parents used signs when they taught words by pointing at objects or pictures, pantomiming, and demonstrating emotional states with the face and body. "I have often wished for an opportunity to inquire," Pettingill wrote with heavy sarcasm, " 'Do the teachers employed in those institutions never smile?' " A smile was a sign not unlike others used in sign language, "one of the most important and expressive known to pantomimists." How could oralists claim to do without the language of signs, of which smiling was an unalienable part? The simple truth for Pettingill was this: "If no signs were employed in their instruction," deaf students remained in utter ignorance; "if the signs were few and poor, their progress in attaining to a knowledge was slow; if the signs were many and good, their progress was more rapid." He was clearly exasperated that the opponents of sign language failed to understand something so obvious.[2]

Pettingill tried to address what he knew of the oralist argument on this point. Oralists, he wrote, "would probably here inform us that it is not natural signs that they object to and disuse, but the artificial and arbitrary signs, which they claim are the medium of communication" in the manualist schools. However, "it is not true," he insisted, "that purely artificial and arbitrary signs are used in any of our institutions." Their signs all possessed "intrinsic significance, some relation to the idea which they represent; and all of them are as natural as we know how to make them."[3]

Here was the crux of the debate—was the sign language of deaf people natural or not? What distinguished natural signs or gestures from artificial ones? Z. F. Westervelt, principal of the school in Rochester, New York, complained that the way that manualists phrased the central question—"Shall natural signs be abandoned?"—misrepresented the issue, since the sign language they used was in fact not natural. "This assumption," he wrote, "that the sign language is 'natural' covers a very considerable part of the ground of controversy." While ordinary gestures could be described as "impulsive," "natural," and "common to all men," he argued, and while deaf children might first learn to communicate at home through gestures and pantomime, these "natural signs" were not sign language. In manualist schools, on the other hand, deaf children learned a complex and "artificial, conventional sign language." Therefore, the "question asked by the advocates of the sign system, 'Shall the natural signs of the deaf mute be given up?' is answered by their own practice," he concluded. Westervelt did not see gesture, pantomime, and sign language as points on a single and unified continuum, as the manualists did, but rather as two distinct forms of communication: the one natural, spontaneous, and simple, and the other artificial, conventional, and complex, with a wide gulf separating them.[4]

At an 1890 convention of teachers, an exchange between Alexander Graham Bell and J. L. Noyes, manualist principal of the Minnesota School for the Deaf, exemplified the distance that lay between the manualist and oralist ways of thinking about nature. Bell told the convention that there was a vast difference between the "natural signs" that oralist teachers used in their schools—those gestures commonly used by hearing people, such as pointing and waving—and "conventional signs, which constitute the Sign language."[5] For Noyes, however, to draw such a line right down the middle of the natural language of signs, dividing what had been considered an indivisible whole, was utter nonsense, and he responded with bafflement: "If I understand Dr. Bell's position in regard to the use of signs, if he was teaching his child geometry, he would object to the use of models or diagrams, in order to illustrate geometry." This, he concluded angrily, "shows the logic of his position."[6] To Noyes and other manualists, the drawings of a geometry class, the expressions of the face, the attitudes of the body, the gestures of the hands, and the sign language of the deaf were all of a kind, and to divide them into separate classes of things, to say that one was acceptable but another not, was an absurdity. Noyes could not make the distinction that Bell wanted him to. For the manualists, the difference between natural pantomime and gesture on the one hand and sign language on the other was one of degree; the latter was the former cultivated to a higher level. For the oralists, however, it was a difference of kind.

While some oralists, such as Emma Garrett, opposed the use of any hand gestures at all with deaf children on the basis of a slippery-slope theory of signing, most saw no harm in ordinary gestures. Samuel G. Davidson of the Pennsylvania Institution, for example, suggested that teachers use gestures no "more than one naturally would in speaking to an audience of hearing people."[7] Bell urged oralists to keep the distinction clear by using the term "sign language," never "signs," to refer to the language used in manualist schools. While it was fine to use "those natural 'signs' employed by hearing and speaking people to express their emotions or to emphasize a point," he wrote, "there is great objection to a language of signs, whereby ideas can be imparted without the use of words at all."[8] When the *American Annals of the Deaf* charged a committee in 1892 with creating definitions for the various methods of instruction in use in the United States, Bell objected to their proposed definition for the oral method (and complained that the committee was dominated by the pro–sign language faction) because it included the sentence "Signs are used as little as possible." He wanted to substitute "Sign-Language [is] discarded altogether." The difference in wording points to the different understanding manualists and oralists had of these terms. Manualists believed it was impossible for oralists to ever truly eliminate the use of signs (or sign language, which to them was the same thing), so it made sense to them to say that oralists used signs "as little as possible." Oralists believed that they used no sign language, even though they did use "natural signs," and wanted to make that distinction.[9]

These uses of the word "natural" by the oralists suggest a definition fundamentally different from the "natural" of the manualist world. At the 1884 Convention of Articulation Teachers of the Deaf, a participant asked a panel whether teachers should always vocalize when teaching articulation or whether it was all right to mouth words silently. Alexander Graham Bell replied to the questioner, and in his reply he encapsulated the evolving understanding of the "natural" (emphases added):

> I think we should aim to be as *natural* as we can. I think we should get accustomed to *treat our deaf children as if they could hear,* and if we get into the habit of articulating to deaf children without voice in this way we make a distinction between them and hearing persons. We should try ourselves to *forget that they are deaf.* We should *teach them to forget that they are deaf.* We should speak to them *naturally* and *with the same voice that we speak to other people,* and avoid *unnatural* movements of the mouth or *anything that would mark them out as different* from others.[10]

For oralists, "natural" did not have the *a priori* definition the manualists gave it but an empirical one. Indeed, it was coming to be indistinguishable from "normal." Samuel G. Davidson urged his fellow teachers that "pupils should always be taught and required to speak naturally. People do not generally talk after the abbreviated manner permitted by many teachers."[11] Here the intended meaning of "naturally" corresponded with the "generally" of the second sentence, and both would be interchangeable with "normally." Similarly, a writer in the *Scientific American* explained that in oral schools "every child is taught to speak in the natural way by means of the vocal organs."[12] When oralists spoke of natural signs or gestures, they meant those signs or gestures *normally* used by *normal* people.

The definition of naturalness as normality was used not only to support the teaching of spoken English, it also became the chief, sometimes the sole, criterion in arguments over *how* it should be taught. Oralists championed the new "natural method" of learning English, for example, which J. D. Kirkhuff explained was "founded upon the manner in which hearing children acquire it." While manualist teachers had taught English in the same way that they had been taught Latin—through the rules of grammar—Kirkhuff objected that this was "unnatural and contrary to the processes by which hearing children learn speech."[13]

An 1884 convention of speech teachers heard the oralist David Greenburger urge them to make their method "conform to the natural." Since hearing children did not "learn to speak by practicing on blows and hisses like p, f, s, sh," but instead by saying entire words, neither should deaf children. Bell responded that he would go even further—while Greenburger "commences with simple words, I commence with complete sentences"; his sole argument for this method was his assertion that hearing children learned language in this way. It was an article of faith to him, needing little or no justification, that teachers "should bring the method of teaching deaf children to speak as nearly as possible to correspond to the methods of teaching ordinary children to speak."[14] The question remained how "ordinary children" actually did learn. Emma Garrett agreed that of course teachers of the deaf ought to determine their methods by observing how hearing children learned, but disputed both Bell and Greenburger on the lessons such observations offered. She insisted that teachers should teach syllables rather than words or sentences because "hearing children's first efforts at speech are syllables—pa, pa, da, da, na, na."[15]

Whatever the actual merits of the methods, Greenburger, Bell, and Garrett all felt it sufficient to argue for their own method chiefly by saying that it was more natural because closer to how hearing children learned. This indeed was the key question asked of any teaching method. The consensus of the convention was that "the best principles of work with other children are best also for the deaf." All that was required, Garrett maintained, was that "we should talk to deaf-born pupils, all the while, in the same manner that we should to a hearing child, using the same language."[16] Responding to manualist arguments that the oralist regimen seriously delayed the acquisition of elementary knowledge and that deaf children should therefore be educated via sign language before they tackled lip-reading and speech, Greenburger argued that since hearing children learned about the world around them simultaneously with learning to speak, it must therefore be "unnatural to separate mental progress and articulation." Greenburger also insisted that since the "hearing child does not learn to write until years after he has learned to *speak* and *think* in spoken language," deaf children should be denied writing skills "till they have learned to speak so well as to be able to express themselves on ordinary topics as readily as hearing children do when they enter school."[17] Sadie Keeler agreed that teaching deaf children new words through writing violated the "first principle" of oral education: "all words which a hearing child learns through the ear, whether before or after entering school, should be learned by deaf-mutes through lip-reading."[18]

The argument from nature-as-normality appeared in many contexts. Mary and Emma Garrett admonished teachers to be "careful to avoid [silent] mouthing, using their arms in talking to the children and everything that is unnatural."[19] Day schools were promoted by some as more natural than boarding schools because "the family life . . . is the natural life." On the other hand, a boarding school's policy of permitting "no interruption, by vacation, of the children's training in speech and language" could be justified by arguing that since hearing children never took a vacation from the learning of speech and language, neither should deaf children.[20]

In certain contexts oralists *appeared* to use also the older definition of "natural." For example, the model they most often held up for the teacher to follow was not the trained professional, the experienced instructor, or the professor of pedagogy, but the one for whom caring for children came "naturally": the mother. "Does a mother commence by giving elementary sounds or syllables to her hearing child?" Bell asked. "No, she gabbles complete sentences, and the child listens."[21] Emma Garrett insisted on "natural ways of treating our little ones"; if "no mother of a hearing infant ever taught her child to lisp the dear words 'father' and 'mother' in detached sounds," this was clear evidence that the phonetic method was less "natural" than the word method. And if "mothers teach their hearing infants to understand spoken language before they understand written speech," teachers of the deaf should "follow the same natural plan."[22] According to Harriet Rogers, furthermore, natural signs were harmless if teachers confined themselves to "those few and simple ones used by intelligent mothers and nurses to explain the meaning of new words and phrases" to their hearing children.[23]

This use of "natural" appears similar to the manualist use of the term, commending the spontaneous activities of mothers *because* they were spontaneous and instinctive, arising from some deep place beyond culture and convention. What is more striking in oralists' rhetoric, however, is not the mother's connection with nature, but her identification with normality. A. L. E. Crouter, for example, advised that "the mother of the *normal* child and the oral teacher of the deaf child should follow the same order of teaching" (emphasis added).[24] They were more concerned with how *normal* mothers behaved under *normal* circumstances than with what mothers did from instinct, a subtle yet fundamental distinction. Oralists generally did not trust mothers of deaf children to make instinctively the right decisions; they suspected that such mothers were prone to be led astray by their maternal urges to coddle deaf children, to be too sympathetic and too ready to turn to gestures when oral communication failed. As Katherine Bingham explained it, the mother "must be assisted to do consciously for her deaf baby what she does unconsciously for her hearing one." Similarly, *deaf* mothers were never mentioned. The normal mother of normal children was the exemplar of proper nurturance. Only the *normal* behaved *naturally*.[25]

A *New York Times* account of the 1880 graduation exercises of the New York Institution (still mostly manualist) indicates that this new use of natural to mean normal was becoming common by that time, and was not confined to teachers of the deaf. The reporter described a portion of the ceremony in which a ten-year-old student told a story in sign language: "The representation of the tree came first; then the bird was represented as alighting on the tree; then the lad retired a few feet and gave the representation of a hunter taking aim with a fowling-piece; then the report of a musket was interpreted, and finally the fall and gasping of the bird." One of the teachers at the ceremony, Isaac Lewis Peet, informed the assembled guests that the boy had "followed the natural mode of conception in telling the story" by doing "exactly what an artist would have done in putting the story upon canvas," and concluded by noting that the "natural mode of intellectual conception is the pictorial one." The *Times* reporter took issue with this explanation in a revealing way. Peet had formed his opinion from "pathological phenomenon," he contended; had his experiences and study been among "healthy children" he would have seen that this "mode of ideation" could not "be insisted upon as the normal one." The reporter had automatically translated Peet's word, "natural," into "normal." To Peet and other manualists, "natural" denoted the essential, uncorrupted core of humanity; this reporter and others of his generation gave to the term the empirical denotation of a "healthy," non-"pathological" norm. For the manualists, deafness resulted in a person who was *more* natural because more pristine. For the oralists, deaf people and sign language were *unnatural* because they were *abnormal*.

While oralists kept possession of "natural" as a synonym for "normal," by the turn of the century they increasingly turned to the latter word itself, using the concepts interchangeably. Crouter, for example, wrote that the "wise oral teacher follows mother nature's lead and learns to teach the deaf by studying the manner in which the normal child acquires speech."[26] The key to unlocking the secrets of "mother nature" was not to study the internal thoughts and feelings of the untutored, supposedly uncorrupted, and therefore natural deaf child, as the manualists had done, but to observe and chart the central tendency of nature's creations, to map the bell-curve of normal behavior.

At first oralists used the concept of normality most often to describe practices—what people "normally" did—but they increasingly used it as a label for people as well. Hearing people became "normal people." Educators compared the development of deaf children—their speech, their English skills, their social behavior—to that of "normal children," and they discussed how their techniques, as teachers "of the abnormal child," compared with those of teachers engaged in "ordinary work with the normal child."[27] While deaf people never accepted this use of the term "normal" and continued to use "hearing" or "speaking," the concept of normality came to dominate the way that professionals and the public thought and spoke about deaf people—and much else besides.

The word *normal* first took on its modern meaning of typical or usual in the early decades of the nineteenth century. Georges Canguilhem has described how it was initially confined to medical discourse: the organ or organism in its "normal state" was healthy, in its "abnormal state," pathological. Auguste Comte then made sociological use of the concept to describe the healthy state of a society, Balzac made humorous use of it to parody medical descriptions (Mlle d'Aubrion had a nose that was "yellowish in the normal state, but completely red after dinner, a sort of plant-like phenomenon"), and the term with its new definition began to enter popular use. Throughout its modern career, the word has been used to describe how things are, as well as to prescribe how they ought to be—often both at once.[28]

In America the concept of normality lacked much cultural force until the post–Civil War era. By then, however, it was on its way to becoming one of the most powerful principles of the modern world. The philosopher Ian Hacking has argued that in the late nineteenth century, normality "displaced the Enlightenment idea of human nature as a central organizing concept" in Western societies. We no longer seriously discuss human nature; we ask instead what it is normal for people to do. "Research foundations are awash with funds for finding out what is normal," Hacking notes. "Rare is the patron who wants someone to investigate human nature."[29]

The ascendance of the idea of the normal, as François Ewald has noted, grew out of the "technological transformations that accompanied industrialization" and modern warfare: the need for standardized measurements, interchangeable parts (and workers), a common technical language, and compatible products and technologies. But the concept was not confined to the industrial or military world; rather it became central to the organization of modern society. The result, he argues, was a "new way of judging individuals." As human nature lost "its metaphysical status," people came to be "judged only with reference to the social and, more precisely, with reference to the average man."[30]

What has not been noticed is how the advancement of the concept of normality toward its twentieth-century position of dominance was at first an advance under cover—not as normality per se but in the guise of the natural. As we have seen, in deaf education the word "natural" gradually took on the denotation of "normal" before the word "normal" itself became common. It could do so because both concepts, while originating within different worldviews, functioned similarly. Hacking, Canguilhem, and others have noted how "normal" is used to both describe and prescribe—how, in Hacking's words, "the magic of the word is that we can use it to do both things at once." Its magic in this is not unique, however. "Natural" also shared this quality, but in terms of discourse so different from those surrounding the twentieth-century concept of normality that the similarity is not immediately apparent.[31]

We have seen that the oralists used normality as a measure of what existed—ostensibly an objective description of humanity based upon empirical observation—and that they then used it also as a standard.[32] It established not just the existing, but the desirable and the right. Naturalness was also clearly prescriptive for the manualists, as when they fought to keep sign language as natural as possible. Less immediately apparent is the way it also functioned as description, since it did not describe the typical behavior of people. Instead, "natural" described what humans were in their essence, stripped of the accoutrements of civilization.[33] Manualists did not think in terms of statistical averages. When they spoke of the nature of humanity they meant the essence of humanity rather than its visible surfaces. Further, as the unsullied embodiment of God's will, the natural was ultimately more real, more *existent* to them.

This is evidenced by the use of the word "universal," commonly paired with "natural" by the manualists and with "normal" by the oralists. Oralists argued that speech was "the normal and universal method of communication," meaning that speaking was typical behavior the world over and therefore desirable behavior. For the manualists, on the other hand, sign language could be described as natural and universal even though, in its cultivated form as deaf people used it, it was a distinctly unusual way to communicate.[34] For the manualists, typical behavior was irrelevant to the question of what was natural or universal; since the majority of people were encumbered with artificial custom and particularism, most typical behavior would be merely an expression of those superficial qualities. What human beings everywhere had in common, the natural and universal, existed at a deeper level, partook of the transcendent, and was not so easily discovered. To see the natural—the "hidden glory veiled from vulgar eyes," in the painter Thomas Cole's words—required discernment.[35]

Both natural and normal, then, served as descriptions of the actually existing and of the ideal. The assumption behind the earlier idea of the natural, as the manualists used it, was that humans could discern in nature what God intended and use it as a guide. The assumption behind the idea of normality, as evidenced by the oralists, was that one could discern from the observation of behavior what natural selection "intended" and use *it* as a guide. The locus of faith had shifted. The rise of the normal as a central organizing principle signaled the decline of natural theology and the rise of natural science (or scientific naturalism, terms that themselves contain the shift in the meaning of "natural"). It came with the advent of statistical thinking and the social sciences. It signified a shift from a culture that looked backward to origins to one that looked forward to an ever higher ascent; from one that looked within to a core to one that looked outward to behavior; from a culture that valued character to one that valued personality; from a culture that sought essences to one that increasingly gazed upon surfaces.

The normality argument could be historicized as well by positing an *evolutionary* normality. Oralists did so in response to the manualist claim that sign language was not only a natural language but also specifically the natural language of the deaf (which suggested that deaf people were essentially different from hearing people). Katherine Bingham, for example, maintained that deaf children's speech was "aided by the cumulative inheritance of a thousand generations of ancestors who have employed this means of communicating their thoughts. They have an undoubted constitutional tendency toward speech." Mary Garrett agreed that deaf children had a "hereditary tendency to talk." After all, "even the deaf children of deaf parents with many deaf relatives have more hearing ancestors who talked than who did not."[36] This form of argument—especially common at the turn of the century but still common today—determined the normal according to a particular construction of the direction of evolution; whatever diverged from that direction was abnormal and therefore undesirable. In a way it was not new, representing in its prescriptive aspect a new twist on the argument from tradition. But, consistent with the ability of the concept of normality to function as both description and prescription, it goes beyond the argument from tradition to state not only that people *should* do what has been done by past generations but that they *will* do so out of an inborn tendency—unless, that is, they are somehow corrupted and turned away from their evolutionary heritage.

This was exactly what oralists claimed had happened to deaf people. Sign language, they charged, was in fact not the natural and spontaneous creation of the deaf community but rather the invention of manualist teachers. Bell asserted that the sign language of the American deaf had been "devised by the Abbé de l'Epée" in the eighteenth century and subsequently imported to the United States; he began referring to it as "de l'Epée sign language." Westervelt likewise contended that "this language can not be considered the outgrowth of the deaf-mute mind, but the result of the accumulated labor of three generations of learned men." Frank Booth argued that sign language was merely an "invented" pedagogical tool that had outlived its usefulness; it therefore could and should be done away with by fiat of hearing educators.[37]

The claim received no support from those credited with the invention. Manualists had always maintained that modern sign language had come from deaf people themselves; teachers merely put to good use, and perhaps refined, what deaf people used as a matter of natural inclination. The teacher, they said, learned "the language of his pupils."[38] This was clearly true, and modern linguists confirm the manualist account. But if sign language were the original and spontaneous creation of deaf people, that fact would be testimony to the proposition that deaf people were fundamentally different from hearing people. This the oralists were loathe to accept, for their entire project was predicated on the belief that any such differences as did exist between hearing and deaf were not essential differences, that deaf people had a natural tendency, desire, and ability to communicate orally if given the chance to do so. It was not that deaf people were different and therefore created sign language as a result of that difference, but rather that they were *made* different by sign language. Sign language had to be the *cause* not the *product* of difference. The manualists with their invented language were at fault. They had created the deaf community; it could therefore be unmade.

In contrast, manualists had seen a clear difference in kind between hearing and deaf people. They were perfectly comfortable asserting that deaf people were "not exactly as other people," that they were "with them, not of them," and that the deaf child therefore "must be set apart for his education."[39] Manualists referred to deaf people as members of a "peculiar class" and spoke of sign language as a "peculiar language." What they meant—what the word had meant for their generation—was that deaf people and sign language were out of the ordinary, remarkable, perhaps unique. They might also say that sign language was "peculiarly fitted for devotion," meaning that it was particularly so, or discuss the "peculiarities" of a system of teaching, meaning its distinctive aspects.[40] "Peculiarity" did not carry negative connotations.

Peculiarity acquired powerfully different connotations in the age of oralism, however, implying not merely distinctiveness but the dreaded condition of abnormality. Oralists were outraged that "because a child is deaf he is . . . considered peculiar, with all the unpleasant significance possible attached to the word."[41] The advantage of an oral education, a teacher noted, was that "when in public, the oral graduate is not constantly attracting to himself undesired and embarrassing attention by a peculiar method of talking, either by signs or writing."[42] "To go through life as one of a peculiar class," oralists asserted, "is the sum of human misery. No other human misfortune is comparable to this."[43]

In matters of deaf education and socialization, the attainment of normality came to dictate both means and ends. Oralists argued that "the best principles of work with other children are best also for the deaf," that they were "trying to make our children like ordinary hearing children," and would therefore try anything that came "nearer to making them like hearing people."[44] Emma Garrett wrote that her "theory has been that the children should be treated just as hearing children," in the faith that they would then grow to be like hearing children. Her fundamental pedagogical principle was simply this: "from the beginning we talk to them just as though they could hear."[45] While Garrett wrote in 1882 that the "oral method does not make the deaf just like hearing people—as some of its too enthusiastic advocates would have us suppose—but it brings them nearer to us than any method known," only eight months later she described the Oral Branch of the Pennsylvania Institution, of which she was head teacher at the time, as "our school for making the deaf like hearing people."[46] "Our first and foremost aim," wrote another oralist teacher in 1907, "has been the development of the deaf child into as nearly a normal individual as possible."[47]

While most oralists reluctantly acknowledged that deafness precluded *complete* attainment of the ideal of normality, they held it to be a goal worthy of unending pursuit nevertheless. Even if deaf people inevitably fell short of normal, they might nevertheless be made more nearly so—or, at the least, less *obviously* abnormal. With continued advances in educational technique, deaf people would move ever closer to the norm, and each advance, however short of the ideal, was of great worth. Accordingly, the experience of which deaf people were encouraged to feel most proud was to converse with hearing people without being known to be deaf. An optimistic writer for *Scientific American* proclaimed in 1907 that, with oral instruction, "congenital mutes are . . . able to speak so perfectly, that it is difficult to distinguish their voices from those of normal persons." When Congressman Galusha A. Grow wanted the House of Representatives to provide money for the training of oral teachers, he argued that according to Mary Garrett children born deaf could be taught "to converse so well that the person conversing with them would not know of their deafness." Mabel Bell was paid the highest compliment of this new era when a speaker at a meeting of special education teachers claimed that he "was surprised after conversing with her to discover that she was a deaf woman" (an unlikely claim, since her speech was in fact often difficult for new acquaintances to understand). This was the new ideal—the deaf person who could *pass* for hearing.[48]

The quest for normality did not reflect merely an unthinking conformity on the part of the oralists. In common with many reformers of their time (and since), they equated equality with sameness. While oralists have been portrayed in recent years most often as oppressors of deaf people, it is important to remember that they thought of their work in precisely the opposite terms, as undoing oppression. The goal of deaf education for Mary and Emma Garrett was not mere sameness for its own sake, but for deaf people to be "like normal people in their ability to communicate with their fellows"; it was, they believed, "entirely possible to make them so, by giving them equal advantages with the normal people."[49] So enthusiastic was the teacher Katherine Bingham about the potential of early oral education for the deaf child that she believed the "whole problem of his education will be solved by the time he finishes his kindergarten course, so that he will no longer require special instruction." When that was achieved, she told a meeting of the National Education Association, deaf people could "assume their natural place among the hearing."[50] Albert G. Lane, a school superintendent from Chicago, responded eagerly that "the suggestions given in Miss Bingham's paper, if followed, would in time make the deaf equal to the normal child."[51]

At first glance it appears paradoxical that oralists used the terms "deaf" and "normal"—an opposition that would seem to emphasize difference—while at the same time ostensibly striving to make difference disappear in the name of equality. As a concept that prescribed as well as described, however, normality stigmatized the abnormal and established a standard toward which deaf people were supposed to strive. If the concept of normality drew attention to difference, it compensated for that by simultaneously encouraging greater exertions on the part of the abnormal to conform. By contrast, the terms "deaf" and "hearing," as the manualists used them, existed as independent and relatively fixed categories with no intrinsic imperative that one should become more like the other. The ideology of normality, however—like the terms "handicapped" and "retarded," both of which suggested a race in which deaf people were lagging behind their "normal" competitors—assumed that all either *were* running in the same direction, or, if not, *should* be, and was intended to stimulate the stragglers to greater effort. Deaf people who communicated only by oral means might not finish in the lead, nor even with the pack, but they might narrow the gap. They at least would be on the same track.

The response of deaf people was often similar to what Nancy Cott has called the "double-lensed view" or "doubleness" of the late-nineteenth-century women's movement, "its simultaneous affirmation of women's human rights [on the basis of their commonality with men] and women's unique needs and differences."[52] Deaf people too argued that they were no different from hearing Americans while at the same time maintaining that they were very different inasmuch as they necessarily formed a distinct language community. Thus, Thomas Francis Fox, a deaf teacher at the New York Institution for Deaf-Mutes, argued before the World Congress of the Deaf in 1904 that "a fundamental error was made in the past by considering the deaf as a special class, to be regarded, discussed, and legislated for as such, instead of plain human beings"; on the other hand, deaf people quite naturally "seek the society of their own kind . . . to talk freely in signs and the manual alphabet"; those who denied children the freedom to do so were "enemies of the deaf."[53] Deaf people were the same as hearing people in that they deserved the same kinds of rights and privileges, but different in that they claimed as one of their rights—a "birthright"—the use of sign language.[54] They claimed equality in difference.

If the oralists failed to achieve this "double-lensed view," the manualists had failed to do so as well. Manualists accepted difference, oralists sought equality, but neither was able to both accept deaf people as different *and* treat them as equals. The manualists had seen deaf people as fundamentally different from hearing people and saw no need to try to undo that difference. They should not, however, be confused with twentieth-century pluralists or multiculturalists, for this they were assuredly not. They were candidly paternalistic; they unabashedly favored hearing people for positions of authority in their schools. Like many Americans of their time, they saw no contradiction between acceptance of difference and acceptance of inequality. Oralists, on the other hand, like many other turn-of-the-century reformers, advocated equality and at the same time were intolerant of difference. Indeed, the two varied inversely—maximal equality implied minimal difference. A simple equation with a complex array of cultural forces driving it, this assumption of the essential similarity of all people, which has driven so much of twentieth-century reform, was an important source for the campaign to eradicate sign language.

Manualists and oralists both could not but fail, for equality cannot be achieved without attention to difference, and difference is not safe when it is accompanied by inequality. When the Reverend James H. Cloud, principal of the Gallaudet School for the Deaf in St. Louis and twice president of the National Association of the Deaf, affirmed that "We are not secondary to the hearing, but separate from them," he affirmed the only route to genuine equality. This was the route never taken in the schools for the deaf.[55]

The Trap of Paternalism

Oralists and manualists appeared in all respects to be opposing forces. Oralists portrayed themselves as "progressive" reformers seeking to free deaf children from the clutches of entrenched and "old-fashioned" traditionalists who were afraid of change and willing to doom deaf children to stunted and narrow lives. Manualists saw themselves as the defenders of deaf people and their language against intolerance and bigotry. Clearly they differed on matters of import, but were they so different after all?

The deaf community certainly saw a clear choice, siding with the manualists and opposing with all its resources the changes in educational practice that the oralists sought. One reason was that manual schools employed deaf teachers and staff while oral schools generally did not. However, while deaf people were permitted to teach in manualist schools, they generally found positions of authority closed to them. Few became principals or superintendents, and probably no deaf person ever sat on a school governing board.[1] The result was that when the hearing society refashioned its images of deafness and turned toward oralism, the deaf community had limited means of resistance.

Resist it did through that combination of open and subterranean means commonly resorted to by beleaguered minorities. From the beginnings of oralism until its decline in the 1970s, deaf people organized to lobby legislatures and school boards in support of sign language in the schools.[2] The National Association of the Deaf passed resolutions at each of its conventions, sending printed copies to every school for the deaf in the country, condemning the proscription of sign language. Deaf leaders such as George Veditz, one-time president of the National Association of the Deaf, vowed that despite efforts to "banish signs from the schoolroom, from the churches, and from the earth . . . as long as we have Deaf people on earth, we will have signs."[3] Deaf parents passed sign language on to their children, and those children who were deaf and attended schools where sign language was banned surreptitiously taught others. Those prevented from learning sign language as children learned it as best they could as adults when they found themselves free to associate with whomever they pleased, however they pleased; over 90 percent continued to marry other deaf people, and deaf clubs and associations continued to thrive.[4] Nevertheless, their means of resistance within the educational establishment were scant, a legacy at least in part of the paternalism of the manualist educators.

Paternalism was what nineteenth-century manualists and oralists had in common. Both of them saw deafness through their own cultural biases and sought to shape deaf people in accordance with those biases. Both used similar clusters of metaphors to forge images of deaf people as fundamentally flawed, incomplete, isolated, and dependent. And both used that imagery to justify not only methods of education but the authority of the hearing over the deaf. This was constant.

Still, deaf people sided with the manualists. We do not yet know precisely how deaf people responded to the images created by either manualists or oralists, to what extent they internalized them, rejected them, or adapted them to their own purposes. The creation of alternative meanings for deafness by the deaf community has a complex history all its own, one that is still largely unwritten.[5] But while the reception of the manualist *message* by deaf people is not yet clear, the manualist *medium*—sign language within a sign-using community— was clearly welcomed by most.

Whatever metaphors of deafness manual*ists* may have used, manual*ism* allowed the possibility of alternative constructions of deafness by deaf people themselves. So long as deaf people had their own language and community, they possessed a cultural space in which to create alternative meanings for their lives. They could resist the meanings that hearing people attached to deafness, adopt them and put them to new uses, or create their own. Oralism, whose ideal was the thoroughly assimilated deaf person, sought to do away with that alternative. Oralism failed in its larger purpose, finally, and sign language survived, because deaf people themselves chose not to relinquish the autonomous cultural space that their community and language made possible.

This tenacious and enduring resistance to the oralist vision did not mean, however, that oralism did little damage. Oralism meant that many deaf people had access only to limited or simplified language during the crucial early years of language development. The belief that oralism must be a total system, that it could not work unless a pure "speech atmosphere" was maintained, meant that a child might go for years with relatively little linguistic input.[6] Oliver Sacks has described the "dramatic deterioration in the educational achievement of deaf children and in the literacy of the deaf generally" that followed upon the oralist triumph. Indeed, Sacks suggests that cerebral development itself may be delayed or arrested by a paucity of exposure to language during the critical period of language learning. Fortunately, such damage can be mitigated, according to Sacks, by educational intervention or by "discovery of the deaf world," including American Sign Language (ASL), during adolescence. This latter is what saved a great many deaf children from severe linguistic impoverishment.[7]

Ruth Sidransky, a hearing daughter of deaf parents, has recently described how her father "never in his lifetime recovered from early verbal neglect compounded by a school system that tried to create an incomplete language system in imitation of normal human sound for deaf children." Her father once told her, " 'I try my life, all my life, to understand hearing people. It is hard.' He banged the sign for the word *hard* on his tightly clenched left fist. Language came into his life too late. He never read a book page by page, nor did my mother. . . . Language denied in childhood is impossible to resurrect in adulthood."[8] Sidransky's parents, like most of their generation, attended an oral school.

Many readers at this point probably look forward to a more or less happy ending to the story. After all, recent years have seen sign language return to the schools. Sign language interpreters are increasingly common at public events, deaf actors appear on television and in the movies, scholarly and popular books and articles are regularly published on ASL and deaf culture, and sign language courses have proliferated in schools, colleges, and universities. In short, there has been a dramatic emergence of the deaf community and their language into public consciousness.

These positive signs are, unfortunately, misleading. Today another campaign to rescue deaf children from what is perceived as their lonely isolation is under way. The practice known as "mainstreaming" or, more recently, "inclusion," which entails the integration of deaf students into local public schools, has increased dramatically in the last decade. While oral schools and programs still exist, and a relatively new technique known as "cued speech" has in a few places given oralism renewed life, the debate in deaf education today is chiefly between those who support mainstreaming, in most cases with interpreters who use a manually coded English system rather than ASL, on the one side, and those who advocate a bilingual and bicultural education employing both ASL and English, on the other. Supporters of the latter (which includes most organizations of deaf people, such as the National Association of the Deaf) generally also argue for more or less separate schooling with deaf people occupying at least some positions of authority.

In many residential schools, deaf teachers are once again being hired in significant numbers; in some deaf superintendents run the schools. Innovative schools such as the Indiana School for the Deaf and the California School for the Deaf at Fremont are trying a bilingual/bicultural approach. Residential schools such as these, however, have fewer and fewer students to work with. In addition to the other pressures working against these schools, legislators often see mainstreaming as an opportunity to cut state budgets; some residential schools have been closed after a century or more of service, much to the anguish of alumni, who have stronger attachments to their schools than hearing people can easily appreciate. Approximately 80 percent of deaf students now attend local public schools.

Alexander Graham Bell maintained that the ideal school "would contain only one deaf child," and Emma Garrett believed that the "ideal education for a deaf child was that he should never see another deaf child." Nearly one hundred years later, mainstreaming is making their dream a reality: thousands of deaf children now sit in classrooms where all the other students and every teacher is hearing.[9] While "mainstreaming" and "inclusion" cover a wide variety of actual circumstances—in some large cities, "magnet schools" might have several dozen deaf children in attendance—for the majority of deaf children, mainstreaming means being the only deaf student in the class. For many, it means being the only deaf student in the entire school.

Even during the long years of oralism's ascendancy, most deaf students continued to attend residential schools, and if they attended day schools they were still with others who were deaf. They had true peers, some of whom were sure to know sign language from somewhere, who could teach the others, and so in private and away from adults they could steal moments of genuine, relaxed, free, and easy communication. Today this is no longer the case. Thousands grow up with no or few deaf friends; most encounter no deaf adults to look up to. They have no access to the deaf community, with its collective knowledge, accumulated over generations, of how to live happy and productive lives in a mostly hearing world. Often the only person they can communicate directly with in school is their interpreter, who, because of the shortage of trained interpreters and the low pay offered by most school districts, is frequently barely competent in a manually coded English system and not at all in ASL.

In a *New York Times* opinion piece, Leah Hager Cohen, a sign-language interpreter, described the beginning of the school day for a deaf high-school student:

> It's a few minutes before the class will start. Everyone's fishing notebooks from knapsacks and sharpening pencils, and it's all "What did you put for the last answer on the algebra?" and "Tomorrow's the last day for yearbook money, right?" and "If we want to stay for the game, Tony says she can give us a ride." All of the eleventh-graders are speaking or listening, directly or indirectly. Except for one student, sitting down in front. She is neither speaking or listening; she is not involved; she is deaf.

Cohen cannot supply the links between the deaf girl and her hearing classmates that only a shared language could provide. Since simultaneous interpreting is a difficult and imprecise art, she cannot always convey even the ordinary goings-on of the classroom—the conversation sometimes occurs too quickly for her to keep pace, several students try to talk at once, or the teacher points at visual aids while continuing to lecture, which means that the student can choose to see the interpreter or what the teacher is pointing to but not both. Most often the girl spends lunch period by herself—in the library or the gym rather than at a lunch table with conversation swirling around her. Most extracurricular activities are closed to her.[10] What teachers sometimes call the "unwritten curriculum," the casual conversation that takes place outside the classroom and that accounts for perhaps 90 percent of all learning, is lost.[11]

Joseph Innes, professor of education at Gallaudet University, and many others have argued that interpreters cannot make classrooms "inclusive" for deaf children. Indeed, "given what is known about the dynamics and limitations of even high-quality interpreting," he writes, "the constant use of an interpreter actually represents a situation that is *inherently unequal*" [emphasis his]. He worries also about the emotional and developmental effects of placing a child "in an environment where he or she requires constant intervention in order to engage in basic social activities." To expect an adolescent to feel comfortable as part of a group while having to speak always through an adult interpreter is expecting a great deal.[12]

The angriest objection to mainstreaming from deaf people is that in the name of liberating children from their supposed "isolation" in the deaf community, a true and potentially devastating isolation is risked. In the name of inclusion in "the" community, deaf children are frequently denied true inclusion in any community. For the sake of an abstraction known as the "mainstream," deaf children are denied the solid and tangible fellowship, culture, language, and heritage of the deaf community.

The sentiment behind mainstreaming shares much in common with the oralist movement. Advocates insist it is "a matter of social justice and human rights . . . of equity and full citizenship."[13] Supplying deaf students with interpreters in public schools is framed as making classrooms "accessible" to them. The latest development in the movement is the demand for "total inclusion," an insistence that special schools and programs be shut down, that *all* children with disabilities, including all deaf children, regardless of parental, professional, or community judgment, be enrolled in regular classrooms in local schools.[14] The concept of "total inclusion" bears striking and uncomfortable resemblance to the "pure oralism" of the nineteenth century. In both cases, activists push a total solution based on abstract ideals. Indeed, the warm-sounding metaphor of "inclusion" in the "mainstream" is nothing more than the concept of "normality," so important to the oralists, now dressed up in new and as-yet-untarnished words.

If the sentiment is similar to oralism, why is the movement not identical with oralism? Why is sign language now acceptable? The decline of public and professional support for oralism came about as quickly and unexpectedly as the reaction against manualism in the late nineteenth century. New research in the 1960s demonstrated convincingly that oralism was a profound failure, but the evidence was available long before for anyone who wanted to see it. What made educators *want* to see that particular evidence at that particular time and begin to view sign language as a promising alternative?

The cultural changes of the 1960s and 1970s that allowed Westerners to see sign language with new eyes need a book of their own. Suffice it to say here that the changing attitudes toward sign language coincided with a profound shift in attitudes toward both the body and the emotions. This shift was manifested in such things as new and more sensuous forms of dance, a greater openness concerning sexuality, and an expanded tolerance for nudity and celebration of the body (the best exemplar being the musical *Hair*). A renewed fascination with "body language" generally and the publication of both scholarly and popular books on the subject accompanied the new popularity of sign language. Moreover, the advocacy beginning in the 1960s of freer, more open expressions of passion and personal feelings made more acceptable a mode of communication typically associated with emotion. The popularity of new psychotherapies that emphasized the importance of unfettering the emotions was but one manifestation of a changing valuation of emotional expression. Expressions of the new ethos ranged from the sublimity of what were seen as emotionally liberating art forms to the banality of "if it feels good, do it." The heart was once again elevated in the esteem of Westerners, and sign language rose with it.

Conversely, the negative associations that sign language held for earlier twentieth-century generations lost their cultural resonance. The notion that sign language was connected with "lower" humans or animals, for example, no longer carried the same connotations. The old idea of an ascending "scale of being," along with rigid hierarchies of all kinds, were being increasingly challenged. Race and species became far more ambiguous as markers of worth and status.

Indeed, with the reemergence of a romantic "noble savage" image in popular thinking, the association of sign language with American Indians was as likely to be a positive association as a negative one—or, at the least, a more ambiguous and complex one. The relative status of nonhuman animals also changed, one expression of which was the reinvigoration of the animal welfare movement and the emergence of philosophies of animal rights. As regard for nature and the natural has risen again (in ways both new and old), so has the twentieth-century reverence for normality faced increased skepticism.

All of this signaled a new romanticism similar in some respects to that of the early nineteenth century. The beliefs and values that made sign language repugnant to hearing Americans for most of the twentieth century either lost cultural force or changed their significance. The important associations that sign languages have traditionally held for most hearing people—with the body, with emotion as opposed to reason, with "primitive" peoples and "lower" animals—no longer carried the meanings that propelled the oralist movement. Instead, the meanings they held now resembled in many ways those of the nineteenth-century manualist era.

If American culture was returning to a higher estimation of the heart in relation to the mind, the national language continued to be central, however, to the way many Americans defined themselves, especially in the presence of yet another "new" immigration and divisive debates over bilingualism in public policy. So while cultural permission might have been forthcoming for people to speak with their hands and bodies, hearing Americans were nevertheless more comfortable if such expression was represented as a manual form of English rather than as a distinct language. Manual English systems and the continued repression of ASL have been the result.

When sign language returned to the schools in the 1970s, then, it was not ASL. Instead, schools turned to various, reinvented manually coded English systems (not "resurrected," since few if any teachers were aware that "methodical signs" had been tried and rejected more than a century before). In most classrooms today, while deaf children are no longer required to rely solely upon the *mode* of communication used by the majority—that is, speech—most are still required to use exclusively the *language* of the majority.

Manually coded English systems are artificially contrived and simplified representations of spoken English on the hands (although, as linguists have pointed out, they more accurately represent *written* English than *spoken,* making them less than efficient for face-to-face communication).[15] Whether they help deaf children to learn English has not been demonstrated. What is significant is that this experiment in language planning, implemented across the country with an alacrity surpassing even the oralist revolution, has taken place with virtually no evidence to support the proposition that a representation of English on the hands would help children to learn spoken and written English. Many linguists have serious doubts, and there is some evidence that it does not. Its value, however, is more symbolic than otherwise. As Frank Bowe has written, both oralism and the use of manually coded English found easy support because they "sounded right"; they seemed to satisfy "common sense" (meaning, of course, common to the hearing world). Claire Ramsey has described support for manual English systems as a matter of "faith," a faith founded on "the symbolic needs of the hearing society" rather than the "linguistic and educational needs of deaf children." Their rapid and widespread acceptance has resulted from their "compatibility with the sociolinguistic values of its main clientele, hearing parents and teachers."[16]

Mainstreaming seems to have similar cultural imperatives driving it. After 175 years of mostly separate education, in less than two decades a radical notion based on little research or experience has become the new orthodoxy. Ironically, it is the acceptance of sign language in public education that has made the widespread mainstreaming of deaf children feasible. Despite the hopes of early oralists such as Emma and Mary Garrett, it was impossible that more than a tiny fraction of deaf children could succeed in a local public school so long as they were confined to oral communication. It was the provision of sign language interpreters that made mainstreaming possible. Thus, one goal of the oralists, an end to the separate education of deaf people, has been achieved by the abandonment of their other chief goal, an end to sign language.

I noted in the beginning of this book that deaf people appear in some respects to belong to that category of people labeled "disabled," while in others they more closely resemble an ethnic group. Much of the drive for mainstreaming has come from deaf people being metaphorically associated with these two categories. Deaf people usually argue that they form a cultural and linguistic minority, more akin to an ethnic group than to people with disabilities. As M. J. Bienvenu, a Deaf activist and cofounder of the Bicultural Center in Riverdale, Maryland, recently said: "For some deaf people, being deaf is a disability. Those who learn forced English while being denied sign emerge semilingual rather than bilingual, and they are disabled people. But for the rest of us, it is no more a disability than being Japanese would be."[17]

Like all metaphors, however, the metaphor of ethnicity carries risks by linking deafness with something it is not. Being Japanese can indeed be a disability in American society, especially during periods of heightened nativism. So long as diversity is valued and celebrated, ethnicity might seem a protective coloration to take on. But an association with ethnicity can in nativistic times turn quickly against deaf people, as it did at the end of the nineteenth century. Even in the absence of overt nativism, there is still a very strong sentiment in America that ethnic groups ought to assimilate with the majority. The greatest social movement in recent American history, the Civil Rights movement, was in large part a struggle against segregation. The Supreme Court decided three decades ago that separate educations are inherently unequal, and the courts as well as majority public opinion have held to that principle ever since. Integration is generally accepted as an unquestionable good (even by the majority of Americans who continue to live in de facto segregated neighborhoods), and the *idea* of segregation is generally abhorred. Arguments for separatism by members of minority groups themselves are considered scarcely more acceptable than calls for segregation by white supremacy groups. Integration has become a powerful symbol of fairness and decency, and segregation a powerful symbol of injustice. When deaf people try to make the case for separate education on the basis of their "ethnic" or cultural identity, they struggle against a powerful current.

It is far more common, however, for hearing people to think of deaf people as disabled people than to think of them as members of a cultural minority. In movie and television portrayals, deaf people are nearly always isolated individuals, either lonely and pitiable or, more often recently, bravely struggling and succeeding in a hearing world. Rarely are they portrayed as members of a rich and closely knit deaf community.[18] Likewise, most hearing people prefer the term "hearing impaired," a construction that emphasizes commonality with hearing people except for a negative characteristic, an impairment or lack—as opposed to "deaf," a term that emphasizes difference (and is freighted for deaf people with rich connotations of culture, history, and heritage). Indeed, the argument of deaf people that they are not disabled is usually incomprehensible to hearing people.

Conceptualizing deafness as disability does have certain advantages for the deaf community, such as greater political clout gained by association with the large number of Americans with disabilities, and the protections of laws such as the Americans with Disabilities Act. That it carries powerful disadvantages as well has been demonstrated by the mainstreaming phenomenon. Those who fight for disability rights have, with some exceptions, generally supported mainstreaming, seeing it as a tremendous improvement over the separate and usually inferior education commonly afforded to children with disabilities. The struggle for the inclusion in local schools of children with disabilities, who in past generations were sent away to institutions, in some cases to be educated and in others to be warehoused, has been long and difficult. Disability rights activists rightfully see inclusion as a matter of justice and, to the extent that inclusion is now practiced, as a great victory.

Ironically, the theorizing of disability as a social construction has also tended to encourage the mainstreaming of deaf children. For example, Gary Bunch, an educator of the deaf and an advocate of inclusion, maintains that "disability is a social construct . . . a creation of those who have regarded, measured, and categorized others, not on the basis of who or what those others are, but on the basis of one particular aspect of difference." This construct, he argues, identifies persons as unacceptably different and sets them apart, unnecessarily stigmatizing them and diminishing the whole community by lessening its natural diversity. For Bunch, inclusion rests on the conviction that "all students are to be seen to be part of the normal, daily, diverse citizenship of our cities, towns, and villages. There is only one set of effective teaching practices, not one set for regular learners and another for special learners."[19]

Here again, the similarities with oralism are striking: notwithstanding the vocabulary of "diversity," the imperative is unity and a denial of difference. Oralists also believed that deafness could be redefined in such a way as to fully integrate deaf people into hearing society on an equal basis. They too believed passionately in the almost infinite plasticity of human beings. If deafness were, indeed, *nothing but* a social construction, if deafness were *merely* a cultural creation, then it might make sense to fashion policies on the basis of abstract principles of rights and equality and proclamations of sameness. Being deaf, however, is more than a cultural construction. It means most fundamentally that one occupies a different sensory world from those who hear, and this has certain consequences that cannot be *constructed* away. This physical reality (upon which culture works, certainly, and with which culture intertwines and interacts) transcends culture.

The concrete, unreconstructable reality of deafness is also beyond the experiential knowledge of hearing people. The metaphors employed by hearing people to come to some understanding of deafness are indispensable; however, they also mislead. By associating deafness with other things, metaphorical understanding makes questions of vital import to deaf people subject to the shifting winds of other, largely irrelevant, cultural issues. The deaf community is not quite like any ethnic group; issues such as bilingual education or mainstreaming are matters significantly different for deaf people than for ethnic minorities. Nor are deaf people identical with people with disabilities; they do not have identical interests. The existence of the conceptual category of "disability" does not mean that those who we place into it are indeed similar in significant or useful ways. Education for deaf children is not the same matter as education for blind children or for children who are quadriplegic or who have mental retardation, just as it is not the same as bilingual education for children from Spanish-speaking homes.

Upon the basis of such metaphors, however, again a great experiment is being tried on deaf children, and again deaf adults are warning that it will be a great tragedy. Leo Jacobs, a prominent deaf educator and author of *A Deaf Adult Speaks Out,* fears mainstreaming will result in "a new generation of educational failures." Mervin Garretson, deaf educator and past president of the National Association of the Deaf, warns that deaf children could be "educationally, vocationally, and emotionally mutilated." Patrick Graybill, a deaf actor and former member of the National Theatre of the Deaf, worries that mainstreamed students will be "lost between two worlds," unable to speak well enough to be understood by hearing people and unfamiliar with ASL and deaf culture. Jacobs, Garretson, and Graybill are all temperate, responsible, and representative leaders in the deaf community, by no means given to alarmism.[20] Yet the collective cultural wisdom that sees a tragedy in the making is not consulted. It is not even recognized as wisdom.

The deaf community finds itself endlessly on the defensive, trying to find hearing educators willing to listen to them. It is difficult to fathom why the delegates to the 1904 convention of the National Association of the Deaf would have to craft a resolution asserting that deaf people "feel that it is their privilege to discuss and pass upon questions of educational methods, inasmuch as they are the results of these methods, and that their opinions therefore should have the weight of authority."[21] Given the wealth of experience that deaf adults have to draw on, it is a constant source of both puzzlement and pain how little their advice is heeded. Only deaf people are able to deal with deafness per se rather than with the shadows of things that at a distance might resemble or remind one of deafness. Yet the education of each generation of deaf children operates almost entirely in ignorance of, or in conscious opposition to, what deaf adults themselves advise. When a generation of deaf children grow up to become deaf adults and attempt to bear witness to the strengths and faults of their education, they are ignored. Today's deaf children will, if history is any guide, grow up with resentment and sometimes open contempt for the way they were raised and educated. They will wonder why their parents and educators did not heed what deaf adults told them. They themselves will try to improve the lot of the next generation. If nothing has changed, they will also be ignored.

This is not to say that deaf people agree on all issues, nor should it suggest that deaf people have not also used metaphor to explain their own lives to themselves. When they have discussed sign language and the education of deaf children, they have often used the same metaphors and images that hearing writers use. Sharing American culture, it is not surprising that they should. The relationship of the deaf community to sign language is of course also a matter of culture; sign language is the basis for a rich heritage of folklore, theater, stories, and poetry, and has been the medium for a complex system of values and beliefs.

But deaf people have historically focused less on the abstractions and distant analogies that have fascinated hearing people, and have spoken instead of real-life consequences. A woman who signed herself merely "A Semi-Deaf Lady" put the matter most cogently in an 1908 article titled "The Sign Language and the Human Right to Expression": "Has the poet the right to sing? Has the orator the right to sway men, not only by what he says, but by the way he says it? Has the musician the right to charm by melody? . . . Have you . . . the right to chat without effort or strain with your friends, claiming free and unrestrained intercourse in conversation as a natural birthright?"

This is perhaps the most profound, and most mundane, of all arguments for an early introduction to ASL and the deaf community. The deaf person has "a right to some kind of language whose chief power and charm for him shall be in expression." For this right to be exercised, a true language community is necessary, and this does not occur for deaf children in the public schools, in a speech class, or with the use of cumbersome manually coded English systems. It occurs for deaf people in the deaf community with the medium of ASL. Without this community and medium, as this writer pointed out, "it must be accepted as true that at least *pleasure* must be counted out."[22]

"There is, or appears to be, in their relation to the deaf," Sarah Porter wrote a hundred years ago, "a certain condescension in oralists which must, one would think, be somewhat galling to a proud-spirited educated deaf person."[23] Deaf people continue to ask the question: why are hearing people so resistant to listening to deaf adults? In a letter to an organization conducting research into what it called "the hearing impaired community," a deaf woman expressed her reluctance to respond to a questionnaire. "I do not want to co-operate with this research," she wrote,

because hearing politicians and hearing authorities listen to the hearing researchers and hearing parents. They listen to people who do not know the Deaf culture and seek cures for deaf children, ignoring the Deaf community. I was at the Philadelphia Zoo recently and came across the Hippo exhibit. There was a sign which explained different facts related to the social habits of the Hippo. The zoo's social scientists conducted a study which revealed that if the hippo was isolated, its emotional and behavioral health was affected. The study showed that the hippo required other animals for company and emotional health. That made me so sad, because it seems the researchers and social scientists study the welfare of hippos more carefully than they study the welfare of deaf children! . . . We Deaf people have had enough suffering.[24]

The manualists of the nineteenth century paid more attention to the opinions of deaf adults than have any educators since their time. Indeed, they have been the only educators in American history who, as a group, have had daily interaction with deaf adults or who were even *capable* of conversing freely with them. Thomas Hopkins Gallaudet insisted that deaf people "are themselves the original sources of the fundamental processes, so far as language is concerned, of conducting their education." He believed that it was the teacher's task to "find the path which nature points out, and to follow it." While "philosophy and art may often do a great deal to remove some of the roughnesses of this path," the teacher must not leave it, "else those whom you would lead in the way of knowledge, of truth, and of duty, will follow on with irksome and reluctant steps, if, indeed, they follow at all."[25]

Yet the hearing manualists valued sign language chiefly for what turned out to be culturally transient reasons, and when those reasons lost currency, sign language lost its appeal for hearing people. Ever since, to the extent that deaf children have followed where their hearing teachers and parents have led them, they have only done so with "irksome and reluctant steps." Mostly they have not followed at all. Whatever hearing people choose to do, deaf people will continue to use ASL. That seems clear. For more than a hundred years, there was a concerted effort to eradicate any use of sign language in this country, and for all of that time American Sign Language was passed down, from generation to generation, without break, without faltering. Today, deaf children leave school after years of manually coded English and turn to ASL as their primary means of communication. Exposure to ASL can be delayed until adulthood, fluency in it can be thereby impaired, general linguistic competence can be thereby injured, but the great majority of deaf people will continue to use it as best and as soon as they can. Regardless of efforts to do so—regardless of how hearing people try to imagine, reimagine, and reconstruct deafness—ASL and the deaf community, it would seem, will not be undone.

Introduction

1. Italics in original; Gordon Allport, *The Nature of Prejudice* (Cambridge, Mass.: Addison-Wesley, 1954), 31.

2. Harry Markowicz and James Woodward, "Language and the Maintenance of Ethnic Boundaries in the Deaf Community," in *How You Gonna Get to Heaven if You Can't Talk with Jesus: On Depathologizing Deafness,* ed. James Woodward (Silver Spring, Md.: T. J. Publishers, 1982), 6.

3. Within forty years there would be twenty residential schools in the United States; by the turn of the century, more than fifty. "Tabular Statement of Schools for the Deaf, 1897–'98," *American Annals of the Deaf* [hereafter cited as *Annals*] 43 (1898): 46–47.

4. Desloges's short book, *Observations d'un sourd et muet sur "Un Cours elementaire d'education des sourds et muets"* (Amsterdam and Paris, 1779), is translated in Harlan Lane, ed., *The Deaf Experience: Classics in Language and Education,* trans. Franklin Philip (Cambridge: Harvard University Press, 1984), 36.

5. Nora Ellen Groce, *Everyone Here Spoke Sign Language: Hereditary Deafness on Martha's Vineyard* (Cambridge: Harvard University Press, 1985).

6. An excellent account of the contemporary American Deaf community can be found in Carol Padden and Tom Humphries, *Deaf in America: Voices from a Culture* (Cambridge: Harvard University Press, 1988). For anyone wishing to understand the world of deaf people, this small but rich and insightful book is a fine place to start. For an excellent, concise history of the community in the nineteenth century, see John Vickrey
Van Cleve and Barry Crouch, *A Place of Their Own: Creating the Deaf

Community in America (Washington, D.C.: Gallaudet University Press, 1989); see also Jack Gannon, *Deaf Heritage: A Narrative History of Deaf America* (Silver Spring, Md.: National Association of the Deaf, 1981), a popular history written by a deaf man and published by the National Association of the Deaf; Harlan Lane, *When the Mind Hears: A History of the Deaf* (New York: Random House, 1984); John Vickrey Van Cleve, ed., *Deaf History Unveiled: Interpretations from the New Scholarship* (Washington, D.C.: Gallaudet University Press, 1993); Harlan Lane and Renate Fischer, eds., *Looking Back: A Reader on the History of Deaf Communities and Their Sign Languages* (Hamburg: Signum, 1993).

7. Olof Hanson, "Circular of Information No. 7, National Association of the Deaf: Oral Teaching of the Deaf" (Washington, D.C.: National Association of the Deaf, 1912), 4.

8. Of the total, 23.7 percent "taught wholly by oral methods"; 14.7 percent "taught also by Manual Spelling (no Sign-language)"; 53.1 percent "with whom speech is used [in at least some classes] as a means of instruction." Alexander Graham Bell, "Address of the President," *Association Review* 1 (October 1899): 78–79 (in 1910 renamed the *Volta Review*). Bell's figures differ somewhat from those provided by the *American Annals of the Deaf*—see, for example, Edward Allen Fay, "Progress of Speech-Teaching in the United States," *Annals* 60 (January 1915): 115. Bell's method of counting, as explained by him in the same issue, is more precise in that he distinguishes between those taught wholly by oral methods and those taught in part orally and in part manually.

9. "Statistics of Speech Teaching in American Schools for the Deaf," *Volta Review* 22 (June 1920): 372.

10. See, for example, J. C. Gordon, "Dr. Gordon's Report," *Association Review* 1 (December 1899): 213; "Teaching Deaf-Mutes to Speak," *Scientific American* 96 (June 8, 1907): 473; Mary McCowen, "Educational and Social Work for the Deaf and Deafened in the Middle West," *Oralism and Auralism* 6 (January 1927): 67.

11. Henry Kisor, *What's That Pig Outdoors? A Memoir of Deafness* (New York: Hill and Wang, 1990), 259; Kisor was orally educated, never learned sign language, and has been very successful communicating orally all his life. Nevertheless, he condemned "the history of oralism, the unrelenting and largely unsuccessful attempt to teach *all* the deaf to speak and read lips without relying on sign language" (9).

The reintroduction of sign language into the classroom has been even more rapid than its banishment at the turn of the century; it occurred amidst widespread dissatisfaction with oralism and after a series of studies demonstrated that sign-language use had no negative effect on speech skills and positive effects on English acquisition as well as social and intellectual development. See Donald F. Moores, *Educating the Deaf: Psychology, Principals and Practices* (Boston: Houghton Mifflin, 1987), 10–13; Julia M. Davis and Edward J. Hardick, *Rehabilitative Audiology for Children and Adults* (New York: John Wiley and Sons, 1981), 319–25; Mimi WheiPing Lou, "The History of Language Use in the Education of the Deaf in the United States," in *Language Learning and Deafness,* ed. Michael Strong (Cambridge: Cambridge University Press, 1988), 88–94; Leo M. Jacobs, *A Deaf Adult Speaks Out* (Washington, D.C.: Gallaudet College Press, 1980), 26, 41–50.

12. Deaf people frequently pointed out that deaf adults almost universally opposed oralism; oralists did not try to rebut these claims. See, for example, Amos G. Draper, "The Attitude of the Adult Deaf towards Pure Oralism," *Annals* 40 (January 1895): 44–54; Sarah Porter, "The Suppression of Signs by Force," *Annals* 39 (June 1894): 171; anonymous ["A Semi-Deaf Lady"], "The Sign Language and the Human Right to Expression," *Annals* 53 (March 1908): 148–49. See also Van Cleve and Crouch, *A Place of Their Own,* 128–41; Lane, *When the Mind Hears,* 371–72; Padden and Humphries, *Deaf in America,* 110–12; Beryl Lieff Benderly, *Dancing without Music: Deafness in America* (Garden City, N.Y.: Doubleday, 1980), 127–29; Oliver Sacks, *Seeing Voices: A Journey into the World of the Deaf* (Berkeley: University of California Press, 1989), 25–28.

13. Quoted in Lane, *When the Mind Hears,* 371.

14. Hanson, "Circular of Information No. 7," 3.

15. Quoted in Lane, *When the Mind Hears,* xvi.

16. Ibid., 301–2. Lane presents strong evidence that this was the case for some supporters of oralism, such as Horace Mann.

17. Richard Winefield, *Never the Twain Shall Meet: Bell, Gallaudet, and the Communications Debate* (Washington, D.C.: Gallaudet University Press, 1987), 81–96; see also Van Cleve and Crouch, *A Place of Their Own,* 114–27; Lane, *When the Mind Hears,* 353–61. Winefield writes perceptively on aspects of the nineteenth-century debate over sign language, but his focus is almost entirely upon Edward Miner Gallaudet and Alexander Graham Bell. This at times distorts his depiction of the debate. For instance, he argues that the family backgrounds of both men had a decisive influence upon their attitudes toward sign language. While this is doubtless true, it does little to explain manualism and oralism as the social and cultural phenomena that they were. These were not the personal philosophies of two individuals, but rather social ideologies with generational, gender, and class dimensions. Overemphasizing the importance of two leaders, he tends to treat the controversy as primarily

a contest between two strong egos. Winefield also suggests that Gallaudet and his generation of teachers were more concerned with the well-being of deaf people as individuals, while Bell and his fellow oralists tended to place the good of society above the good of the individual. While I think this is to a limited extent true, it is far too ambiguous a formulation. First, the manualists were also very concerned with the good of society—but their conception of how to benefit society was quite different from that of the oralists. They, like other evangelical Christians of their time, saw social improvement as coming about through the improvement of individuals. One led to the other. Similarly, the oralists clearly believed that deaf people as individuals would benefit from their reforms. Nowhere do their words suggest that they thought it best to sacrifice the interests of deaf people as individuals for the good of the society as a whole. The central conflict was not so much concern for the individual versus concern for society as it was a conflict between different ways of imagining society and its relationship with the individual.

18. Van Cleve and Crouch, *A Place of Their Own,* 106–7, 119, 126. Van Cleve and Crouch emphasize the role of Bell (his eugenics research, his skill as a promoter, his prestige and wealth), the desire of hearing parents to see their children communicate in a "normal" manner, state legislators' preference for the new oralist day schools over the more expensive, traditional residential schools, and the belief among many hearing teachers that sign language "interfered with the socialization of deaf children, as the use of languages other than English supposedly interrupted the socialization of immigrant children" (107). While brief, the two chapters by Van Cleve and Crouch on the oralist movement and the resistance of the deaf community to it are the most reliable narrative introduction to the subject.

19. Lane, *When the Mind Hears,* xiii, 283–85. Lane writes compellingly of the oralist campaign as the oppression of a linguistic minority and of the deaf community's resistance to that campaign. His work is especially strong in exploring Bell's role. Lane, however, tends to attribute twentieth-century motives to nineteenth-century actors, missing the specificity of historical circumstances. He attributes to turn-of-the-century oralists motives similar to today's oralists and Manually Coded English advocates, while nineteenth-century manualists in his account often sound like today's ASL advocates. While they are in some ways analogous, Lane's conclusion that "nothing fundamental has changed in these matters since 1900" (xv) is based on a misleading kind of synecdoche: attitudes toward a minority language are assumed to stand for an unchanging constellation of beliefs. In the nineteenth century, however, attitudes toward ASL were part of different constellations from those of

today. Manualists, for example, were tolerant of certain kinds of diversity (at least as regards deaf people and their language), but at the same time were not interested, as ASL supporters today are, in social equality for deaf people. Oralists, on the other hand, like their contemporaries in the movements for the "Americanization" of Indians and immigrants, advocated social equality for deaf people and believed it could come about only through assimilation (as I discuss in chapter 6).

20. Training in speech and lip-reading is still included in nearly all educational programs for deaf and hearing-impaired children. Current orthodoxy and nineteenth-century manualism have in common the use of sign language, but ASL was most often used in nineteenth-century classrooms, while today some form of Manually Coded English, sometimes delivered simultaneously with speech, is most common. The integration of deaf pupils into the public schools, using interpreters, is now the norm (see the epilogue for a discussion). The central debate today is not between oralism and manualism (although this debate still exists), but between signed English and American Sign Language, and between mainstreaming and separate residential schooling. See Moores, *Educating the Deaf*, 1–28.

21. For examples of the manualist version, see Harvey P. Peet, "Memoir on the History of the Art of Instructing the Deaf and Dumb," *Proceedings of the Fifth Convention of American Instructors of the Deaf, 1858* (Jacksonville, Ill., 1859), 338; Job Williams, "A General View of the Education of the Deaf in the United States," *Proceedings of the Thirteenth Convention of American Instructors of the Deaf, 1893* (Washington, D.C., 1893), 10. For the oralist version, see Fred DeLand, *Dumb No Longer: Romance of the Telephone* (Washington, D.C.: Volta Bureau, 1908), 54; "Prof. Bell Spoke for Deaf Mutes, and Was Intently Listened to in the House Committee," *Detroit Journal* (Apr. 12, 1899), Alexander Graham Bell Family Papers, Manuscript Division, Library of Congress, Container 178, Folder: Deaf—Day Schools, Mich. Another oralist version of the story was that Gallaudet had to accept training in manual methods because he had no money and oralists in Britain charged for their training; recounted in *Proceedings of the Fourteenth Biennial Convention of the Minnesota Association of the Deaf* (St. Paul: 1917), 22.

22. Edward Miner Gallaudet, "The Intermarriage of the Deaf, and Their Education," *Science* 16 (Nov. 28, 1890): 296. Gallaudet was responding directly to an article that appeared in the same journal the month before, in which the author made precisely the statement that Gallaudet decried. See Bernard Engelsman, "Deaf-Mutes and Their Instruction," *Science* 16 (Oct. 17, 1890): 220.

23. Edward Miner Gallaudet, "The American System of Deaf-Mute Education, Its Incidental Defects and Their Remedies," *Proceedings of the*

First Conference of Principals of Institutions for the Deaf and Dumb, 1868 (Washington, D.C., 1868), 48.

24. Ibid.

25. According to Lane, Mann knew very little about deaf education but wrote the report at the urging of Howe; *When the Mind Hears,* 295.

26. This view, that it is in the *nature* of deaf people to create signed languages, has been given support by linguistic research into language acquisition by deaf infants. Susan Goldin-Meadow, for example, has found that deaf children born to hearing parents and not yet exposed to sign language nevertheless use their hands to communicate and that they develop idiosyncratic gestural communication systems that have linguistic properties similar to the oral language of hearing children of the same age. See Susan Goldin-Meadow and Heidi Feldman, "The Development of Language-like Communication without a Language Model," *Science* 197 (1977): 401–3; Susan Goldin-Meadow and Carolyn Mylander, "Beyond the Input Given: The Child's Role in the Acquisition of Language," *Language Journal of the Linguistic Society of America* 66 (June 1990): 323–55.

27. *Proceedings of the Ninth Convention of the National Association of the Deaf and the Third World's Congress of the Deaf, 1910* (Philadelphia: Philocophus Press, 1912), 30.

28. Susan D. Rutherford, "The Culture of American Deaf People," *Sign Language Studies* 59 (Summer 1988): 133; James Woodward, "Historical Bases of American Sign Language," in *Understanding Language through Sign Language Research,* ed. Patricia Siple (New York: Academic Press, 1978), 333–48; L. A. Friedman, "Formational Properties of American Sign Language," in *On the Other Hand: New Perspectives on American Sign Language,* ed. L. A. Friedman (New York, 1977), 3.

29. See Joseph D. Stedt and Donald F. Moores, "Manual Codes on English and American Sign Language: Historical Perspectives and Current Realities," in *Manual Communication: Implications for Education,* ed. Harry Borstein (Washington, D.C.: Gallaudet University Press, 1990), 1–20; Woodward, "Historical Bases," 333–48; Groce, *Everyone Here Spoke Sign Language,* 67–74. Recent research has cast into doubt the efficacy of Manually Coded English systems for teaching English to deaf children; see Brenda Schick and Mary Pat Moeller, "What is Learnable in Manually Coded English Sign Systems," *Applied Linguistics* 13 (1992): 313–40.

Chapter One

1. Luzerne Rae, "Introductory," *American Annals of the Deaf* [hereafter cited as *Annals*] 1 (October 1847): 4.

2. Thomas H. Gallaudet, "The Natural Language of Signs—I," *Annals* 1 (October 1847): 55–56.

3. Thomas H. Gallaudet, "The Natural Language of Signs—II" *Annals* 1 (January 1848): 80.

4. Ibid., 82, 88.

5. Ibid., 82–85.

6. Paul E. Johnson, *A Shopkeeper's Millennium: Society and Revivals in Rochester, New York, 1815–1837* (New York: Hill and Wang, 1978), 97.

7. Gallaudet, "Natural Language of Signs—II," 88–89; see also Lucius H. Woodruff, "Moral Education of the Deaf and Dumb," *Annals* 3 (January 1851): 66, 70. The emphasis on the heart rather than the intellect was a commonplace of Second Great Awakening evangelicalism. Reason and knowledge were not, however, seen as opposed to religion and were also highly valued; see Jean V. Matthews, *Toward a New Society: American Thought and Culture, 1800–1830* (Boston: Twayne, 1991), 35.

8. Gallaudet, "Natural Language of Signs—II," 86.

9. Lucius Woodruff, "The Motives to Intellectual Effort on the Part of the Young Deaf-Mute," *Annals* 1 (April 1848): 163–65.

10. Harvey P. Peet, "The Personal Character of the Teacher," *Proceedings of the Third Convention of American Instructors of the Deaf, 1853* (Columbus, 1853), 187.

11. David Walker Howe, "The Evangelical Movement and Political Culture in the North during the Second Party System," *Journal of American History* 77 (March 1991): 1220.

12. Collins Stone, "The Religious State and Instruction of the Deaf and Dumb," *Annals* 1 (April 1848): 144.

13. Henry B. Camp, "Claims of the Deaf and Dumb upon Public Sympathy and Aid," *Annals* 1 (July 1848): 213–14.

14. Collins Stone, "Address upon the History and Methods of Deaf Mute Instruction," *Annals* 14 (April 1869): 96.

15. Gallaudet, "Natural Language of Signs—II," 82–83.

16. Stone, "Religious State," 133–34, 137.

17. Luzerne Rae, "Thoughts of the Deaf and Dumb before Instruction," *Annals* 1 (April 1848): 150–51.

18. Camp, "Claims of the Deaf," 210–15. See also Woodruff, "Motives to Intellectual Effort," 163–65.

19. Stone, "Religious State," 136–37.

20. Woodruff, "Motives to Intellectual Effort," 165–66.

21. J. A. Ayres, "An Inquiry into the Extent to which the Misfortunes of Deafness May Be Alleviated," *Annals* 1 (April 1848): 224.

22. John Carlin, "The Mute's Lament," *Annals* 1 (October 1847): 15.

Carlin, a successful artist, was known for expressions of what today might be termed "self-hatred." A contradictory individual, he married a deaf woman, used sign language, and supported the establishment of Gallaudet College, but claimed to prefer the company of hearing people and expressed contempt for deaf people and sign language. While he did not himself speak or lip-read, he became one of the small minority of deaf adults who supported the oralist movement. Carlin once derided proposals for a separatist community of deaf people on the grounds that "it is a well known fact that the majority of them [deaf people] show little decision of purpose in any enterprise whatever." *Annals* 10 (April 1858): 89. See also John Vickrey Van Cleve and Barry Crouch, *A Place of Their Own: Creating the Deaf Community in America* (Washington, D.C.: Gallaudet University Press, 1989), 66, 76–78; Harlan Lane, *When the Mind Hears: A History of the Deaf* (New York: Random House, 1984), 245–46, 275–76, 325.

23. Anon., *Annals* 1 (July 1848): 209.

24. Carol Padden and Tom Humphries identify the use of "silence" in reference to deaf people as metaphorical. Their argument is complementary but somewhat different from mine here. Their contention (to simplify) is that sound directly and indirectly plays an important role in the lives of deaf people and has important meanings for them, albeit quite different ones than for the hearing; *Deaf in America: Voices from a Culture* (Cambridge: Harvard University Press, 1988), 91–109.

25. Clara Cahill Park, "Mary Garrett," *American Magazine* 74 (September 1912): 552–53.

26. Frank Booth, "The Association Magazine," *Association Review* 1 (October 1899): 4.

27. Alexander Graham Bell, "Address of the President," *Association Review* 1 (October 1899): 78–79 (see note 8 in the introduction above); "Statistics of Speech Teaching in American Schools for the Deaf," *Volta Review* 22 (June 1920): 372.

28. Percentage of deaf teachers by year: 1852, 38; 1858, 41; 1870, 41; 1880, 29; 1890, 26; 1900, 17; 1910, 17; 1920, 15; compiled from periodic reports of schools for the deaf, published in the *American Annals of the Deaf* in the January issue of the years indicated under the heading "Tabular Statement of American Schools for the Deaf."

29. Richard Winefield, *Never the Twain Shall Meet: Bell, Gallaudet, and the Communications Debate* (Washington, D.C.: Gallaudet University Press, 1987), 48.

30. John Van Cleve, "Nebraska's Oral Law of 1911 and the Deaf Community," *Nebraska History* 65 (Summer 1984): 208.

31. Edward M. Gallaudet, "Must the Sign-Language Go?" *Annals* 44

(June 1899): 221–29; the predominance of oralism in the twentieth century is sometimes obscured by the fact that many schools called themselves "combined system schools" rather than "oral schools." By the twentieth century, however, this usually meant starting all students in oral classes and only transferring to manual departments those students who clearly could not function at all in an oral class. In addition to being labeled "oral failures," they were often labeled mentally deficient as well.

32. Edward M. Gallaudet, " 'Deaf-Mute' Conventions, Associations, and Newspapers," *Annals* 18 (July 1873): 200–206.

33. John M. Tyler, "The Teacher and the State," *Association Review* 1 (October 1899): 9, 12–13.

34. Katherine T. Bingham, "All along the Line," *Association Review* 2 (February 1900): 27, 29; Edward C. Rider, "The Annual Report of the Northern New York Institution for the Year Ending September 30, 1898," reprinted in the *Association Review* 1 (December 1899): 214–15; S. G. Davidson, "The Relation of Language to Mental Development and of Speech to Language Teaching," *Association Review* 1 (December 1899): 132; Gardiner G. Hubbard, "Introduction of the Articulating System for the Deaf in America," *Science* 16 (Dec. 19, 1890): 337; see also Alexander Graham Bell, *Proceedings of the Twelfth Convention of American Instructors of the Deaf* (New York, 1890), 181.

35. Joseph C. Gordon, *The Difference between the Two Systems of Teaching Deaf-Mute Children the English Language: Extracts from a Letter to a Parent Requesting Information Relative to the Prevailing Methods of Teaching Language to Deaf-Mutes in America* (Washington D.C.: Volta Bureau, 1898), 1.

36. Z. F. Westervelt, "The American Vernacular Method," *Annals* 34 (July 1889): 205, 207.

37. Letter from Bell to Miss Mary E. Bennett of Los Angeles, Aug. 30, 1913, in the Alexander Graham Bell Family Papers, Library of Congress, Manuscript Division, Container 173, Folder-Gen. Correspondence A–C.

38. Draft of a letter from Bell to the editor of the *Educator* (Philadelphia), titled "The Question of Sign Language: Some Remarks upon Mr. Jenkins Letter," February 1894, Alexander Graham Bell Family Papers, Manuscript Division, Library of Congress, Container 198. See also Bell, "Discussion," *Proceedings of the Twelfth Convention of American Instructors of the Deaf, 1890* (New York, 1890), 181.

39. J. D. Kirkhuff, "The Sign System Arraigned," *Silent Educator* 3 (January 1892): 88a.

40. S. G. Davidson, "The Relation of Language Teaching to Mental Development," *National Educational Association: Journal of Proceedings and Addresses of the 37th Annual Meeting* (Washington, D.C., 1898), 1044; see

also Westervelt, "American Vernacular," 202: sign language made deaf people "like the Jews, a people without a country."

41. Frederick E. Hoxie, *A Final Promise: The Campaign to Assimilate the Indians, 1880–1920* (Lincoln: University of Nebraska Press, 1984), 12.

42. Alexander Graham Bell, *Memoir upon the Formation of a Deaf Variety of the Human Race* (Washington, D.C.: Government Printing Office, 1884), 194.

43. Bell, *Memoir*, 194, 217–18, 223.

44. Bell, *Memoir*, 220–21.

45. Mary S. Garrett, "The State of the Case," *National Educational Association: Journal of Proceedings and Addresses of the Thirty-Ninth Annual Meeting* (Washington, D.C., 1900): 663; Bell, *Memoir*, 221–22.

46. Alexander Graham Bell, "A Few Thoughts Concerning Eugenics," *Association Review* 10 (April 1908): 173.

47. Bell, *Memoir*, 217, 221–23.

48. Edward Allen Fay, "An Inquiry Concerning the Results of Marriages of the Deaf in America," *Annals* 42 (February 1897): 100–102; see also the discussion of this issue in Van Cleve and Crouch, *A Place of Their Own*, 150–52.

49. On the influence of eugenics upon Bell's work in deaf education, see Winefield, *Never the Twain Shall Meet*, 82–96; Lane, *When the Mind Hears*, 353–61; Van Cleve and Crouch, *A Place of Their Own*, 145–52; for a more sympathetic view of Bell's eugenic concerns about deafness, see Robert V. Bruce, *Bell: Alexander Graham Bell and the Conquest of Solitude* (Ithaca, N.Y.: Cornell University Press, 1973), 409–12.

50. "Public Instruction of the Deaf: Professor Alexander Graham Bell Speaks before Board of Education," *Inter-Ocean* [newspaper] (Chicago, March 7, 1895): 6; see also the account given in the *Tribune* (Chicago, March 7, 1895): 6; both of these articles can be found in the Alexander Graham Bell Family Papers, Manuscript Division, Library of Congress, Container 173.

51. See, for example, *Detroit Evening News* (Mar. 8, 1895), *Detroit Tribune* (Mar. 8, 1895), in Alexander Graham Bell Family Papers, Manuscript Division, Library of Congress, Container 178; Mary S. Garrett, "Helps and Hindrances of Deaf Children in Acquiring Speech and Language at the Natural Age," *Association Review* 10 (June 1908): 276.

52. Quoted in Padden and Humphries, *Deaf in America*, 36.

53. Helen Taylor, "The Importance of a Right Beginning," *Association Review* 1 (December 1899): 159.

54. Ibid.

55. Fred DeLand, *Dumb No Longer: Romance of the Telephone* (Washington, D.C.: Volta Bureau, 1908), 20.

56. Bingham, "All along the Line," 28–29.

57. Ibid. See also J. C. Gordon, "Dr. Gordon's Report," *Association Review* 1 (December 1899): 204. Mary Garrett, "The Next Step in the Education of the Deaf," in *Congress of Women,* ed. Mary Kavanaugh Oldham Eagle (Chicago, 1893), 444. Gordon, "Dr. Gordon's Report," 213.

58. Gallaudet, "Natural Language of Signs—II," 89; J. D. Kirkhuff, "Sign System Arraigned," 88a.

59. Davidson, "Relation of Language," 132.

60. Emma Garrett, "A Plea that the Deaf 'Mutes' of America May be Taught to Use Their Voices," *Annals* 28 (January 1883): 18.

61. Bingham, "All along the Line," 29; see also Emma Garrett, "A Plea," 18.

62. From extracts reprinted in Alexander Graham Bell, "Historical Notes Concerning the Teaching of Speech to the Deaf," *Association Review* (April 1902): 151.

63. Stone, "Religious State," 137.

64. Ibid.; Camp, "Claims of the Deaf," 214. Philip G. Gillett, superintendent of the Illinois school, wrote in 1890 that while deafness had at one time consigned a person to "dense ignorance for life," "what was once a calamity is now only a serious inconvenience." Philip G. Gillett, *Science* 16 (Oct. 31, 1890): 249–50.

65. Bingham, "All along the Line," 28; Taylor, "Importance of a Right Beginning," 158.

66. J. A. Jacobs, "To Save the Souls of His Pupils, the Great Duty of a Teacher of Deaf-Mutes," *Annals* 8 (July 1856): 211; Susanna E. Hull, "The Psychological Method of Teaching Language," *Annals* 43 (April 1898): 190.

67. Donald G. Matthews, "The Second Great Awakening as an Organizing Process, 1780–1830: An Hypothesis," *American Quarterly* 21 (Spring 1969): 23–43; Richard Carwardine, "The Know-Nothing Party, the Protestant Evangelical Community and American National Identity," in *Religion and National Identity,* ed. Stuart Mews (Oxford: Published for the Ecclesiastical History Society by B. Blackwell, 1982), 449–63.

68. Rivka Shpak Lissak, *Pluralism and Progressives: Hull House and the New Immigrants, 1890–1919* (Chicago: University of Chicago Press, 1989), 50–55.

69. Taylor, "Importance of a Right Beginning," 158. The equation of equality with sameness was a staple of Progressive reform thought; see Lissak, *Pluralism and Progressives,* 153.

70. Lissak, *Pluralism and Progressives;* Hoxie, *A Final Promise;* Joshua A. Fishman, *Language Loyalty in the United States: The Maintenance and*

Perpetuation of Non-English Mother Tongues by American Ethnic and Religious Groups (The Hague: Mouton, 1966).

71. George Lakoff, *Women, Fire, and Dangerous Things: What Categories Reveal about the Mind* (Chicago: University of Chicago Press, 1987), xiv.

72. Leo M. Jacobs, *A Deaf Adult Speaks Out* (Washington, D.C.: Gallaudet College Press, 1980), 90–100; Jerome D. Schein, *At Home among Strangers: Exploring the Deaf Community in the United States* (Washington, D.C.: Gallaudet University Press, 1989), 130; Paul C. Higgins, *Outsiders in a Hearing World: A Sociology of Deafness* (Beverly Hills, Calif.: Sage Publications, 1980), 69–76; James Woodward, *How You Gonna Get to Heaven if You Can't Talk with Jesus: On Depathologizing Deafness* (Silver Spring, Md.: T. J. Publishers, 1982), 11. Collins Stone pointed out over a hundred years ago that it was "vain to say that [deaf people] are 'strangers and foreigners among their own friends,' when we can point to hundreds who will indignantly repel such an intimation"; *The 53rd Annual Report of the Directors and Officers of the American Asylum at Hartford* (Hartford, Conn., 1869), 18–19.

73. The principal of the Western New York Institution for Deaf Mutes at Rochester, Z. F. Westervelt, instituted such a policy and claimed that he had seen students educated this way "acquire the habit of expressing their thought through English, and grow so accustomed to the language that their conversation was fluent, natural, and readily intelligible." Z. F. Westervelt, "The Colloquial Use of English by the Deaf," *Proceedings of the Twelfth Convention of American Instructors of the Deaf, 1890* (New York, 1890), 112.

Chapter Two

1. John M. Tyler, "The Teacher and the State," *Association Review* 1 (October 1899): 19–21, 26.

2. Peter J. Bowler, *Evolution: The History of an Idea* (Berkeley: University of California Press, 1989), 188; John C. Greene, *Science, Ideology, and World View* (Berkeley: University of California Press, 1981), 52. Alvar Ellegård's exhaustive review of the British popular press has shown that by 1870 the basic idea of evolution was widely accepted in Britain. See *Darwin and the General Reader: The Reception of Darwin's Theory of Evolution in the British Periodical Press, 1859–1872* (1958; Chicago: University of Chicago Press, 1990). While in the United States we have no survey as extensive, Richard Hofstadter's more limited survey led him to conclude that, within ten years after the publication of the *Origin,* popular magazines progressed "from hostility to skepticism

to gingerly approval and finally to full-blown praise"; *Social Darwinism in American Thought* (Boston: Beacon Press, 1955), 22.

3. The literature here is vast. To begin, on mental illness and evolution, see Sander L. Gilman, *Disease and Representation: Images of Illness from Madness to Aids* (Ithaca: Cornell University Press, 1988), 129–32; on sin as reversion, see Cynthia Eagle Russett, *Darwin in America: The Intellectual Response* (San Francisco: W. H. Freeman, 1976), 30, and Jon H. Roberts, *Darwinism and the Divine in America: Protestant Intellectuals and Organic Evolution, 1859–1900* (Madison: University of Wisconsin Press, 1988), 199–201; on criminology, see Stephen Jay Gould, *The Mismeasure of Man* (New York: W. W. Norton, 1981), 122–35; see also Daniel Levine, *Jane Addams and the Liberal Tradition* (Madison: University of Wisconsin Press, 1971), 94; as Levine wrote, "social Darwinism was not so much a conservative doctrine as a universal doctrine. The analogy found a home in America with amazing speed and ubiquity." In light of recent work by Peter J. Bowler, among others, Levine's statement should be amended to say that it was social "evolutionism," not Darwinism per se, that became ubiquitous; see Bowler, *The Non-Darwinian Revolution: Reinterpreting a Historical Myth* (Baltimore: Johns Hopkins University Press, 1988).

4. Bowler, *Evolution*, 296–99.

5. Tyler, "Teacher and the State," 22, 26.

6. Ibid., 22–26.

7. See Gordon W. Hewes, "Primate Communication and the Gestural Origin of Language," *Current Anthropology* 14 (February–April 1973): 5; A. S. Diamond, *The History and Origin of Language* (New York: Philosophical Society, 1959), 265; Alf Sommerfelt, "The Origin of Language: Theories and Hypotheses," *Journal of World History* 1 (April 1954): 886–92; Edward B. Tylor, *Researches into the Early History of Mankind* (1865; New York: Henry Holt, 1878), 15.

8. This section of my account of Condillac is based upon James H. Stam, *Inquiries into the Origin of Language: The Fate of a Question* (New York: Harper and Row, 1976), 45–52.

9. Renate Fischer, "Language of Action," in *Looking Back: A Reader on the History of Deaf Communities and their Sign Languages,* ed. Renate Fischer and Harlan Lane (Hamburg: Signum, 1993), 431–33.

10. B. D. Pettingill, "The Sign-Language," *American Annals of the Deaf* [hereafter cited as *Annals*] 18 (January 1873): 9; Remi Valade, "The Sign Language in Primitive Times," *Annals* 18 (January 1873): 31. See also Warring Wilkinson, "The Development of Speech and of the Sign-Language," *Annals* 26 (January 1881): 167–78; Harvey P. Peet, "Notions of the Deaf and Dumb before Instruction," *Annals* 8 (October 1855): 10;

Warren Robinson, "Something about the Sign Language," *Silent Educator* 1 (1890): 216; J. C. Covell, "The Nobility, Dignity, and Antiquity of the Sign Language," *Proceedings of the Seventh Convention of American Instructors of the Deaf, 1870* (Indianapolis, 1870), 133–36. Edward M. Gallaudet claimed that sign language was the "mother language of mankind"; *Speech for the Deaf: Essays Written for the Milan International Congress on the Education of the Deaf, Milan, Sept. 6–11, 1880* (no publisher, n.d., copy located in the Volta Bureau archives, Washington, D.C.): 17, quoted in Margaret Winzer, "An Examination of Some Selected Factors that Affected the Education and Socialization of the Deaf of Ontario, 1870–1900" (Ph.D. diss., University of Toronto, 1981), 118.

11. See Peet, "Notions of the Deaf and Dumb," 20, for a wide-ranging discussion of the issue; while Peet believed humans were created with a spontaneous ability to use spoken language, he recounts here the argument that language developed over time. See also Valade, "Sign Language," 31.

12. See, for example, Peet, "Notions of the Deaf and Dumb," 15; Tyler, "Teacher and the State," 20.

13. Joseph Jastrow, "The Evolution of Language," *Science* 7 (June 18, 1886): 555–56.

14. Stam, *Inquiries*, 242–50.

15. William Dwight Whitney, *The Life and Growth of Language: An Outline of Linguistic Science* (New York: D. Appleton, 1876), 291.

16. Bowler, *Evolution*, 233; Frederick E. Hoxie, *A Final Promise: The Campaign to Assimilate the Indians* (Lincoln: University of Nebraska Press, 1989), 115–45.

17. Tylor, *Researches*, 15, 44; Oliver Sacks notes Tylor's knowledge of sign language and friendships with deaf people in *Seeing Voices: A Journey into the World of the Deaf* (Berkeley: University of California Press, 1989), 75. See also sociologist Charles Horton Cooley, *Social Organization: A Study of the Larger Mind* (New York: Scribner, 1909), 67: it is "probable that artificial gesture language was well organized before speech had made much headway."

18. Garrick Mallery, "The Sign Language of the North American Indians," *Annals* 25 (January 1880): 1–3, 6; Garrick Mallery, "The Gesture Speech of Man," *Annals* 27 (April 1882): 69; Garrick Mallery, *Introduction to the Study of Sign Language among the North American Indians as Illustrating the Gesture Speech of Mankind* (Washington, D.C., 1880), reprinted in *Aboriginal Sign-Languages of the Americas and Australia*, ed. D. Jean Umiker-Sebeok and Thomas A. Sebeok (New York: Plenum Press, 1978), 1:13; see also Tylor, *Researches*, 77–78. In a recent and fascinating book, the anthropologist Brenda Farnell has corrected the

long-held assumption that Indian Sign Language—or "Plains Sign Talk" (PST) as it is more properly called—functioned only as a *lingua franca* for intertribal communication. Farnell discovered that among the Assiniboine people of northern Montana, at least, PST was an integral part of the language for everyday interactions and especially for formal storytelling. *Do You See What I Mean: Plains Indian Sign Talk and the Embodiment of Action* (Austin: University of Texas Press, 1995), 1–3.

19. Mallery, "Gesture Speech," 80.

20. Edward B. Tylor, "On the Origin of Language," *Fortnightly Review* 4 (Apr. 15, 1886): 547.

21. Charles Darwin, *The Expression of the Emotions in Man and Animals* (1872; Chicago: University of Chicago Press, 1965), 61.

22. Mallery, *Introduction to the Study of Sign Language*, 12–14.

23. Jastrow, "Evolution of Language," 556.

24. Quoted in Thomas Francis Fox, "Speech and Gestures," *Annals* 42 (November 1897): 398, 400. The reporter was noting a common attitude, but he himself disagreed with the modern disdain for gesture.

25. J. C. Gordon, "Dr. Gordon's Report," *Association Review* 1 (December 1899): 206; Gardiner G. Hubbard, "Proceedings of the American [Social] Science Association," *National Deaf Mute Gazette* 2 (January 1868): 5; J. D. Kirkhuff, "Superiority of the Oral Method," *Silent Educator* 3 (January 1892): 139; Susanna E. Hull, "Do Persons Born Deaf Differ Mentally from Others Who Have the Power of Hearing?" *Annals* 22 (October 1877): 236. See also Katherine T. Bingham, "All along the Line," *Association Review* 2 (February 1900): 22: the sign language of deaf people was, according to Bingham, identical to the gestures used by "a people of lowest type" found to exist "in the ends of the earth where no gleam of civilization had penetrated."

26. Emma Garrett, "A Plea that the Deaf 'Mutes' of America May be Taught to Use Their Voices," *Annals* 28 (January 1883): 18. In 1910 oralists were still arguing the same point in the same way, that it was wrong "to leave [deaf people] a few thousand years behind the race in the use of that language of signs from which human speech has been evolved." A. L. E. Crouter, "The Development of Speech in the Deaf Child" (pamphlet, no publisher listed, n.d), Gallaudet Archives; Box: PSD Dr. Crouter's Speeches (reprinted from the *Transactions of the American Laryngological, Rhinological and Otological Society*, 1910).

27. Mallery, "Sign Language," 7; for other accounts of such visits, see "Institution Items: Pennsylvania Institution," *Annals* 19 (January 1874): 48–49; Warring Wilkinson, "The Development of Speech and of the Sign-Language," *Annals* 26 (January 1881): 171; Garrick Mallery, "The Gesture Speech of Man," *Annals* 27 (April 1882): 75.

28. Harvey P. Peet, "Preliminary Remarks—Signs versus Articulation," *National Deaf Mute Gazette* 2 (February 1868): 4, 6–7; see also Robinson, "Something about the Sign Language," 216; Thomas H. Gallaudet, "On the Natural Language of Signs—I," *Annals* 1 (October 1847): 59.

29. Gallaudet, "Natural Language of Signs—I," 59.

30. Peet, "Notions of the Deaf and Dumb," 16.

31. Isaac Lewis Peet, "The Relation of the Sign Language to the Education of the Deaf," *Silent Educator* 1 (January 1890), 214.

32. Warring Wilkinson, "The Development of Speech and of the Sign-Language," *Annals* 26 (January 1881): 167.

33. John Dutton Wright, "Speech and Speech-Reading for the Deaf," *Century Magazine* (January 1897): 332–34.

34. "Discussion," *Proceedings of the Tenth Convention of American Instructors of the Deaf, 1882* (Jacksonville, Ill., 1882), 105–6.

35. Most such schools were never listed—for example, the Georgia and Mississippi schools, both established in 1882—because, even though physically separated from the main school, they were not formally independent but rather "colored departments" under the direction of the white school (see *Annals* 27 (April 1882): 125–26.) In other cases, it may be because such schools were underfunded and lacked the resources to answer the long questionnaires sent out by the *Annals* for their reports. The Texas school for black students, while listed in the *Annals* reports, submitted information only sporadically. Much space in the early reports of the Virginia school for black students, for example, is devoted to describing the needs of the school and the need for increased funding. See Virginia State School for Colored Deaf and Blind Children, "First Biennial Report, 1911," and "Second Biennial Report, 1913" (Newport News, Virginia, 1911 and 1913). Edward Allen Fay, in his *Histories of American Schools for the Deaf, 1817–1893* (Washington. D.C.: Volta Bureau, 1893), reports segregated departments for black students at the schools for the deaf in Arkansas, Tennessee, and Mississippi. See also the discussion in the *Proceedings of the Ninth Convention of American Instructors of the Deaf, 1878* (Columbus, Ohio, 1879), 231–37.

36. "Tabular Statement of American Schools for the Deaf, Oct. 20, 1920," *Annals* 66 (January 1921): 36–37; for Texas and Maryland, figures are taken from the 1919 report, because they did not submit reports in 1920: "Tabular Statement of American Schools for the Deaf, Oct. 20, 1919," *Annals* 65 (January 1920): 4–5.

37. Thomas Flowers, "Education of the Colored Deaf," *Proceedings of the Twentieth Convention of American Instructors of the Deaf, 1914* (Washington, D.C., 1915), 100.

38. Dr. Settles, "Normal Training for Colored Teachers," *Annals* 85 (March 1940): 211. Because of the continued use of sign language in the classroom, however, the ironic result of this policy of discrimination may have been that southern deaf African-Americans, in spite of the chronic underfunding of their schools, received a better education than most deaf white students.

39. Thomas Flowers, "Life after Graduation," draft of an essay, undated and unsigned but the body of the letter identifies it as written by Flowers in 1908, in the Gallaudet University Archives, Box: PSD; Misc.; AGB; Thomas Flowers; letters. His school file identifies him as "partially deaf" and "able to hear loud tones from those he is accustomed to hear speak," so there would have been no question about his suitability for an oral education.

40. "Discussion," *Proceedings of the Tenth Convention of American Instructors of the Deaf, 1882* (Jacksonville, Ill., 1882), 105–6.

41. Letter from Caroline Yale to Mrs. Alexander Graham Bell, dated May 19, 1908, Clarke School for the Deaf, Northampton, Mass., files stored in the president's office, box labeled Dr. and Mrs. Alexander Graham Bell.

42. The Washington, D.C., school for the deaf, however, had "eight or nine" black students out of a total of sixty students in 1886, according to Edward M. Gallaudet: "in the sleeping apartments and at the table they are separated in deference to the caste prejudice, which still continues in our country to a certain extent, but in the classes they come together"; Gallaudet gave no indication, however, of whether they were generally taught by the same methods or followed the same course of study; Joseph C. Gordon, ed., "Education of Deaf Children: Evidence Presented to the Royal Commission of the United Kingdom" (Washington, D.C.: Volta Bureau, 1892): 12.

43. See, for example, Keith Thomas, *Man and the Natural World* (New York: Pantheon Books, 1983); Peter Singer, *Animal Liberation: A New Ethics for Our Treatment of Animals,* (New York: Avon Books, 1975), 192–222; Mary Midgely, *Beast and Man: The Roots of Human Nature* (Ithaca: Cornell University Press, 1978); James Turner, *Reckoning with the Beast: Animals, Pain, and Humanity in the Victorian Mind* (Baltimore: Johns Hopkins University Press, 1980).

44. Quoted in Roberts, *Darwinism and the Divine,* 53.

45. Luzerne Rae, "The Philosophical Basis of Language," *Proceedings of the Third Convention of American Instructors of the Deaf, 1853* (Columbus, 1853): 157–58.

46. Peet, "Notions of the Deaf and Dumb," 19; Harvey P. Peet, "On the Origin and Early History of the Art of Instructing the Deaf and

Dumb," *Proceedings of the First Convention of American Instructors of the Deaf, 1850* (New York, 1850), 107.

47. Peet, "Notions of the Deaf," 9, 20–44.

48. Collins Stone, "On the Religious State and Instruction of the Deaf and Dumb," *Annals* 1 (April 1848): 137–41.

49. Lucius H. Woodruff, "Grace of Expression," *Annals* 2 (July 1849): 195.

50. Henry B. Camp, "Claims of the Deaf and Dumb upon Public Sympathy and Aid," *Annals* 1 (July 1848): "214–15.

51. Ayres, "Inquiry," 223.

52. Isaac Lewis Peet, "Moral State of the Deaf and Dumb Previous to Education, and the Means and Results of Religious Influence among Them," *Annals* 3 (July 1851): 212.

53. Paul F. Boller, "The New Science," in *The Gilded Age: A Reappraisal,* ed. Howard Wayne Morgan (Syracuse: Syracuse University Press, 1970), 247.

54. T. H. Huxley, *Man's Place in Nature* (London: Macmillan, 1906), 104.

55. Charles Darwin, *The Descent of Man and Selection in Relation to Sex* (New York: D. Appleton, 1896), 65–96.

56. Roberts, *Darwinism and the Divine,* 176–79, 2057; Paul A. Carter, *The Spiritual Crisis of the Gilded Age* (DeKalb, Ill.: Northern Illinois University Press, 1971), 85–107; James R. Moore, *The Post-Darwinian Controversies: A Study of the Protestant Struggle to Come to Terms with Darwin in Great Britain and America, 1870–1900* (Cambridge: Cambridge University Press, 1979), 232–33, 266–67, 336–37; Norman Pearson, *The Soul and Its Story: A Sketch* (London: Arnold, 1916), 4–23; D. R. Oldroyd, *Darwinian Impacts: An Introduction to the Darwinian Revolution* (Milton Keynes, England: Open University Press, 1980), 250–52.

57. Huxley, *Man's Place in Nature,* 95–96.

58. Cooley, *Social Organization,* 70; see also Franklin Henry Giddings, *The Elements of Sociology* (1898; New York: MacMillan, 1916), 238–41.

59. Frank Overton, *Applied Physiology: Including the Effects of Alcohol and Narcotics, Advanced Grade* (1897; New York: Macmillan, 1908), 298.

60. Emma Garrett, "Report of the Teacher in Charge; Branch for Oral Instruction [Pennsylvania Institution for the Deaf and Dumb]," Jan. 1, 1882; Gallaudet Archives; Box: PSD Sundry Reports, Communications, etc., dating prior to 1890.

61. Mary McCowen, "How Best to Secure Intelligent Speech for Deaf Children," *Association Review* 9 (February–April 1907): 258–59.

62. Lewis J. Dudley, "Report of the Corporation," *Seventeenth An-*

nual Report of the Clarke Institution for Deaf-Mutes (Northampton, Mass., 1884), 7.

63. Lewis J. Dudley, "Address of Mr. Dudley in 1880," *Fifteenth Annual Report of the Clarke Institution for Deaf-Mutes* (Northampton, Mass.: 1882), 7.

64. Pettingill, "Sign-Language," 4; Sarah Harvey Porter, "The Suppression of Signs by Force," *Annals* 39 (June 1894): 171. Porter repeated this observation in 1913, when she stated, "the oralists cried to us, derisively: 'Your children, making signs, look like monkeys!'" *Annals* 58 (September 1913): 284; R. W. Dodds, "The Practical Benefits of Methods Compared," *Annals* 44 (February 1899): 124; Wright, "Speech and Speech-Reading," 337–38; see also Edward M. Gallaudet, "How Shall the Deaf Be Educated," *International Review* (December 1881), reprinted in *Education of Deaf Children: Evidence of Edward Miner Gallaudet and Alexander Graham Bell Presented to the Royal Commission of the United Kingdom,* ed. Joseph C. Gordon (Washington, D.C.: Volta Bureau, 1892), 101.

65. For a concise review of nineteenth-century writings on expression, see the introduction to Darwin's *Expression;* Sir Charles Bell, *The Anatomy and Philosophy of Expression as Connected with the Fine Arts* (1806; London: George Bell and Sons, 1885); Gallaudet, "Natural Language of Signs—II," 80; see also Robert J. Richards, *Darwin and the Emergence of Evolutionary Theories of Mind and Behavior* (Chicago: University of Chicago Press, 1987), 230–34.

66. Charles P. Turner, "Expression," *Annals* 1 (January 1848): 77.

67. Gallaudet, "Natural Language of Signs—II," 81.

68. See, for example, Turner, "Expression," 77–78; see also Harlan Lane, *When the Mind Hears: A History of the Deaf* (New York: Random House, 1984), 174–75.

69. Darwin, *Expression,* 10.

70. Jastrow, "Evolution of Language," 555–56.

71. Anon., "The Perversity of Deaf-Mutism," *Annals* 18 (October 1873): 263.

72. Pettingill, "Sign-Language," 4. This was not an entirely new concern, but it carried different connotations for the oralist generation than it had for the manualists. In 1849 Lucius Woodruff complained of the "tendency to *grimace* in the natural language of the deaf and dumb." His concern was that such "uncouth expression" was "ungraceful" and would "betoken ill-breeding" and "offend against good taste." There was, however, an "inherent beauty in the language of signs, which cannot but be favorable to the development of pleasing expression" if correct instruction were provided. "Grace of Expression," *Annals* 2 (July 1849): 193, 195–96.

73. Samuel Gridley Howe, et al., *Second Annual Report of the Board of State Charities* (Boston, 1866), liii–liv.

74. Unsigned excerpt from the *Kentucky Mute,* "Vulgarity in Signing," *Silent Educator* 1 (January 1890): 91.

75. B. Engelsman, "Deaf Mutes and Their Instruction," *Science* 16 (Oct. 17, 1890): 220.

76. See Gilman, *Disease and Representation,* 129–32; Darwin (*Expression,* 131) indicated that exaggerated expression was characteristic of insanity. He may also have subscribed to the theory that insanity was reversion to a more primitive state of evolution. "This loss of control" of facial expression, according to Gilman, "would be the absence of civilized standards of behavior and a return to earlier modes of uncontrolled expression."

77. Gallaudet, "Natural Language of Signs—II," 86.

78. Ibid., 80.

79. Susanna E. Hull, "The Psychological Method of Teaching Language," *Annals* 43 (April 1898): 190; Hull was British but had an important following in the United States.

80. *Proceedings of the Fifth National Conference of Principals and Superintendents of Institutions for Deaf-Mutes* (St. Paul, Minn., 1884), 178.

Chapter Three

1. Myra Strober and David Tyack, "Why Do Women Teach and Men Manage? A Report on Research on Schools," *Signs: Journal of Women in Culture and Society* 5 (Spring 1980): 494.

2. Ibid., 495, 497. See also Thomas Woody, *A History of Women's Education in the United States* (1929; New York: Octagon Books, 1974), 460–518; Maris Vinovskis and Richard Bernard, "The Female School Teacher in Ante-Bellum Massachusetts," *Journal of Social History* 10 (March 1977): 332–45; Thomas Morain, "The Departure of Males from the Teaching Profession in Nineteenth-Century Iowa," *Civil War History* 26 (1980): 161–66; Myra H. Strober and Audri Gordon Lanford, "The Feminization of Public School Teaching: Cross-sectional Analysis, 1850–1880," *Signs: Journal of Women in Culture and Society* 11 (Winter 1986): 212–35; Jill K. Conway, "Politics, Pedagogy, and Gender," *Daedalus* 116 (Fall 1987): 137–52.

3. Strober and Tyack, "Why Do Women Teach and Men Manage?" 496.

4. Quoted in Kathryn Kish Sklar, *Catherine Beecher: A Study in American Domesticity* (New Haven: Yale University Press, 1973), 312–13.

5. "The History of the Pennsylvania Institution for the Deaf: Extracts from a Thesis Written by Miss Rose E. Huston," *Mt. Airy World* 47

(January 1932): 97. The Pennsylvania Institution was the first state residential school to open a separate branch for oral instruction. Of twenty-two teachers employed during its first ten years, only two were men, and they remained there a total of three years between them. See *Annual Report of the Board of Directors of the Pennsylvania Institution for the Deaf and Dumb* (Philadelphia) for the years 1881 to 1890.

6. Franklin Sanborn, review of "Eleventh Annual Report of the Columbian Institution for the Deaf and Dumb," *North American Review* 109 (July 1869): 288.

7. Amos G. Draper, "The Education of the Deaf in America," *American Annals of the Deaf* [hereafter cited as *Annals*] 49 (May 1904): 359; Edward P. Clarke, "The Training of Teachers of the Deaf in the United States," *Annals* 45 (September 1900): 352.

8. Figures derived from "Tabular Statement of American Schools for the Deaf, 1900–1901," *Annals* 46 (January 1901): 84–93. See also Edward P. Clarke, "An Analysis of the Schools and Instructors of the Deaf in the United States," *Annals* 45 (April 1900): 232–33.

9. Draper, "Education of the Deaf," 359.

10. Harvey P. Peet, "Progress in Deaf-Mute Education," *Proceedings of the Seventh Convention of American Instructors of the Deaf* (Indianapolis, 1870): 230.

11. *Proceedings of the Twelfth Convention of American Instructors of the Deaf, 1890* (New York, 1890), 34. Letter dated Jan. 30, 1882, from Mary Garrett to the Board of Directors, Pennsylvania Institution for the Deaf, Gallaudet University Archives, Box: PSD Reports Building Committee . . . Employment Committee; packet labeled Oral Branch Reports.

12. Alexander G. Bell, *Upon the Formation of a Deaf Variety of the Human Race* (Washington, D.C.: Government Printing Office, 1884), 211–16; this increase in the proportion of adventitiously deafened children to congenitally deaf children probably had some impact upon the growth of the oral method. Children deafened after learning spoken English naturally have less difficulty with speech and lip-reading; during oralism's early years, then, a proportionately greater number of children would have been found to be successful with the method than would normally be the case.

13. J. W. Blattner, "Some Reflections Occasioned by the Growth of Speech Teaching," *Annals* 46 (1901): 520–22, 525; see also *Proceedings of the National Conference of Principals of Institutions for the Deaf and Dumb, 1868* (Washington, 1868): 80.

14. Harvey P. Peet, "Notes of a Visit to the Clarke Institution," *Annals* 14 (April 1869): 87–88.

15. Sklar, *Catherine Beecher,* 182.

16. "Appendix to the Report on Deaf-Mute Education in Massachusetts," *Massachusetts Senate Joint Special Committee on the Education of Deaf-Mutes, Senate Document No. 265* (Boston, May 1867), 8.

17. As with female teachers, this was often justified on the basis of supply and demand. See, for example, Philip G. Gillett, "The Organization for an Institution for the Deaf and Dumb," *Annals* 15 (October 1870): 209.

18. Amos G. Draper, "The Attitude of the Adult Deaf towards Pure Oralism," *Annals* 40 (January 1895): 51. In the first five years of Gallaudet College (1869 to 1874), a liberal arts college exclusively for deaf students, 75 percent of its graduates became teachers at schools for the deaf; from 1894 to 1899, fewer than a third did so; see Clarke, "Analysis," 228–29.

19. Caroline Yale, "A Report on the Third International Congress for the Amelioration of the Condition of Deaf-Mutes," *Sixteenth Annual Report of the Clarke Institution for Deaf-Mutes* (Northampton, Mass., 1883), 59; see also F. W. Booth, "The Passing of the Deaf Teacher," *Association Review* 8 (December 1906): 496; A. G. Bell considered deaf teachers "another element favorable to the formation of a deaf race—to be therefore avoided" (*Formation of a Deaf Variety*, 224).

20. This was a common argument for the lower salaries of both deaf and female teachers; see, for example, Gillett, "Organization," 209; Edward Miner Gallaudet, "President Gallaudet's Address," *Proceedings of the Nineteenth Convention of American Instructors of the Deaf, 1911* (Washington, D.C., 1912), 41; see also Sylvia Chapin Balis, *Proceedings of the Twelfth Convention of American Instructors of the Deaf, 1890* (New York, 1890), 35.

21. Discussion following the paper of Weston Jenkins, "The Standard of Teachers," *Proceedings of the Twelfth Convention of American Instructors of the Deaf 1890* (New York, 1890), 34–39. This was an issue of over thirty years standing. At the 1853 convention, and again in 1858, a deaf teacher raised the issue; hearing teachers argued, however, that "men of liberal education were required for the more advanced classes, as well as to be in training for the post of principal"; this meant hearing men and justified their higher pay. *Proceedings of the Third Convention of American Instructors of the Deaf, 1853* (Columbus, 1853), 210–12; Samuel Porter, "Fifth Convention of American Instructors of the Deaf," *Annals* 10 (October 1858): 196. The opening of Gallaudet College in 1864, which meant that deaf men too could be "men of liberal education" (deaf women were not admitted until 1886), did not result, however, in the equalization of deaf and hearing salaries.

22. Emma Garrett, "Report to the Committee on the Branch for

Oral Instruction" (Pennsylvania Institution for the Deaf) for Jan. 28, 1882, and Sept. 29, 1882 (Gallaudet University Archives, Box: PSD Reports Building Committee . . . Employment Committee, packet labeled Oral Branch Reports); Emma Garrett, letter to Committee on Oral Branch, Pennsylvania Institution for the Deaf, dated Jan. 30, 1882 (Gallaudet University Archives, Box: PSD Reports Building Committee . . . Employment Committee; packet labeled Oral Branch Reports, envelope addressed to Dr. Seiss, Chairman Committee on Branch for Oral Instruction, Pa. Ins. D. & D. [sic].)

23. Cornelia Trask, "Women as Teachers of Mutes," *Proceedings of the National Conference of Principals of Institutions for the Deaf and Dumb, 1868* (Washington, D.C., 1868), 129, reprinted in "Conference of the Principals of the American Institutions," *Annals* 13 (1868): 242–54.

24. Walter Angus, "We Are Not Retrograding," *Annals* 16 (1871): 169; "Proceedings of the Conference of the Principals of the American Institutions," *Annals* 13 (1868): 145. See also, "Proceedings of the First Convention of American Instructors of the Deaf," *Annals* 3 (1850): 25–26; "Reports of the American Institutions for the Deaf and Dumb," *Annals* 18 (1873): 178.

25. Fred DeLand noted this connection in his celebratory history of the oralist movement, *Dumb No Longer: Romance of the Telephone* (Washington, D.C.: Volta Bureau, 1908), 24.

26. W. A. Cochrane, "Articulation as a Means of Instruction," *Proceedings of the Seventh Convention of American Instructors of the Deaf, 1870* (Indianapolis, 1870), 236–37; Mary Garrett, "Report of Principal and Secretary," *Second Report of the Home for the Training in Speech of Deaf Children before They Are of School Age* (Philadelphia, 1893), 11–13; see also "Superintendent's Report for March 1893 [Pennsylvania Institution for the Deaf and Dumb]," Gallaudet University Archives (Box: PSD, Principal and Superintendent Reports): "it is generally conceded that for best results under Oral Methods the age of six years affords the best opportunities for good speech and lip-reading"; Rose E. Huston, "The History of the Pennsylvania School for the Deaf," *Mt. Airy World* 47 (February 1932): 123.

27. W. H. Latham, "Difficulties Connected with Deaf-Mute Instruction," *Annals* 15 (1870): 109; Benjamin Talbot, "The Proper Age for the Admission of Pupils to Institutions for the Deaf and Dumb," *Proceedings of the National Conference of Principals of Institutions for the Deaf and Dumb, 1868* (Washington D.C., 1868), 45–46. The Convention of American Instructors of the Deaf had resolved in 1850 that it was "inexpedient to receive deaf and dumb children as pupils into our Institutions, except in special cases, under the age of ten years; and that in our opinion, twelve

would be a more suitable age for admission" (the "special cases" were children growing up surrounded by "corrupting influences"). *Proceedings of the First Convention of American Instructors of the Deaf, 1850* (New York, 1850), 223–25, reprinted in *Annals* 3 (1850): 25–26. William W. Turner, "On the Proper Age for the Admission of Pupils into Institutions for the Deaf and Dumb," *Annals* 5 (April, 1853): 147–48. See also Henry W. Syle, "A Summary of the Recorded Researches and Opinions of Harvey Prindle Peet, Ph.D., LL.D.—II," *Annals* 18 (October 1873): 213. Latham, "Difficulties Connected with Deaf-Mute Instruction," 109; Angus, "We Are Not Retrograding," 169–70, argued that the kind of work a deaf child must undertake in school "requires a mental effort to which at best he is not fairly equal until he reaches the age of nine to twelve years."

28. William W. Turner, "On the Proper Age for the Admission of Pupils into Institutions for the Deaf and Dumb," *Annals* 5 (April 1853): 147–48. Turner and others sometimes suggested that if deaf students were not limited to five or six years of school by state legislatures, the schools would be happy to admit younger students. There is little evidence, however, that manualists fought for the lifting of this limit, suggesting that they in fact were not eager to teach young children. Oralists, on the other hand, did fight for it and succeeded; see F. B. Sanborn, "Report of the Corporation," *Tenth Annual Report of the Clarke Institution for Deaf-Mutes, 1877* (Northampton, Mass., 1869), 6. For discussions of admission age, see also, "Reports of American Institutions for the Deaf and Dumb," *Annals* 18 (July 1873): 176–81; *Proceedings of the Ninth Convention of American Instructors of the Deaf, 1878* (Columbus, 1879), 69–74.

29. Jacob Van Nostrand, "Necessity of a Higher Standard of Education for the Deaf and Dumb," *Proceedings of the First Convention of American Instructors of the Deaf, 1850* (New York, 1850), 245, 247; William W. Turner, "High School for the Deaf and Dumb," *Proceedings of the Second Convention of American Instructors of the Deaf, 1851* (Hartford, 1851), 21–36; William W. Turner and J. Van Nostrand, "Report of a Committee on a High School for the Deaf and Dumb," *Proceedings of the Third Convention of American Instructors of the Deaf, 1853* (Columbus, 1853), 79–85.

30. "Report of the Corporation," *Fifteenth Annual Report of the Clarke Institution for Deaf-Mutes, 1882* (Northampton, Mass., 1882), 9.

31. Warring Wilkinson, "Day-Schools, Their Advantages and Their Disadvantages," *Annals* 50 (1905): 79, 93.

32. Katherine T. Bingham, "All along the Line," *Association Review* 2 (February 1900): 21.

33. A. L. E. Crouter, "Address of the President before the Seventh

Summer Meeting [of the American Association to Promote the Teaching of Speech to the Deaf]," issued as a Circular of Information to members of the Association (Washington, D.C., 1906), Gallaudet University Archives, Container: PSD, Dr. Crouter's Speeches (reprinted in *Association Review* 8 [October 1906]: 301–17); see also Bingham, "All along the Line," 24.

34. Emma Garrett, "Principal's Report," *First Report of the Home for the Training in Speech of Deaf Children before They Are of School Age* (Philadelphia, 1892), 11; Mary Garrett, "Report of Principal and Secretary," *Second Report of the Home for the Training in Speech* (Philadelphia, 1893), 13; S. Edwin Megargee, "President's Report," *Second Report of the Home for the Training in Speech* (Philadelphia, 1893), 9; Mary S. Garret, "Helps and Hindrances of Deaf Children in Acquiring Speech and Language at the Natural Age," *Association Review* 10 (1908): 275 (a paper read before a meeting of the First International Council of Mothers, March 14, 1908, Washington, D.C.).

35. "Tabular Statement of American Schools for the Deaf, 1889," *Annals* 35 (January 1890): 62; The McCowen Oral School for Young Deaf Children was opened in Chicago in 1883 by Mary McCowen; the Sarah Fuller Home School for Little Deaf Children, attached to the Boston Day School for the Deaf (later known as the Horace Mann School), was opened in 1888; the Albany Home School for the Oral Instruction of the Deaf in New York was begun in 1889 by Anna Black; and the Home for the Training in Speech of Deaf Children before They Are of School Age, was established in Philadelphia by Emma and Mary Garrett in 1892.

36. Mary S. Garrett, "Report of Secretary and Principal," *Third Report of the Home for the Training in Speech* (Philadelphia, 1893), 12–13.

37. In 1868, when most schools still set their minimum age of admission at ten or twelve, the minimum age for admission at the Clarke School was five. The median age of admittance was just over nine years of age; "Names, Residences, Etc, of Pupils in the Clarke Institution for Deaf Mutes, December 31st, 1868," *Second Annual Report of the Clarke Institution for Deaf-Mutes, 1869* (Boston, 1869), 12–13; see also, Gardiner G. Hubbard, "Report of the Corporation," *Eighth Annual Report of the Clarke Institution for Deaf-Mutes, 1875* (Cambridge, 1875), 16; Sanborn, "Report of the Corporation," *Tenth Annual Report,* 6.

At the Pennsylvania Institution, a separate "oral branch" was established in 1881; that year at the main branch, where sign language was still used, the admission age was ten, having been lowered from age twelve a few years before, but at the new oral branch the age of admission was six years. When in 1893 the entire school was converted to oralism, the admission age was made uniform at six; see "Report," *Annual Report of the Board of Directors for the Pennsylvania Institution for the Deaf and Dumb for the Year 1881* (Philadelphia, 1881), 10. See also Cochrane, "Articulation as a Means of Instruction," 236–37.

38. Gardiner G. Hubbard, "Report of the Corporation," *Eighth Annual Report of the Clarke Institution for Deaf Mutes, 1875* (Cambridge, 1875), 17.

39. Trask, "Women as Teachers," 129–30. Women during this period who argued for an enlarged sphere of action for women typically did so in terms of traditional, essentialist understandings of gender; see George Cotkin, *Reluctant Modernism: American Thought and Culture, 1880–1900* (New York: Twayne, 1992), 75.

40. Clarke, "Analysis," 232.

41. See John V. Van Cleve and Barry Crouch, *A Place of Their Own: Creating the Deaf Community in America* (Washington, D.C.: Gallaudet University Press, 1989), 117–20; Harlan Lane, *When the Mind Hears: A History of the Deaf* (New York: Harvard University Press, 1984), 362–65; John Vickrey Van Cleve, "The Academic Integration of Deaf Children: A Historical Perspective," in *Looking Back: A Reader on the History of Deaf Communities and their Sign Languages,* ed. Renate Fischer and Harlan Lane (Hamburg: Signum Press, 1993), 333–47.

42. Bingham, "All along the Line," 29. At a recent conference on sign language in the schools (Seventh Annual Conference on Issues in Language and Deafness—"The Use of Sign Language in Educational Settings: Current Concepts and Controversies," Boys Town National Research Hospital, Omaha, Nebraska, Oct. 3–4, 1992), this was still prominent in the rhetoric of opponents of ASL in the schools who advocate, instead, the use of some form of signed English. ASL, it was argued, alienates children from parents and encourages them to identify with the deaf community more than with their own families.

43. Catherine E. Beecher, "How to Redeem Woman's Profession from Dishonor," *Harper's New Monthly Magazine* 31 (November 1865): 716, quoted in Dorothy Hayden, *The Grand Domestic Revolution: A History of Feminist Designs for American Homes, Neighborhoods, and Cities* (Cambridge: MIT Press, 1989), 56.

44. "From Separation to Togetherness: The Social Construction of Domestic Space in American Suburbs, 1840–1915," *Journal of American History* 76 (September 1989): 508.

45. Ann Douglas, *The Feminization of American Culture* (New York: Knopf, 1977), 12.

46. DeLand, *Dumb No Longer,* 32.

47. "Public Instruction of the Deaf: Professor Alexander Graham Bell

Speaks before Board of Education," *The Inter-Ocean* [newspaper], Chicago, Mar. 7, 1895, 6 (this article can be found in the Alexander Graham Bell Family Papers, Manuscript Division, Library of Congress, Container 173).

48. "Appendix to the Report on Deaf-Mute Education in Massachusetts," 32; see also R. C. Spencer, "Work of the Wisconsin Phonological Institute and the Wisconsin Public Day-Schools for the Deaf," *Proceedings of the Fourteenth Convention of American Instructors of the Deaf, 1895* (Flint, 1895), 134: the day school system, he told the convention, "obviates the necessity of violating home ties and affections by moving children to institutions, thus dwarfing the filial sentiments."

49. Pennsylvania Institution for the Deaf, Draft of Annual Report, 1890; Gallaudet Archives: PSD Sundry Communications, 1890–94. See also, Emma Garrett, "Principal's Report," *First Report of the Home for the Training in Speech of Deaf Children before They Are of School Age* (Philadelphia, 1892), 18; S. Edwin Megargee, "President's Report," *Second Report of the Home for the Training in Speech,* 7; see also Emma Garrett, "A Plea that the Deaf-Mutes of America May be Taught to Use Their Voices," *Proceedings of the Tenth Convention of American Instructors of the Deaf, 1882* (Springfield, Ill., 1882), 67: "day-schools are best for the deaf; but if boarding-schools are a necessity anywhere, I think they should be on the cottage plan."

50. Sylvia Chapin Balis, "A Woman's View," *Annals* 45 (September 1900): 315–16. Men were no longer interested in teaching deaf children, she wrote, because they "distrust the methods employed and escape all responsibility for their furtherance" (316).

51. Strober and Lanford, "Feminization of Public School Teaching," 218–19.

52. See *Annual Report of the Board of Directors of the Pennsylvania Institution for the Deaf and Dumb* (Philadelphia, 1891), 37–38.

53. Fred DeLand, "The Real Romance of the Telephone, or Why Deaf Children Need No Longer Be Dumb," *Association Review* 7 (October 1905): 320. Such references appear to have been so common, in fact, that it became an analogy used by teachers in other fields. In 1900 the superintendent of Indian education for the federal government explained that the "Indian teacher must deal with the conditions similar to those that confront the teacher of the blind or the deaf. She must exercise infinite patience." Quoted in Frederick E. Hoxie, *A Final Promise: The Campaign to Assimilate the Indians, 1880–1920* (Lincoln: University of Nebraska Press, 1984), 195.

54. Franklin B. Sanborn, "Proceedings of the Sixth Summer Meeting of the American Association to Promote the Teaching of Speech to the Deaf—Address of Welcome," *Association Review* 1 (October 1899): 58.

55. A. J. Winnie, "What a Study of the Deaf Child will do for the Hearing Child," *Association Review* 7 (April 1905): 138.

56. Franklin B. Sanborn, *15th Annual Report of the Clarke Institution for Deaf-Mutes* (Northampton, Mass., 1882), 11. See also *Proceedings of the Fourth Conference of Principals of Institutions for the Deaf, 1880* (Northampton, Mass., 1880), 25.

57. Peet, "Progress in Deaf-Mute Instruction," 230; Harvey P. Peet, "Notions of the Deaf and Dumb before Instruction," *Annals* 8 (October 1855): 4; J. A. Ayres, "An Inquiry into the Extent to which the Misfortune of Deafness May Be Alleviated," *Annals* 1 (April 1848): 225–26.

58. Luzerne Rae, "Thoughts of the Deaf and Dumb before Instruction," *Annals* 1 (April 1848): 150–51; Thomas H. Gallaudet, "The Natural Language of Signs—I," *Annals* 1 (October 1847): 55–59; and see chapter 5 below.

59. Emphasis in original; Lucius Woodruff, "The Motives to Intellectual Effort on the Part of the Young Deaf-Mute," *Annals* 1 (January 1848): 159; Woodruff, "Moral Education of the Deaf and Dumb," *Annals* 3 (January 1851): 9.

60. *Proceedings of the Ninth Convention of American Instructors of the Deaf, 1878* (Columbus, 1879), 63; see also 249, 252.

61. DeLand, "Real Romance of the Telephone," 321.

62. Trask, "Women as Teachers," 134–35.

63. Of ninety-four delegates present, twenty-two were women. Eleven of these, however, appear to have been wives of male teachers or principals. In subsequent *Proceedings,* spouses were listed with the honorary members, but in this one that does not seem to be the case. How many of these were not themselves teachers and would not therefore be likely to speak in any case, and how many were teachers could not be told from the *Proceedings. Proceedings of the Seventh Convention of American Instructors of the Deaf, 1870* (Indianapolis, 1870), 12–13.

64. Nineteen papers were read, three of them specifically on the topic of articulation training; although 30 percent of the official delegates and the vast majority of articulation teachers were women, they presented no papers; *Proceedings of the Eighth Convention of American Instructors of the Deaf, 1874* (Toronto, 1876).

65. The two were Sarah Fuller and Harriet B. Rogers, both of them school principals and prominent leaders of the oralist movement; none of twenty-two motions were made by women; see *Proceedings of the Ninth Convention of American Instructors of the Deaf, 1878* (Columbus, 1879), 258, 280. Figures taken from list of members reported to be present at the meeting, excluding honorary members.

66. *Proceedings of the Ninth Convention,* 19.

67. At the 1851 convention, the Reverend Thomas Gallaudet (eldest

son of Thomas H.) moved that voting be by hand "in order that the deaf-mute members of the Convention may participate." In 1853 a motion to vote by hand was debated and, on the second day, adopted. The issue does not reappear in the records until 1890, when it was again suggested that voting be by hand instead of voice, and again this rule was adopted. It is unclear what the practice had been in the intervening years, but the fact that the issue had to be raised again suggests that voting by hand had not become customary. *Proceedings of the Second Convention of American Instructors of the Deaf, 1851* (Hartford, 1851), 37; *Proceedings of the Third Convention of American Instructors of the Deaf, 1853,* (Columbus, 1853), 13; *Proceedings of the Twelfth Convention of American Instructors of the Deaf, 1890* (New York, 1890), 18.

68. Garrick Mallery, "The Gesture Speech of Man," *Annals* 27 (April 1882): 82.

69. Laura Sheridan, "Some Embarrassments of Our Work and Possible Remedies," *Proceedings of the Ninth Convention of American Instructors of the Deaf, 1878* (Columbus, 1879), 107; Laura Sheridan, "Religious Instruction of Deaf Mutes," *Proceedings of the Tenth Convention of American Instructors of the Deaf, 1882* (Jacksonville, Ill., 1882), 15.

70. Garrett, "A Plea," 64.

71. *Proceedings of the Eleventh Convention of American Instructors of the Deaf, 1886* (Sacramento, 1887), 18, index. Of 145 official delegates, sixty-one were women; women made seventeen of the 503 "Remarks and Addresses." Women delivered five papers, compared to sixteen for the men—less than a quarter of the total, at a convention where women were over 40 percent of the official delegates—but a higher percentage than was usual before or after.

72. *Proceedings of the Twelfth Convention of American Instructors of the Deaf, 1890* (New York, 1890), i–v, 345–46. Only three women are recorded as having spoken more than once during the course of the five-day meeting: Sylvia Chapin Balis spoke four times; Caroline Yale, principal of the flagship school of the oralist movement, the Clarke Institution, did so three times; and a teacher visiting from France spoke twice.

73. Sylvia Chapin Balis, "A Woman's View," *Annals* 45 (September 1900): 313.

74. *Convention of Articulation Teachers of the Deaf—1884: Official Report* (Albany, 1884), 9, 155–62.

75. Balis, "A Woman's View," 313–14.

76. Quoted in Karlyn Kohrs Campbell, *Women Public Speakers in the United States, 1800–1925* (Westport, Conn.: Greenwood Press, 1993), 120.

77. Elizabeth Cady Stanton before the U.S. Senate Committee on Woman Suffrage, Feb. 20, 1892, in Mary Jo Buhle and Paul Buhle, *The Concise History of Woman Suffrage* (Urbana: University of Illinois Press,

1978), 325–27. See also Stanton in Ellen Carol Dubois, ed., *Elizabeth Cady Stanton, Susan B. Anthony: Correspondence, Writings, Speeches* (New York: Schocken Books, 1981), 210, 211, 215, 225.

78. Barbara Bardes and Suzanne Gossett, *Declarations of Independence: Women and Political Power in Nineteenth-Century American Fiction* (New Brunswick: Rutgers University Press, 1990), 11–12, 69.

79. *Proceedings of the National Association of the Deaf and the World's Congress of the Deaf, Colorado Springs, 1910* (Los Angeles, 1910), 38–39, 88–89; "Discussion," *Proceedings of the Fifth Conference of Principals and Superintendents of Institutions for Deaf-Mutes, 1884* (St. Paul, 1884), 162–80.

80. Draper, "Attitude of the Adult Deaf," 44.

81. "Oral Teaching of the Deaf," National Association of the Deaf Circular of Information No. 7 (Washington, D.C. 1912).

82. David Tillinghast, quoted in Olof Hanson, "Superintendents Defend the Sign Language," National Association of the Deaf Circular of Information No. 4 (Washington D.C., ca. 1910).

83. Ibid.

84. S. M. Freeman, "Pure Oralism vs. the Combined System," *Proceedings of the National Association of the Deaf and the World's Congress of the Deaf, Colorado Springs, 1910* (Los Angeles, 1910), 41.

85. Mary Ryan, "The American Parade: Representations of the Nineteenth-Century Social Order," in *The New Cultural History,* ed. Lynn Hunt (Berkeley: University of California Press, 1989), 149–50.

86. Freeman, "Pure Oralism vs. the Combined System," 41; R. P. MacGregor, "The Social Side of Oralism," *Proceedings of the National Association of the Deaf and the World's Congress of the Deaf, Colorado Springs, 1910* (Los Angeles, 1910), 38.

87. Helen Taylor, "The Importance of a Right Beginning," *Association Review* 1 (December 1899): 161.

88. Edward C. Rider, "Kindergarten Work in the Schools for the Deaf," *Association Review* 1 (October 1899): 39.

89. DeLand, *Dumb No Longer,* 20.

90. "Report of the Corporation" and "Address of Mr. Dudley in 1880," in *The Fifteenth Annual Report of the Clarke Institution for Deaf-Mutes* (Northampton, Mass., 1882), 5, 6.

91. Clarke, "Analysis," 228–29; Draper, "Attitude of the Adult Deaf," 50–51.

Chapter Four

1. Edward Miner Gallaudet, "Our Profession," *American Annals of the Deaf* [hereafter cited as *Annals*] 37 (January 1892): 1–5.

2. Reported later in Edward P. Clarke, "An Analysis of the Schools

and Instructors of the Deaf in the United States," *Annals* 45 (April 1900): 235–36. In the year of the study, 1893, 138 of 833 teachers, or 16 percent, were college graduates.

3. Benjamin Talbot, "Changes in Our Profession," *Annals* 40 (June 1895): 173–74.

4. See, for example, Harvey P. Peet, "Progress in Deaf-Mute Instruction," *Annals* 15 (October 1870): 212, 216.

5. Cornelia Trask, "Women as Teachers of Mutes," *Proceedings of the First Conference of Principals of Institutions for the Deaf and Dumb, 1868* (Washington, D.C., 1868), 134.

6. In 1900 Edward P. Clarke, a teacher at the Pennsylvania Institution, reported the following survey results for male principals:

Year	Male Principals	College Graduates	Percentage of College Graduates
1869	23	19	82
1870	26	21	80
1880	43	26	60
1890	48	26	54
1900	59	30	50

Since his figures were for male principals only, they were not the result of the proliferation of small day schools, most of which were headed by women, and where one might expect fewer college educated principals. (In 1900 there were fifty-four female principals, one of them a college graduate, the great majority of them in day schools.) Clarke noted additionally that in the eleven *largest* schools in the country, "a majority of the principals or superintendents are not college-bred men." Clarke, "Analysis," 235.

7. Max Weber, *From Max Weber: Essays in Sociology,* ed. and trans. by H. H. Gerth and C. Wright Mills (New York: Oxford University Press, 1958), 243.

8. Collins Stone, "Address upon the History and Methods of Deaf Mute Instruction," *Annals* 14 (April 1869): 112; Isaac Lewis Peet, "Remarks," *Proceedings of the Third Convention of American Instructors of the Deaf, 1853* (Columbus, 1853), 213.

9. Lawrence A. Cremin, *American Education: The National Experience, 1783–1876* (New York: Harper and Row, 1980), 403–5.

10. "Miscellaneous: Yale Graduates," *Annals* 24 (January 1879): 193.

11. Clarke, "Analysis," 235–36.

12. See, for example, Andrew West, "Must the Classics Go?" *North American Review* 138 (February 1884): 151–62, reprinted in David N.

Portland, *Early Reform in American Higher Education* (Chicago: Nelson-Hall, 1972), 47–60.

13. See, for example, J. M. Francis, "The Difficulties of a Beginner in Learning the Sign Language," *Proceedings of the Fifth Convention of American Instructors of the Deaf, 1858* (Alton, Ill., 1859), 101; having compared sign language with painting, Francis goes on to say, however, that "by its very terms it is a language, and therefore, capable of expressing, and that without the intervention of arbitrary written symbols, the various thoughts and emotions of the soul."

14. Harvey P. Peet, "Preliminary Remarks—Signs versus Articulation," *National Deaf Mute Gazette* 2 (February 1868): 4.

15. Stone, "Address," 97.

16. Harvey P. Peet, *Proceedings of the First Convention of American Instructors of the Deaf, 1850* (New York, 1850), 104, 113, 115, 117–18, 124; see also Robert Paterson, "The Legitimate Use of Pantomime in the Education of the Deaf and Dumb," *Proceedings of the Ninth Convention of American Instructors of the Deaf, 1878* (Columbus, 1879), 165.

17. J. Addison Cary, "On Significant Action in the Pulpit," *Proceedings of the First Convention of American Instructors of the Deaf, 1850* (New York, 1850), 171.

18. J. M. Francis, "The Difficulties of a Beginner in Learning the Sign Language," *Proceedings of the Fifth Convention of American Instructors of the Deaf, 1858* (Alton, Ill., 1859), 101.

19. Harvey P. Peet, "Memoir," *Proceedings of the First Convention of American Instructors of the Deaf, 1850* (New York, 1850), 104; Peet, "Preliminary Remarks," 4.

20. William Turner, "Discussion," *Proceedings of the Third Convention of American Instructors of the Deaf, 1853* (Columbus, 1853), 73.

21. Lucius H. Woodruff, "Moral Education of the Deaf and Dumb," *Annals* 3 (January 1851): 66, 69; see also Thomas Hopkins Gallaudet, "The Natural Language of Signs—II," *Annals* 1 (January 1848): 93.

22. Gallaudet, "Natural Language of Signs—II," 88–89; Cary, "On Significant Action," 171; see also J. Addison Cary, "Deaf-Mute Idioms," *Proceedings of the Second Convention of American Instructors of the Deaf, 1851* (Hartford, 1851), 103.

23. Henry B. Camp, "Claims of the Deaf and Dumb upon Public Sympathy and Aid," *Annals* 1 (July 1848): 211.

24. Thomas Gallaudet, "On Articulating and Reading on the Lips," *Proceedings of the Third Convention of American Instructors of the Deaf, 1853* (Columbus, 1853), 242; J. Van Nostrand, "On the Cultivation of the Sign Language as a Means of Mental Improvement to the Deaf and Dumb," *Proceedings of the Third Convention of American Instructors of the Deaf, 1853* (Columbus, 1853), 43.

25. Gallaudet, "Natural Language of Signs—II," 89; see also Nostrand, "On the Cultivation of the Sign Language," 43; see also Camp, "Claims of the Deaf," 211.

26. Stone, "Address," 110.

27. W. A. Cochrane, "Articulation as a Means of Instruction," *Proceedings of the Seventh Convention of American Instructors of the Deaf, 1870* (Indianapolis, 1870), 232; Harvey P. Peet, "Notes of a Visit to the Clarke Institution," *Annals* 14 (April 1869): 87; Peet, "Preliminary Remarks," 3; Collins Stone, "Report of the Principal," *Fiftieth Annual Report of the American Asylum for the Deaf and Dumb* (Hartford, 1866), 20–21.

28. Quoted in Fred DeLand, *Dumb No Longer: Romance of the Telephone* (Washington, D.C.: Volta Bureau, 1908), 40.

29. Peet, "Preliminary Remarks," 3.

30. "Appendix to the Report on Deaf-Mute Education in Massachusetts," *Massachusetts Senate Joint Special Committee on the Education of Deaf-Mutes, Senate Document No. 265* (Boston, May 1867), 175.

31. Peet, "Preliminary Remarks," 6. On the similarities of sign language to ancient languages, see also Cary, "Deaf-Mute Idioms," 105, 110–13; John R. Keep, "The Language of Signs," *Annals* 14 (April 1869): 94–95. On the "inverted and arbitrary forms of written language," see also Collins Stone, "On the Difficulties Encountered by the Deaf and Dumb in Learning Language," *Proceedings of the Third Convention of American Instructors of the Deaf, 1853* (Columbus, 1853), 129, 135. See chapter 5 below for more on this topic.

32. Edward M. Gallaudet, "Must the Sign Language Go?" *Annals* 44 (June 1899): 221–29; Andrew West, "Must the Classics Go?" *North American Review* 138 (February 1884): 151–62, reprinted in David N. Portland, *Early Reform in American Higher Education* (Chicago: Nelson-Hall, 1972), 49.

33. Kenneth Cmiel, *Democratic Eloquence: The Fight over Popular Speech in Nineteenth-Century America* (New York: William Morrow, 1990).

34. Quoted in James Woodward, "Historical Bases of American Sign Language," in *Understanding Language Through Sign Language Research,* ed. Patricia Siple (New York: Academic Press, 1978), 336.

35. Lewis Weld, "Suggestions on Certain Varieties of the Language of Signs as Used in the Instruction of the Deaf and Dumb," *Proceedings of the Second Convention of American Instructors of the Deaf, 1851* (Hartford, 1851), 80.

36. L. H. Woodruff, "Grace of Expression," *Annals* 2 (July 1849): 193–98.

37. Ibid., 193–98; Fritz Graf, "The Gestures of Roman Actors and

Orators," in *A Cultural History of Gesture,* ed. Jan Bremmer and Herman Roodenburg (Ithaca: Cornell University Press, 1992), 44–47.

38. Graf, "Gestures of Roman Actors and Orators," 36–58; unlike the manualists, however, Roman orators thought pantomimic gesture appropriate for the stage but not for oration (43).

39. Gallaudet, "Natural Language of Signs—II," 80.

40. Cary, "On Significant Action," 175.

41. Gallaudet, "Natural Language of Signs—II," 80.

42. Francis, "Difficulties," 101.

43. J. C. Covell, "The Nobility, Dignity, and Antiquity of the Sign Language," *Proceedings of the Seventh Convention of American Instructors of the Deaf, 1870* (Indianapolis, 1870), 136; Covell could not see in 1870 that sign language was beginning a long decline in status among hearing people; more than a hundred years later, however, his prediction seems to be coming to pass, as ASL is added to the curricula of an increasing number of universities and has become already a respected topic in linguistic departments.

44. Gallaudet, "Natural Language of Signs—II," 89; William W. Turner, *Proceedings of the First Conference of Principals of Institutions for the Deaf and Dumb, 1868* (Washington, D.C., 1868), 68; Paterson, "Legitimate Use of Pantomime," 165.

45. On the decline in status of college education and on the changes in the curriculum, see Lawrence R. Veysey, *The Emergence of the American University* (Chicago: University of Chicago Press, 1965), 4–6, 57–120. See also Charles W. Eliot, "What Is a Liberal Education," *Century* 28 (June 1884): 203–12; and West, "Must the Classics Go?" 151–62. Andrew Carnegie, *The Empire of Business* (New York, 1902), 79–81, quoted in Raymond E. Callahan, *Education and the Cult of Efficiency: A Study of the Social Forces That Have Shaped the Administration of the Public Schools* (Chicago: University of Chicago Press, 1962), 9.

46. Edward P. Clarke, "The Training of Teachers of the Deaf in the United States," *Annals* 45 (September 1900): 350–54, 360. The normal department established at Gallaudet College in 1891 was a partial exception to the trend. One purpose of Gallaudet College Normal Department was to try to continue older standards; it recruited men and women with college degrees and specifically worked to attract men to the profession. From its founding in 1891 until 1908, it awarded teaching certificates to fifty-two men and twenty-seven women. Of these, forty-seven of the men and twelve of the women held college degrees. While the program did not admit deaf students, it never advocated "pure oralism," instructing students in both oral and manual methods. See Percival Hall, "The Normal Department of Gallaudet College," *Annals* 53 (September 1908): 294.

47. Frank W. Booth, "Normal Training for Oral Teachers of the Deaf," *Association Review* 9 (February–April 1907): 208.

48. Callahan, *Education and the Cult of Efficiency*, 2.

49. Frank W. Booth, "Normal Training for Oral Teachers," 206.

50. Frederick Winslow Taylor, *The Principles of Scientific Management* (1911; New York: Norton, 1967), 8.

51. Callahan, *Education and the Cult of Efficiency*, 43; Cecelia Tichi, *Shifting Gears: Technology, Literature, Culture in Modernist America* (Chapel Hill: University of North Carolina Press, 1987), 75–96.

52. Lawrence R. Veysey, *The Emergence of the American University* (Chicago: University of Chicago Press, 1965), 61; Callahan, *Education and the Cult of Efficiency*, 9; see also Lawrence A. Cremin, *The Transformation of the School: Progressivism in American Education, 1876–1957* (New York: Vintage Books, 1964), 23–57.

53. James L. Smith, "Making Education More Practical," *Annals* 59 (November 1914): 425.

54. J. W. Jones, "One Hundred Years of History in the Education of the Deaf in America and Its Present Status," *Proceedings of the Twenty-First Convention of American Instructors of the Deaf, 1917* (Washington, D.C. 1918), 189–90; R. O. Johnson, "Discussion," *Proceedings of the Twentieth Convention of American Instructors of the Deaf, 1914* (Washington, D.C., 1915), 188; Rose E. Huston, "The History of the Pennsylvania Institution for the Deaf: Emphasis Placed upon Better Trades Teaching, 1870–1896," *Mt. Airy World* 47 (February 1932): 121–23. James W. Trent has documented a similar trend in institutions for people with mental retardation in the 1880s and 1890s, where education shifted from intellectual development to vocational training; *Inventing the Feeble Mind: A History of Mental Retardation in the United States* (Berkeley: University of California Press, 1994), 82–83.

55. E. J. Heckler, "Let Us Be Something," *Proceedings of the Fourteenth Convention of American Instructors of the Deaf, 1895* (Flint, 1895), 196–97.

56. E. A. Gruver, "Correlation of Liberal and Vocational Education for the Deaf," *Proceedings of the Twentieth Convention of American Instructors of the Deaf, 1914* (Washington, D.C., 1915), 167.

57. Carl N. Werntz, "Why Art," *Proceedings of the Nineteenth Convention of American Instructors of the Deaf, 1911* (Washington, D.C., 1912), 58, 61.

58. C. P. Cary, "Address of Welcome for Educational Wisconsin, Supt. C. P. Cary," *Proceedings of the Nineteenth Convention of American Instructors of the Deaf, 1911* (Washington, D.C., 1912), 18–19.

59. Emma Garrett, "A Plea that the Deaf Mutes of America May Be Taught to Use Their Voices," *Proceedings of the Tenth Convention of Amer-*

ican Instructors of the Deaf, 1882 (Jacksonville, Ill., 1882), 66; R. C. Spencer, "Work of the Wisconsin Phonological Institute and the Wisconsin Public Day-Schools for the Deaf," *Proceedings of the Fourteenth Convention of American Instructors of the Deaf, 1895* (Flint, 1895), 137–39.

60. Frances Wettstein, "Education of the Deaf in Day Schools," *Proceedings of the Twentieth Convention of American Instructors of the Deaf, 1914* (Washington, D.C., 1915), 106.

61. Cornelia Trask, "Articulation and Lip-Reading," *Annals* 14 (July 1869): 147.

62. Mrs. S. G. Davidson, "The Orally Taught Deaf after Graduation," *Proceedings of the Thirteenth Convention of American Instructors of the Deaf, 1893* (Washington, D.C., 1893), 181–84; see also James L. Smith, "Making Education More Practical," *Annals* 59 (November 1914): 425. Deaf people frequently disputed this point of view, arguing that an education based solely on speech was itself impractical, and that writing was a much more practical and reliable means of communication in the work place than speech and lip-reading. See "Discussion," *Proceedings of the Fifth Conference of Principals and Superintendents of Institutions for Deaf-Mutes, 1884* (St. Paul, 1884), 162–80; E. Henry Currier, *The Deaf: By Their Fruits Ye Shall Know Them* (New York, 1912).

63. *Proceedings of the Fifth Conference of Principals and Superintendents of Institutions for Deaf-Mutes, 1884* (St. Paul, 1884), 162–80.

64. Wettstein, "Education of the Deaf," 107.

65. DeLand, *Dumb No Longer*, 15–16.

66. Ibid., 20, 24, 32.

67. Quoted in "Teaching Mutes," *Detroit Journal* (Mar. 8, 1895), Alexander Graham Bell Family Papers, Manuscript Division, Library of Congress, Container 178, Folder—Deaf-Day Schools, Michigan.

68. Letter from Alexander Graham Bell to F. H. Wines, Jan. 26, 1889, Alexander Graham Bell Family Papers, Manuscript Division, Library of Congress, Container 173.

69. Mary S. and Emma Garrett, "The Possibilities of the Oral Method for the Deaf and the Next Steps Leading towards Its Perfection," *Silent Educator* 3 (January 1892): 65.

70. Emlen Hutchinson, *Annual Report of the Board of Directors of the Pennsylvania Institution for the Deaf and Dumb for the Year 1893–1894* (Philadelphia, 1894), 11; Grace C. Green, "The Importance of Physical Training for the Deaf," *Association Review* 9 (February–April 1907): 183. The word was first adopted by oralists, but some deaf people also believed "handicapped" to be preferable to "afflicted"; see Laura McDill Bates, *Annals* 59 (March 1914): 148.

71. James L. Smith, "Making Education More Practical," *Annals* 59 (November 1914): 425; Trask, "Articulation," 147.

72. Collins Stone, "On the Religious State and Instruction of the Deaf and Dumb," *Annals* 1 (April 1848): 133; Thomas Gallaudet and Thomas Machinator, "Discussion," *Proceedings of the Ninth Convention of American Instructors of the Deaf, 1878* (Columbus, 1879), 131, 133. On deafness as an affliction decreed by God, and/or indirectly brought about by human sin, see also J. A. Ayres, "An Inquiry into the Extent to Which the Misfortune of Deafness May Be Alleviated," *Annals* 1 (April 1848): 221; William W. Turner, "Scheme for a Commonwealth of the Deaf and Dumb," *Annals* 8 (1856): 120.

73. R. O. Johnson, "Discussion," *Proceedings of the Twentieth Convention of American Instructors of the Deaf, 1914* (Washington, D.C., 1915), 186; see also William N. Burt, "Address of Welcome for the East," *Proceedings of the Nineteenth Convention of American Instructors of the Deaf, 1911* (Washington, D.C., 1912), 25-26.

74. Frank W. Booth, "Discussion of Dr. Crouter's Paper," *Proceedings of the Nineteenth Convention of American Instructors of the Deaf, 1911* (Washington, D.C., 1912), 151; Frank W. Booth, "The Sign-Language—Neither a Cause nor a Preventive of Deaf-Mutisms," *Association Review* 8 (December 1906): 498.

75. John Dutton Wright, "Why Speech Teaching Fails Sometimes," *Annals* 60 (September 1915): 323; A. L. E. Crouter, "Discussion," *Proceedings of the Twentieth Convention of American Instructors of the Deaf, 1914* (Washington, D.C., 1915), 191-93.

76. Emma Garrett, "A Few Thoughts on Several of the Topics for Consideration," *Convention of Articulation Teachers of the Deaf, 1884* (Albany, 1884), 41; Alice E. Worcester, "How Shall Our Children Be Taught to Read," *Convention of Articulation Teachers of the Deaf, 1884* (Albany, 1884), 81; J. H. Brown, "Irregularities of English Spelling," *Convention of Articulation Teachers of the Deaf, 1884* (Albany, 1884), 133-35; on the spelling reform movement, see Kenneth Cmiel, *Democratic Eloquence: The Fight over Popular Speech in Nineteenth-Century America* (New York: William Morrow, 1990), 158; Dennis E. Baron, *Grammar and Good Taste: Reforming the American Language* (New Haven: Yale University Press, 1982), 89-98.

77. See J. H. Brown, "Irregularities of English Spelling," *Convention of Articulation Teachers of the Deaf, 1884* (Albany, 1884), 135; Gertrude Burton, "Line Writing and Kindergarten," *Convention of Articulation Teachers of the Deaf, 1884* (Albany, 1884), 142.

78. Emma Garrett, letter dated Aug. 21, no year (probably 1881), addressed to Dr. Seiss (member of the Pennsylvania Institution for the Deaf and Dumb Board of Directors), Gallaudet University Archives, Container: Pennsylvania School for the Deaf Reports, Building Committee . . . Employment Committee.

79. E. F. Pike, "How Science Might Force a Spelling Reform," letter to the editor, *Scientific American* 97 (Nov. 23, 1907): 379; Mabel G. Bell, "Visible Speech," *Scientific American* 98 (Jan. 18, 1908): 43.

80. Sylvia Chapin Balis, "A Visit to Rochester and Mt. Airy," *Annals* 40 (January 1895): 36.

81. *Association Review* 10 (April 1908): 202.

82. Garrett, "A Plea," 67; Frances Wettstein, "Articulation in the Intermediate Grades," *Association Review* 9 (February–April 1907): 154.

83. DeLand, *Dumb No Longer,* 61.

84. Garrick Mallery, "The Gesture Speech of Man," *Annals* 27 (April 1882): 69, 76.

85. Bruce A. Kimball, *The True Professional Ideal in America: A History* (Cambridge: Harvard University Press, 1992), 222.

86. Robert Crunden, *Ministers of Reform: The Progressives' Achievement in American Civilization, 1889–1920* (Urbana: University of Illinois Press, 1982), 69; Jane L. Russell, "Observation of Oral Work in German Schools," *Proceedings of the Fifteenth Convention of American Instructors of the Deaf, 1898* (Washington, D.C., 1899), 153.

87. Emma Garrett, Pennsylvania Institution for the Deaf, Oral Branch, Monthly Report (Mar. 31, 1882), Gallaudet University Archives, Container: PSD Reports—Building Committee . . . Employment Committee.

88. "Teaching Deaf Mutes," *Detroit Tribune,* Mar. 9, 1895, in Alexander Graham Bell Family Papers, Manuscript Division, Library of Congress, Container—178, Folder—Deaf-Day Schools, Michigan. *Daily Eastern Argus* (Portland, Maine), Jan. 19, 1894, and Mar. 2, 1894, Alexander Graham Bell Family Papers, Manuscript Division, Library of Congress, Container—178, Folder—Deaf-Day Schools, Michigan. Z. F. Westervelt, "The Colloquial Use of English by the Deaf," *Proceedings of the Twelfth Convention of American Instructors of the Deaf, 1890* (New York, 1890), 113. Caroline A. Yale, *Years of Building: Memories of a Pioneer in a Special Field of Education* (New York: Dial Press, 1931), 48. See also, Franklin B. Sanborn, "Address of Welcome," *Association Review* 1 (October 1899): 57.

89. West, "Must the Classics Go?" 48.

90. "Discussion," *Proceedings of the Twelfth Convention of American Instructors of the Deaf, 1890* (New York, 1890), 182–83.

Chapter Five

1. See, for example, Nancy Frishberg, "Arbitrariness and Iconicity: Historical Change in American Sign Language," *Language* 51 (September 1975): 696.

2. See, for example, Thomas H. Gallaudet, "The Natural Language of Signs—I," *American Annals of the Deaf* [hereafter cited as *Annals*] 1 (October 1847): 59; Collins Stone, "Address upon the History and Methods of Deaf Mute Instruction," *Annals* 14 (April 1869): 107–8.

3. The first chapter of Condillac's *Grammar* was reprinted in the *Annals* in 1886 after Edward Miner Gallaudet came across the book in his late father's collection; Susan Gallaudet, Edward's second wife, translated the chapter for publication; "The Language of Action," *Annals* 31 (January 1886): 35–41.

4. Stone, "Address upon the History," 106.

5. Ibid., 107; J. C. Covell, "The Nobility, Dignity, and Antiquity of the Sign Language," *Proceedings of the Seventh Convention of American Instructors of the Deaf, 1870* (Indianapolis, 1870), 135; R. H. Kinney, "A Few Thoughts on the Universality and Power of the Language of Signs," *Proceedings of the Fifth Convention of American Instructors of the Deaf, 1858* (Jacksonville, Ill., 1858), 85; Gallaudet, "Natural Language of Signs—I," 58; Thomas H. Gallaudet, "The Natural Language of Signs—II" *Annals* 1 (January 1848): 91.

6. Luzerne Rae, "The Philosophical Basis of Language," *Proceedings of the Third Convention of American Instructors of the Deaf, 1853* (Columbus, 1853), 157–62.

7. Rae, "Philosophical Basis of Language," 157–62.

8. B. D. Pettingill, "The Sign Language," *Annals* 18 (January 1873): 1.

9. Ibid., 6, 10–11.

10. See, for example, Frishberg, "Arbitrariness and Iconicity," 717–18.

11. Ibid., 696–719.

12. J. A. Ayres, "An Inquiry into the Extent to Which the Misfortune of Deafness May Be Alleviated," *Annals* 1 (April 1848): 223.

13. Lewis Weld, "Suggestions on Certain Varieties of the Language of Signs as Used in the Instruction of the Deaf and Dumb," *Proceedings of the Second Convention of American Instructors of the Deaf, 1851* (Hartford, 1851), 78.

14. Gallaudet, "Natural Language of Signs—I," 57–58.

15. Pettingill, "Sign Language," 3.

16. See, for examples, "Institution Items: Pennsylvania Institution," *Annals* 19 (January 1874): 48–49; Warring Wilkinson, "The Development of Speech and of the Sign-Language," *Annals* 26 (January 1881): 171; Garrick Mallery, "The Gesture Speech of Man," *Annals* 27 (April 1882): 75; Collins Stone, "Address upon the History," 107–8; William Turner, "Discussion," *Proceedings of the Third Convention of American Instructors of the Deaf, 1853* (Columbus, 1853), 73.

17. Lucius Woodruff, "Primary Instruction of the Deaf and Dumb," *Annals* 1 (October 1847): 54.

18. The anthropologist Brenda Farnell argues that a bias against iconicity in Western thought has worked to make sign languages appear to be less than true languages. She is certainly correct that this bias exists, and it probably accounts for the tendency of modern linguists, in their desire to establish the legitimacy of sign languages, to ignore or minimize their iconicity. Farnell, however, tends to describe this bias as a constant, a legacy of the Cartesian mind-body dualism in Western culture. As I hope to show here, attitudes toward iconicity have been anything but constant over time; *Do You See What I Mean: Plains Indian Sign Talk and the Embodiment of Action* (Austin: University of Texas Press, 1995), x–xi, 41–57.

19. This is what the historian Leo Marx referred to as the "middle landscape" in his classic work, *The Machine in the Garden* (New York: Oxford University Press, 1964), 73–144; see also Philip G. Terrie, "Wilderness: Ambiguous Symbol of the American Past," in *Dominant Symbols in Popular Culture,* ed. Ray B. Browne et al. (Bowling Green, Ky.: Bowling Green State University Press, 1990), 134.

20. Merle Curti, *Human Nature in American Thought: A History* (Madison: University of Wisconsin Press, 1980), 183; Henry Nash Smith, *Virgin Land: The American West as Symbol and Myth* (Cambridge: Harvard University Press, 1950), 123–24.

21. Harvey P. Peet writing in 1833, quoted in Edward Miner Gallaudet, "Our Profession," *Annals* 37 (January 1892): 2.

22. Collins Stone, "On the Difficulties Encountered by the Deaf and Dumb in Learning Language," *Proceedings of the Third Convention of American Instructors of the Deaf, 1853* (Columbus, 1853), 129, 135; see also William Turner, "Discussion," *Proceedings of the Third Convention of American Instructors of the Deaf, 1853* (Columbus, 1853), 72–73; Harvey P. Peet, "Preliminary Remarks—Signs Versus Articulation," *National Deaf-Mute Gazette* 2 (February 1868): 6; Woodruff, "Primary Instruction," 51–52.

23. Benjamin Talbot, "Discussion," *Proceedings of the Seventh Convention of American Instructors of the Deaf, 1870* (Indianapolis, 1870), 60.

24. John R. Keep, "Natural Signs—Shall They Be Abandoned?" *Annals* 16 (January 1871): 22. Keep's explanation was a common one among nineteenth-century manualists. It is also very similar to an explanation once offered to me by a deaf friend. He told me that ASL adjectives usually followed nouns because it was impossible to visualize an attribute before one had an object to attach that attribute to. This may just be a kind of explanation that readily springs to mind, or it could possibly

have become a traditional explanation passed down within the deaf community.

25. Harvey P. Peet, "Notions of the Deaf and Dumb before Instruction," *Annals* 8 (October 1855): 19. This belief was not unique to teachers of the deaf; on the various theories of the Adamic language, see Maurice Olender, *The Languages of Paradise: Race, Religion, and Philology in the Nineteenth Century* (Cambridge: Harvard University Press, 1992), 1–20; Hans Aarslef, *From Locke to Saussure: Essays on the Study of Language and Intellectual History* (Minneapolis: University of Minnesota Press, 1982), 282.

26. J. Addison Cary, "Deaf-Mute Idioms," *Proceedings of the Second Convention of American Instructors of the Deaf, 1851* (Hartford, 1851), 110; see also Peet, "Preliminary Remarks," 6; "Discussion," *Proceedings of the Seventh Convention of American Instructors of the Deaf, 1870* (Indianapolis, 1870), 59–60; Lucius Woodruff, "Primary Instruction of the Deaf and Dumb," *Annals* 1 (October 1847): 51.

27. Harlan Lane, *When the Mind Hears: A History of the Deaf* (New York: Harvard University Press, 1984), 61–63; see also Renate Fischer, "Language of Action," in *Looking Back: A Reader on the History of Deaf Communities and their Sign Languages,* ed. Renate Fischer and Harlan Lane (Hamburg: Signum, 1993), 433–36.

28. Similar, albeit simpler, systems (known today as Manually Coded English, or MCE) are once again being widely experimented with in schools, with the important difference that manualists never saw methodical sign language as anything more than a supplement to natural sign language, whereas many today attempt to use MCE as a replacement for the natural language, American Sign Language.

29. Lane writes (*When the Mind Hears,* 63) that "by the 1830s, methodical signs had disappeared on both sides of the Atlantic." This was clearly not true in America, although the precise extent to which they continued to be used is less clear. The debate over methodical signs at the 1851 and 1853 conventions of American Instructors of the Deaf demonstrates that, while controversial, they were still in use to some degree; *Proceedings* (Hartford, 1851), 92–102; *Proceedings* (Columbus, 1853), 63–74. H. P. Peet argued in 1856 that they should be used only to a very limited extent, and reported in 1858 that most schools were moving away from their use; "Discussion," *Proceedings of the Fourth Convention of American Instructors of the Deaf, 1856* (Richmond, Va., 1857), and "Memoir on the History and Art of Instructing the Deaf and Dumb," *Proceedings of the Fifth Convention of American Instructors of the Deaf, 1858* (Jacksonville, Ill., 1859), 339. Job Williams, principal of the Hartford school, stated in 1893 that "methodical signs were mostly abandoned forty years ago"; *Proceedings of the Thirteenth Convention of American Instructors of the Deaf, 1893* (Washington, D.C., 1893), 11. Laurent Clerc,

the central subject of Lane's account, appears to have been still using them to some degree in 1856, since according to the minutes of an instructors' meeting, he "said that while teaching, he always used the signs for the tenses of the indicative, potential, imperative, subjunctive, and infinitive moods," signs that would only exist within a methodical sign system; *Proceedings of the Fourth Convention of American Instructors of the Deaf, 1858* (Richmond, Va., 1857), 152. See also Lane's discussion in *The Mask of Benevolence: Disabling the Deaf Community* (New York: Knopf, 1992), 112, 264–65.

30. Weld, "Suggestions," 82–84; J. A. Ayres, "Discussion," *Proceedings of the Third Convention of American Instructors of the Deaf, 1853* (Columbus, 1853), 68.

31. H. P. Peet, "Discussion," *Proceedings of the Fourth Convention of American Instructors of the Deaf, 1856* (Staunton, Va., 1857), 147, 150–51; Thomas Gallaudet, "Methods of Perfecting the Sign-Language," *Proceedings of the Fifth Convention of American Instructors of the Deaf, 1858* (Alton, Ill., 1859), 189. See also, "Discussion," *Proceedings of the Second Convention of American Instructors of the Deaf, 1851* (Hartford, 1851), 92–102; "Discussion," *Proceedings of the Third Convention of American Instructors of the Deaf, 1853* (Columbus, 1853), 63–74; William Turner, "On the Deaf-Mute Language," *Proceedings of the Fifth Convention of American Instructors of the Deaf, 1858* (Alton, Ill., 1859), 183–84.

32. *Proceedings of the Fifth Convention of American Instructors of the Deaf, 1858* (Alton, Ill., 1859), 193–213, 251–53. The practice of denoting classes of objects by listing three particulars is still in use—"fruit," for example, is sometimes signified in this manner—but more so among older deaf people than younger. The common use of signed English systems in the schools is causing many such older features of ASL to fade from use.

33. J. M. Francis, "The Difficulties of a Beginner in Learning the Sign Language," *Proceedings of the Fifth Convention of American Instructors of the Deaf, 1858* (Alton, Ill., 1859), 109–10; the Reverend B. M. Fay, "Discussion," *Proceedings of the Fifth Convention of American Instructors of the Deaf, 1858* (Alton, Ill., 1859), 117.

34. Weld, "Suggestions," 84–85. Opinion on this subject varied; for a defense of initialized signs, see Isaac Lewis Peet, "Initial Signs," *Proceedings of the First Conference of Principals of Institutions for the Deaf and Dumb* (Washington, D.C. 1868), 96–104.

35. Benjamin Talbot noted in 1895, "There is now and then one, especially among younger teachers, who calls loudly for signs in the order of words, but this mode of teaching is mostly discarded as too mechanical and as failing to convey the true meaning of the language used"; see "Changes in our Profession," *Annals* 40 (June 1895): 183. For

the argument in favor of signs in English order, see E. Gates Valentine, "The Proper Order of Signs," *Proceedings of the Seventh Convention of American Instructors of the Deaf, 1870* (Indianapolis, 1870), 44–55; see also the discussion following, in which E. M. Gallaudet voices his support for this argument.

36. Robert Patterson, "The Legitimate Use of Pantomime in the Education of the Deaf and Dumb," *Proceedings of the Ninth Convention of American Instructors of the Deaf, 1878* (Columbus, 1879), 160–63.

37. Horace Gillet, "On Language, Considered with Reference to the Instruction of Primary Classes," *Proceedings of the Seventh Convention of American Instructors of the Deaf, 1870* (Indianapolis, 1870), 20–21; John R. Keep, "The Language of Signs," *Annals* 14 (April 1869): 93.

38. Emerson's concerns were related to a sense of anxiety over the artificial and the counterfeit in antebellum culture generally, a sense that the simple republican virtue of the Revolutionary generation was on the wane; loss of linguistic purity was one symptom among many of decline, from unreliable paper money to urban "confidence men and painted women"; see Michael O'Malley, "Specie and Species: Race and the Money Question in Nineteenth-Century America," *American Historical Review* 99 (April 1994): 369–95; Karen Halttunen, *Confidence Men and Painted Women: A Study of Middle-Class Culture in America, 1830–1870* (New Haven: Yale University Press, 1982). Quotations from *Nature* are all taken from chapter 4, "Language."

39. See Barbara Novak, *Nature and Culture: American Landscape and Painting, 1825–1875* (New York: Oxford University Press, 1980), 10–13.

40. Gallaudet, "Natural Language of Signs—I," 56.

41. Cary, "Deaf-Mute Idioms," 103.

42. Stone, "Address upon the History," 110, 119.

43. Patterson, "Legitimate Use," 160–63.

44. Gillet, "On Language," 20–21.

45. See Novak, *Nature and Culture*, 3–17.

46. Russel B. Nye, *Society and Culture in America, 1830–1860* (New York: Harper and Row, 1974), 344–52.

47. Gallaudet, "Natural Language of Signs—I," 54, 56; Gallaudet, "Natural Language of Signs—II," 81; Cary, "Deaf-Mute Idioms," 103; Pettingill, "Sign Language," 7; see also Woodruff, "Primary Instruction," 54.

48. Collins Stone, "Report of the Principal," *The 53rd Annual Report of the Directors and Officers of the American Asylum at Hartford* (Hartford, Conn., 1869), 18–19.

49. Rae, "Philosophical Basis of Language," 161;

50. Harvey P. Peet, "Discussion," *Proceedings of the Third Convention of American Instructors of the Deaf, 1853* (Columbus, 1853), 56, 58; Peet,

"Notions," 42. For other examples of the "awakening" metaphor, see Lucius Woodruff, "Motives to Intellectual Effort on the Part of the Young Deaf-Mute," *Annals* (April 1848): 159; J. Van Nostrand, "On the Cultivation of the Sign Language as a Means of Mental Improvement to the Deaf and Dumb," *Proceedings of the Third Convention of American Instructors of the Deaf, 1853* (Columbus, 1853), 43; R. L. Chittenden, "On the Benefits Conferred upon the Deaf Mute by the Usual Course of Instruction," *Proceedings of the Third Convention of American Instructors of the Deaf, 1853* (Columbus, 1853), 177.

51. Henry B. Camp, "Claims of the Deaf and Dumb upon Public Sympathy and Aid," *Annals* 1 (July 1848): 213; Harvey P. Peet, "The Personal Character of the Teacher Considered in Reference to the Influence of His Example on the Character of the Pupils," *Proceedings of the Third Convention of American Instructors of the Deaf, 1853* (Columbus, 1853), 188. See also Woodruff, "Motives to Intellectual Effort," 159; Isaac L. Peet, "The Use of Grammatical Symbols in the Instruction of the Deaf and Dumb," *Proceedings of the Third Convention of American Instructors of the Deaf, 1853* (Columbus, 1853), 265–66.

52. Rae, "Philosophical Basis of Language," 160–61.

53. J. Addison Cary, "Discussion," *Proceedings of the Second Convention of American Instructors of the Deaf, 1851* (Hartford, 1851), 34.

54. H. P. Peet, "Notions," 1–2.

55. Ibid.

56. Ibid., 10–11. See also, Henry Winter Syle, "Summary of the Recorded Researches and Opinions of Harvey Prindle Peet, Ph.D., LL.D.," *Annals* 18 (1873): 146.

57. H. P. Peet, "Notions," 17–18.

58. Ibid., 15.

59. Ibid., 10–11; See also Syle, "Summary of the Recorded Researches," 146.

60. H. P. Peet, "Notions," 10–11; H. P. Peet, "Discussion," *Proceedings of the Third Convention of American Instructors of the Deaf, 1853* (Columbus, 1853), 61; H. P. Peet, "Discussion," *Proceedings of the First Conference of Principals of Institutions for the Deaf and Dumb, 1868* (Washington, D.C., 1868), 80–81.

61. H. P. Peet, "Notions," 19.

62. Ibid., 12, 15–16.

Chapter Six

1. Katherine T. Bingham, "All along the Line," *Association Review* 2 (February 1900): 22–23.

2. B. D. Pettingill, "The Sign Language," *American Annals of the Deaf* [hereafter cited as *Annals*] 18 (January 1873): 2.

3. Pettingill, "Sign Language," 2–3.

4. Z. F. Westervelt, "The Disuse of Signs," *Proceedings of the Ninth Convention of American Instructors of the Deaf* (Columbus, 1879), 165–71; like that of many others in this debate, Westervelt's terminology was often inconsistent; for example, while his description of sign language made it clear that he distinguished between sign language and pantomime, he still often referred to it, as was customary, as the "language of pantomime." Westervelt was not, technically speaking, an oralist. His school pioneered what became known as the "Rochester method," which combined oral communication with the use of fingerspelled English. Sign language was forbidden.

5. Alexander G. Bell, "Discussion," *Proceedings of the Twelfth Convention of American Instructors of the Deaf, 1890* (New York, 1890), 180; see also Mary Garrett, *National Education Association: Journal of Proceedings and Addresses of the 37th Annual Meeting* (Washington, D.C., 1898), 1033; Fred DeLand, *Dumb No Longer: Romance of the Telephone* (Washington, D.C.: Volta Bureau, 1908), 13, 19, 22, 23; Alexander Graham Bell, letter to the editor of the *Daily Eastern Argus* (Portland, Maine, Jan. 19, 1894), in Alexander Graham Bell Family Papers, Manuscript Division, Library of Congress, Container—178, Folder—Df–Day Schools, Mich.

6. J. L. Noyes, "Discussion," *Proceedings of the Twelfth Convention of American Instructors of the Deaf, 1890* (New York, 1890), 182.

7. Samuel G. Davidson, "Conference on Language Teaching under Oral Methods," *Proceedings of the Nineteenth Convention of American Instructors of the Deaf, 1911* (Washington, D.C., 1912), 166.

8. Letter from Alexander Graham Bell to Mary E. Bennett of Los Angeles, Calif., dated Aug. 30, 1913, in the Alexander Graham Bell Family Papers, Library of Congress, Manuscript Division, Container 173, Folder—General Correspondence A–C.

9. Letter to Miss McDowell, dated Cape Breton, Nova Scotia, Jan. 12, 1893, Alexander Graham Bell Family Papers, Manuscript Division, Library of Congress, Container 178, Folder: The Deaf—Committee on Classification of Methods.

10. *Convention of Articulation Teachers of the Deaf—1884: Official Report* (Albany, 1884), 11.

11. Davidson, "Conference on Language Teaching," 166.

12. Anon., "Teaching Deaf-Mutes to Speak," *Scientific American* 96 (June 8, 1907): 474.

13. J. D. Kirkhuff, "The Natural Method," *Annals* 36 (April 1891): 120, 124, 125; also Westervelt, "Disuse of Signs," 165–71; E. A. Gruver,

"Disputed Points in Oral Instruction," *Proceedings of the Nineteenth Convention of American Instructors of the Deaf, 1911* (Washington, D.C., 1912), 146, 148–49. Some younger manualist teachers by the 1860s had begun to speak of teaching by the natural method. For them this did not mean that deaf children had to learn exactly as hearing children, but it marked the beginnings of the sentiment that a "natural" way of learning could be empirically demonstrated, which made possible its link with the idea of the "normal"; see Isaac Lewis Peet, "Discussion," *Proceedings of the First Conference of Principals of Institutions for the Deaf and Dumb, 1868* (Washington, D.C., 1868), 33.

14. "The Discussion," *Convention of Articulation Teachers of the Deaf— 1884: Official Report* (Albany, 1884), 36.

15. Emma Garrett, "A Few Thoughts on Several of the Topics for Consideration," *Convention of Articulation Teachers of the Deaf—1884: Official Report* (Albany, 1884), 37–38, 40–41.

16. Dwight Elmendorf, "The Discussion," *Convention of Articulation Teachers of the Deaf—1884: Official Report* (Albany, 1884), 81, 95, 96; Garrett, "A Few Thoughts," 37–38, 40–41.

17. D. Greenburger, *Convention of Articulation Teachers of the Deaf— 1884: Official Report* (Albany, 1884): 32–33.

18. Sadie Keeler, "Speech-Reading," *Convention of Articulation Teachers of the Deaf—1884: Official Report* (Albany, 1884): 60.

19. Mary S. Garrett and Emma Garrett, "The Possibilities of the Oral Method for the Deaf and the Next Steps Leading towards Its Perfection," *Silent Educator* 3 (January 1892): 65.

20. Anna E. Schaffer, "Wisconsin State Teachers' Association, Special Education Section Meeting," *Association Review* 8 (February 1906): 66; Mary S. Garrett, "Helps and Hindrances of Deaf Children in Acquiring Speech and Language at the Natural Age," *Association Review* 10 (June 1908): 275.

21. "The Discussion," *Convention of Articulation Teachers of the Deaf— 1884: Official Report* (Albany, 1884), 36.

22. Emma Garret, "Principal's Report," *First Report of the Home for the Training in Speech of Deaf Children before They Are of School Age* (Philadelphia, 1892), 13–14.

23. Harriet B. Rogers, "Report of the Principal," *Second Annual Report of the Clarke Institution for Deaf-Mutes* (Boston, 1869), 14–15.

24. A. L. E. Crouter, "The Possibilities of Oral Methods in the Instruction of the Deaf," *Proceedings of the Nineteenth Convention of American Instructors of the Deaf, 1911* (Washington, D.C., 1912), 139.

25. Bingham, "All along the Line," 21, 26; see also Mary Garrett, "Helps and Hindrances," 274; S. Edwin Megargee, "President's Re-

port," *Second Report of the Home for the Training in Speech* (Philadelphia, 1893), 9; in the draft of a letter from A. G. Bell addressed "To the editors of the *Educator*," dated Mar. 26, 1894 (the date subsequently crossed out by Bell), Bell wrote: "The children and their friends invented such signs at home because their parents didn't know how to teach them English." (In the draft, this sentence was crossed out.) When a mother found that her child was deaf, too often she would begin to "substitute signs for speech"; in such cases, "soon the fatal habit of silence is formed and the pernicious practice of pantomime is confirmed;" Alexander Graham Bell Family Papers, Manuscript Division, Library of Congress, Container 198.

26. Crouter, "Possibilities of Oral Methods," 139–41; for other examples of the use of "normal" to mean *hearing,* see "The Discussion," *Convention of Articulation Teachers of the Deaf—1884: Official Report* (Albany, 1884), 95; J. W. Jones, "The Education of the Deaf-Blind," *Association Review* 9 (February–April 1907): 213; Mary McCowen, "How Best to Secure Intelligent Speech for Deaf Children," *Association Review* 9 (February–April 1907): 259.

27. Mary and Emma Garrett, "The Possibilities of the Oral Method," 65; Richard A. Johnson, "Annual Business Meeting of the Association," *Association Review* 9 (February–April 1907): 281–82; Jennie L. Cobb, "Schoolroom Efficiency," *Annals* 58 (May 1913): 208; Caroline A. Yale, *Formation and Development of Elementary English Sounds* (Northampton, Mass.: Gazette Printing, 1914), 3–4.

28. Georges Canguilhem, *The Normal and the Pathological* (New York: Zone Books, 1989), 39–64, 125; quotations from Ian Hacking, *The Taming of Chance* (Cambridge: Cambridge University Press, 1990), 160–66.

29. Hacking, *Taming of Chance,* xi, 161.

30. François Ewald, "Norms, Discipline, and the Law," *Representations* 30 (Spring 1990): 146, 149–50, 154.

31. Hacking, *Taming of Chance,* 163.

32. "Normality" is also, as Hacking discusses, used to describe the *merely* average upon which people are urged to improve. This sense of the term did not enter into the sign language debate, however, and so need not be explored here. See Hacking, *Taming of Chance,* 168–69.

33. Hacking has noted that Comte used "normal" to describe not only the ordinary healthy state, but also "the purified state to which we should strive, and to which our energies are tending." Normality was the end result of progress. This is of less relevance to the discourse of the oralists, however, than the conception of normality as the typical, so I have omitted consideration of this aspect of the subject; *Taming of Chance,* 168.

34. T. V. Archer, "Conference on Lip Reading as a Means of Communication in Teaching," *Proceedings of the Nineteenth Convention of American Instructors of the Deaf, 1911* (Washington, D.C., 1912), 154.

35. Quoted in Barbara Novak, *Nature and Culture: American Landscape and Painting, 1825–1875* (New York: Oxford University Press, 1980), 38.

36. Bingham, "All along the Line," 22; Mary Garrett, "Helps and Hindrances," 274–75. See also T. V. Archer, who argued that because "speech has been the normal and universal method of communication" for so long, there was probably "in the brain of man a tendency toward this method of communication"; "Conference on Lip Reading as a Means of Communication in Teaching," *Proceedings of the Nineteenth Convention of American Instructors of the Deaf, 1911* (Washington, D.C., 1912), 154.

37. Alexander Graham Bell, letters to the editor, *Daily Eastern Argus* (Portland, Maine), Jan. 19 and Mar. 2, 1894, in Alexander Graham Bell Family Papers, Manuscript Division, Library of Congress, Container 178, Folder: Df—Day Schools, Mich; see also, a letter from Alexander Graham Bell to Mary E. Bennett of Los Angeles, Aug. 30, 1913, Alexander Graham Bell Family Papers, Library of Congress, Manuscript Division, Container 173, Folder—General Correspondence A–C; Alexander Graham Bell, *Memoir upon the Formation of a Deaf Variety of the Human Race* (Washington, D.C., 1884), 219; Westervelt, "Disuse of Signs," 170; Frank Booth "The Sign-Language—Neither a Cause nor a Preventive of Deaf-Mutisms," *Association Review* 8 (December 1906): 498.

38. Harvey P. Peet, "The Personal Character of the Teacher," *Proceedings of the Third Convention of American Instructors of the Deaf, 1853* (Columbus, 1853), 190.

39. Patterson, "Legitimate Use," 159. See also Harvey Peet who, for example, cautioned teachers that "when we see them act precisely like those around them, it is difficult to realize that they do not act from the same motives; or that their thoughts are not of a tissue similar to our own"; Harvey P. Peet, "Notions of the Deaf and Dumb before Instruction," *Annals* 8 (October 1855): 3.

40. Thomas Gallaudet, "On Articulation and Reading on the Lips," *Proceedings of the Third Convention of American Instructors of the Deaf, 1853* (Columbus, 1853), 242; Edward Miner Gallaudet, "President Gallaudet's Address," *Proceedings of the Nineteenth Convention of American Instructors of the Deaf, 1911* (Washington, D.C., 1912), 39; Harvey P. Peet, "Discussion," *Proceedings of the Third Convention of American Instructors of the Deaf, 1853* (Columbus, 1853), 31; Isaac L. Peet, "The Use of Grammatical Symbols in the Instruction of the Deaf and Dumb," *Proceedings of the*

Third Convention of American Instructors of the Deaf, 1853 (Columbus, 1853), 268.

41. Helen Taylor, "The Importance of a Right Beginning," *Association Review* 1 (December 1899): 159.

42. Mrs. S. G. Davidson, "The Orally Taught after Graduation," *Proceedings of the Thirteenth Convention of American Instructors of the Deaf, 1893* (Washington, D.C., 1893), 183.

43. Bingham, "All along the Line," 28–29.

44. Dwight Elmendorf, "The Discussion," *Convention of Articulation Teachers of the Deaf—1884: Official Report* (Albany, 1884), 81, 95, 96.

45. Emma Garrett, "A Plea that the Deaf 'Mutes' of America May Be Taught to Use Their Voices," *Annals* 28 (1883): 17.

46. "Oral Branch Monthly Report, Pennsylvania School for the Deaf" (Mar. 31 and Nov. 30, 1882), Gallaudet University Archives, Container: PSD Reports—Building Committee . . . Employment Committee.

47. Grace C. Green, "The Importance of Physical Training for the Deaf," *Association Review* 9 (February–April 1907): 180–81. See also Taylor, "Importance of a Right Beginning," 158. The ideal would be to have "deaf boys working right along with their hearing brothers," where "no difference is felt by the teacher." The equation of equality with sameness was a staple of Progressive reform thought; see Rivka Shpak Lissak, *Pluralism and Progressives: Hull House and the New Immigrants, 1890–1919* (Chicago: University of Chicago Press, 1989), 153.

48. Anon., *Scientific American* 96 (June 8, 1907): 474; "Miscellaneous: Proposed Congressional Action," *Annals* 41 (January 1896): 126; Emma F. West, "The National Educational Association Meeting—Proceedings of Department XVI," *Association Review* 1 (October 1899): 107; Robert V. Bruce, *Bell: Alexander Graham Bell and the Conquest of Solitude* (Ithaca: Cornell University Press, 1973), 321–22.

49. Mary and Emma Garrett, "Possibilities of the Oral Method," 65.

50. Bingham, "All along the Line," 26–27.

51. West, "National Educational Association Meeting," 108. A California teacher explained in a letter to A. G. Bell the provisions of a new day school bill passed in California in 1903 with Bell's help: "It provides for the Oral method but does not make of the deaf a *special class*. We simply make the classes a part of the public school system and they are on the same plane and have the same advantages as hearing children." Letter dated Mar. 11, 1903, to Bell from Jennie Bright Holden, Alexander Graham Bell Family Papers, Manuscript Division, Library of Congress, Container 178, Folder: The Deaf—Day Schools, Calif.

52. Nancy F. Cott, *The Grounding of Modern Feminism* (New Haven: Yale University Press, 1987), 20, 49.

53. Thomas Francis Fox, "The Social Status of the Deaf in the United States," *Proceedings of the World's Congress of the Deaf and Report of the Seventh Convention of the National Association of the Deaf, 1904* (St. Louis: 1904), 132, 138.

54. *Proceedings of the Ninth Convention of the National Association of the Deaf and the Third World's Congress of the Deaf, 1910* (Philadelphia: Philocophus Press, 1912), 28.

55. *Proceedings of the Ninth Convention of the National Association of the Deaf and the Third World's Congress of the Deaf, 1910* (Philadelphia: Philocophus Press, 1912), 57.

Epilogue

1. John Vickrey Van Cleve and Barry Crouch, *A Place of Their Own: Creating the Deaf Community in America* (Washington, D.C.: Gallaudet University Press, 1989), 128.

2. See W. Earl Hall, "To Speak or Not to Speak: That is the Question behind the Bitter Deaf-Teaching Battle," *Iowan* 4 (February–March 1956), for a brief description of a battle between the Iowa Association of the Deaf and the Iowa School for the Deaf in the 1950s over this issue. See also, John Van Cleve, "Nebraska's Oral Law of 1911 and the Deaf Community," *Nebraska History* 65 (Summer 1984): 195–220; Van Cleve and Crouch, *A Place of Their Own*, 128–41.

3. See *Proceedings of the Ninth Convention of the National Association of the Deaf and the Third World's Congress of the Deaf, 1910* (Philadelphia: Philocophus Press, 1912), 28. George Veditz quoted in Carol Padden and Tom Humphries, *Deaf in America: Voices from a Culture* (Cambridge: Harvard University Press, 1988), 36.

4. Padden and Humphries, *Deaf in America*, 5–6; Beryl Lieff Benderly, *Dancing without Music: Deafness in America* (Garden City, N.Y.: Doubleday, 1980), 218–39; Jerome D. Schein, *At Home among Strangers: Exploring the Deaf Community in the United States* (Washington, D.C.: Gallaudet University Press, 1989), 72–105, 106, 120.

5. Padden and Humphries, *Deaf in America*, 26–38, 110–21, explore the alternative meanings of deafness created by the deaf community; their focus is on the present, but their brief forays into the historical roots of these meanings are suggestive and insightful.

6. See, for example, John Dutton Wright, *Volta Review* 18 (January 1916): 3–4.

7. Oliver Sacks, *Seeing Voices: A Journey into the World of the Deaf* (Berkeley: University of California Press, 1989), 28, 110–11.

8. Ruth Sidransky, *In Silence: Growing Up Hearing in a Deaf World* (New York: St. Martins, 1990), 65.

9. Alexander Graham Bell, *Memoir upon the Formation of a Deaf Variety of the Human Race* (Washington, D.C.: Government Printing Office, 1884), 222; Mary S. Garrett and Emma Garrett, "The Home for the Training in Speech of Deaf Children before They Are of School Age," in Edward Allen Fay, *Histories of American Schools for the Deaf, 1817–1893* (Washington, D.C.: Volta Bureau, 1893), 3:13. John Vickrey Van Cleve has written an excellent brief review and critique of mainstreaming efforts in turn-of-the-century Wisconsin, in which he argues that mainstreaming was far more an ideological issue than a pedagogical one, that the "cultural imperative was more important than academic achievement or occupational success." In the final section of the article, he argues that similar cultural imperatives drive mainstreaming today, such as the desire for cultural homogeneity, the sentimentalization of children and parenthood, and parents' fervent desire for their children to be "normal" at any cost. See "The Academic Integration of Deaf Children: A Historical Perspective," in *Looking Back: A Reader on the History of Deaf Communities and their Sign Languages,* ed. Renate Fischer and Harlan Lane (Hamburg: Signum Press, 1993), 333–47.

10. Leah Hager Cohen, "Schools for All, or Separate but Equal?: An Interpreter Isn't Enough," *New York Times,* Feb. 22, 1994, 21.

11. Mervin Garretson, review of Margaret Walworth et al., *A Free Hand: Enfranchising the Education of Deaf Children,* in *American Annals of the Deaf* [hereafter cited as *Annals*] 138 (December 1993): 386.

12. Joseph J. Innes, "Full Inclusion and the Deaf Student: A Deaf Consumer's Review of the Issue," *Annals* 139 (April 1994): 155.

13. Gary Bunch, "An Interpretation of Full Inclusion," *Annals* 139 (April 1994): 150–51.

14. For a useful discussion of full inclusion, see *Annals* 139 (April 1994): 148–71.

15. Claire Ramsey, "Language Planning in Deaf Education," in *The Sociolinguistics of the Deaf Community,* ed. Ceil Lucas (San Diego, Academic Press, 1989), 137–38.

16. Frank Bowe, "Radicalism vs. Reason: Directions in Educational Uses of American Sign Language," in *A Free Hand: Enfranchising the Education of Deaf Children,* ed. Margaret Walworth, Donald Moores, and Terrence J. O'Rourke (Silver Spring, Md.: T.J. Publishers, 1992), 188; Claire Ramsey, "Language Planning in Deaf Education," in *The Sociolinguistics of the Deaf Community,* ed. Ceil Lucas (San Diego, Academic

Press, 1989), 140, 143, 146. See also Donald Moores, *Educating the Deaf: Psychology, Principles, and Practices* (Boston: Houghton Mifflin, 1987), 207–19; Harlan Lane, *The Mask of Benevolence: Disabling the Deaf Community* (New York: Knopf, 1992), 47, 112, 133–35.

17. Quoted in Andrew Solomon, "Defiantly Deaf," *New York Times Magazine,* Aug. 28, 1994, 62, 65.

18. John Schuchman, *Hollywood Speaks: Deafness and the Film Entertainment Industry* (Urbana: University of Illinois Press, 1988).

19. Gary Bunch, "An Interpretation of Full Inclusion," *Annals* 139 (April 1994): 150. Bunch briefly acknowledges the difficulties deaf children face in mainstreamed environments—such as "minimal social life"—but then quotes another writer that "there are advantages and disadvantages inherent in each educational model." This formulation effectively trivializes the immense potential for harm from social and linguistic deprivation for the mainstreamed deaf child.

20. Edward Dolnick, "Deafness as Culture," *Atlantic Monthly* (September 1993): 46, 52.

21. 1904 resolutions reprinted in *Proceedings of the Ninth Convention of the National Association of the Deaf and the Third World's Congress of the Deaf, 1910* (Philadelphia: Philocophus Press, 1912), 28.

22. [A Semi-Deaf Lady], "The Sign Language and the Human Right to Expression," *Annals* 53 (March 1908): 141–42.

23. Sarah Harvey Porter, "The Suppression of Signs by Force," *Annals* 39 (June 1894): 171.

24. Letter from Donna M. Shinton, "Are Hippos More Important than Deaf Children?" *Bicultural Center News,* no. 46 (April 1992): 7.

25. Thomas Hopkins Gallaudet, "The Natural Language of Signs—II," *Annals* 1 (January 1848): 87–88.

Adam and Eve. *See* Eden
affliction, vs. handicap, 102
African-American deaf. *See* deaf people, African-American
Albany Home School for the Oral Instruction of the Deaf, 65
Allport, Gordon, 2
American Annals of the Deaf
  and classification of educational methods, 136
  and decline of manualism, 25–26
  introduced, 17
  on schools for African-American deaf, 45–46
  types of articles published, 95
American Association to Promote the Teaching of Speech to the Deaf, 25, 36, 77
American Asylum, 30, 64, 83, 85, 118
  and evangelical Protestantism, 20, 33
  founding of, 3, 7, 15
  publisher of *American Annals of the Deaf,* 17
  See also schools for deaf
American Indians
  noble savage image, 156

sign conversations with deaf people, 43–44, 114
  and sign language, 43–45, 73, 109
American School for the Deaf. *See* American Asylum
American Sign Language
  continued repression of, 156–57, 163
  defined, 12–13
  in education, 152, 168n. 20
  as human right, 161–62
  importance of, 151, 162–63
  origins of, 12–13
  transmission of, 2, 150
  See also manually coded English; sign language
Amistad (slave ship), 114–15
analogy, contrasted with metaphor, 23–24
Anatomy and Physiology of Expression, The (Bell), 53
ancient languages
  in college education of manualists, 85
  manualists' view of, 85–86
  as similar to sign language, 44, 89–90, 105, 117

ancient languages (*continued*)
uncorrupted nature of, 117
See also Rome
animals
as "other," 48
and sign language, 49, 52–55,
155–56
what separates humans from,
48–55
See also Darwin, Charles; evolutionary theory
anthropology, 40–41
argument from design, 51, 124–25,
130
art
and practicality movement, 97–
98
sign language as, 86–88
artificial languages, 108
Association Review, 25, 26, 102, 104
automatic, vs. natural, 124
awakening, education as, 125–26
Ayres, J. A., 21, 50, 113, 119

Balis, Sylvia Chapin, 69, 74–75
Bardes, Barbara, 76
Barnard, Frederick A. P., 83
beauty, 94
declining importance of, 98, 101,
104–5
and evolution, 105
significance for manualists, 88–89,
94
of sign language, 88–89, 94, 104–5
and speech, 89
Beecher, Catherine, 57, 59, 67
Bell, Alexander Graham, 6, 8, 75, 95,
101
and American Association to Promote the Teaching of Speech to
the Deaf, 25
on day schools, 67
and eugenics, 6, 30–31
on French and German systems,
106
on gesturing, 135–36

on immigration, 28
on intermarriage of deaf, 30–31
and mainstreaming, 152
on natural and normal, 137–39
on natural signs, 135–36
on sign language as foreign, 28
on value of speech, 55
and Visible Speech, 103, 104
Bell, Charles, 53
Bell, Mabel G., 47
and passing, 146
on Visible Speech, 104
Bienvenue, M. J., 158
bilingual/bicultural education, 152,
156, 160
Bingham, Katherine, 132, 139, 143,
146–47
body, changing attitudes toward,
155–56
Boller, Paul, 50
Booth, Frank, 25, 102, 144
Bowe, Frank, 157
Brown, J. H., 103
Bruce, Robert V., 173n. 49
Bunch, Gary, 159

California School for the Deaf, 12
Callahan, Raymond E., 96, 198n. 51
Camp, Henry B., 21, 50, 88, 125–
26
Canguilhem, Georges, 141–42
Carlin, John, 22, 24, 170–71n. 22
Carnegie, Andrew, 94
Cary, J. Addison, 93, 117, 123, 125
Catholicism, 33
child, image of, 78–81
Cicero, 85, 86, 94
Civil War, 26, 59, 61, 84
clannishness of deaf, 26
Clarke Institution, 43, 47, 57, 64,
70
Clerc, Laurent, 7, 12, 30
and American Asylum, 3
and methodical sign language, 118,
204–5n. 29
on sign language, 91

Cloud, James H., 148
Cmiel, Kenneth, 90–91
Cohen, Leah Hager, 153–54
Cole, Thomas, 123, 143
combined system, 14, 171–72n. 31
    defined, 26, 69
    and gendered teaching assign-
        ments, 69
    meaning of changed, 69
community
    based on language, 9, 15–16, 27–
        35
    based on religion, 9, 15–16, 21, 25,
        33
    deaf (*see* deaf community)
compensation, principle of, 125
Comte, Auguste, 141, 210n. 33
Condillac, Etienne Bonnot de, 38–39,
    109
Conference of Principals and Super-
        intendents of Institutions for
        Deaf-Mutes, 99
Convention of American Instructors
        of the Deaf, 19
    deaf members of, 72–73
    female members of, 72–73
    and natural vs. arbitrary signs,
        120
    and vocational education, 97–
        98
    and women speakers, 73–74
Cooley, Charles Horton, 52
Cott, Nancy, 147
Course of Empire, The (Cole), 123
Covell, J. C., 93, 110
creationism
    defined, 36
    and direction of history, 40
    and facial expression, 53–54, 55
    and manualist generation, 36
    and origin of language, 39–40,
        55
    See also evolutionary theory
Crouch, Barry, 167n. 18
Crouter, A. L. E., 102, 139
cued speech, 152

cultivation, of sign language, 113–16,
    118, 119, 122
cult of domesticity, 67
cultural authority, shift of, 96–97

Darwin, Charles, 36–37, 51
    *Expression of the Emotions in Man
        and Animals, The,* 54
    on facial expression, 54
    on gesture, 42
    Origin of Species, The, 36
    See also evolutionary theory; lin-
        guistic Darwinism
Davidson, Samuel G., 135, 136
day schools, 66, 67–68, 153
    and normality, 138
    and vocational education, 99–100
    See also schools for deaf
deaf community, 35, 153
    defined, 11–12
    formation of, 3–4
    newspapers and periodicals of, 24,
        29, 34
    organizations of, 26, 29–30, 34,
        77, 149–50 (*see also* National
        Association of the Deaf)
    Parisian, 3
    and separatism, 30
    See also deafness; deaf people
Deaf in America (Padden and Hum-
        phries), 164n. 6
deafness
    as absence, 1
    cultural/social construction of,
        1–2, 7, 10–11, 15–16, 34–35,
        160
    essentiality of, 10, 160
    metaphors of (*see* metaphors of
        deafness)
    as social relation, 24
    See also deaf community; deaf peo-
        ple; education, deaf
deaf people
    African-American, 45–48, 179n.
        35, 180n. 38, 180n. 42
    as disabled, 2–3, 157–60

deaf people (*continued*)
  as ethnic group, 2–3, 16, 32, 34,
    157–60
  as foreigners, 26–35
  innocence of, 21–23
  isolation of, 152–54 (*see also* meta-
    phors of deafness)
  marriage patterns of, 30–31, 150
  movie and television portrayals of,
    158
  as staff in schools for deaf, 81
  as teachers (*see* teachers, deaf)
  understanding of equality, 147– 48
  views on mainstreaming, 152, 154,
    160–63
  views on manualism, 150–51
  views on oralism, 4–6, 10, 149–51,
    76–78, 80
  See also deaf community; deafness;
    education, deaf; metaphors of
    deafness; schools for deaf;
    teachers, deaf
decorum, refinement, taste, 91, 92,
    105
degeneration, of races, 44
DeLand, Fred, 100
de Leon, Pedro Ponce, 87
de l'Epée, Abbé Charles, 39, 106, 118,
    144
Descent of Man, The (Darwin), 51
design, argument from, 51, 124–25, 130
Desloges, Pierre, 3
difference, manualist acceptance of,
    144–45, 148, 159. *See also*
    sameness
disability, 3, 157–60
Douglas, Ann, 67
Draper, Amos, 76–77
Dudley, Lewis, 52, 64

Eden, Garden of
  America as, 115–16, 122
  language of, 39, 116–17, 127–30
  See also creationism; evangelical
    Protestantism; language,
    original

education, deaf
  bilingual/bicultural, 152, 160
  business values in, 96–101, 107
  interpreting, limitations of,
    153–54
  vocational, 97–98
  See also education, manualist con-
    ception of; education, oralist
    conception of; mainstreaming;
    manualism; manualists; oral-
    ism; oralists; schools for deaf;
    teachers, deaf; teachers of
    deaf
education, manualist conception of,
    63–64
  and age of admittance, 63–64
  as awakening, 88–89, 125–26
  and dormancy of faculties, 88–89,
    125–26
  and gender, 63–64, 70–71
  as Platonic, 126
  and religion, 15–16, 18–22, 33, 63,
    126
  See also education, deaf, manu-
    alism; manualists; oralism; oral-
    ists; teachers of deaf
education, oralist conception of, 63
  and age of admittance, 62–66
  and gender, 66–70
  as instilling of habits, 63, 64–65
  as science, 96
  See also education, deaf; manu-
    alism; manualists; oralism; oral-
    ists; teachers of deaf
efficiency movement, 96–97, 102–4
Ellegard, Alvar, 175–76n. 2
Emerson, Ralph Waldo, 122–23
English language, 32
  criticism, 90–91
  as inferior to ancient languages,
    90
  and national community, 27–28,
    33–34
  signed (*see* manually coded En-
    glish)
  spelling reform movement, 103–4

equality as sameness. *See* sameness
Essay on the Origin of Human Knowl-
   edge (Condillac), 38
eugenics, 6, 30–31
evangelical Protestantism, 9
   and community, 9, 15–16, 21, 25,
      33
   and creationism, 39–40
   and goals of education, 15–16, 18–
      22, 33, 63, 126
   and nature, 110, 124–25 (*see also*
      nature/natural)
evolutionary theory, 36–38
   acceptance of, 175–76n. 2, 176n. 3
   and beauty, 105
   and concept of handicap, 101–2
   and concept of normality, 143–44
   and inferiority of gestural lan-
      guage, 38–45, 52–55, 105–6
   and oralism, 9, 36–37, 43–45,
      52–55
   and progress, 37–38, 40–45, 105–6
   and social evolutionism, 176n. 3
   and uniqueness of humanity, 50–
      55
   See also Darwin, Charles; eugenics;
      linguistic Darwinism
Ewald, François, 141–42
exhibitions at schools for deaf, 72
experience of deafness, 11, 160–61
Expression of the Emotions in Man and
   Animals, The (Darwin), 54

family, significance to oralists, 66–
   69
Farnell, Brenda, 177n. 18, 203n. 18
feminization of teaching profession,
   56. *See also* teachers of deaf,
   female
finger-spelling, 26, 35, 69, 87, 119,
   208n. 4
Finney, Charles, 18
Fischer, Renate, 39
Flournoy, J. J., 30
Flowers, Thomas, 46–47, 180n. 39
foreignness, metaphor of, 26–35

Fox, Thomas Francis, 147–48
France, status relative to Germany,
   106
Francis, J. M., 87, 93, 121

Gallaudet, Edward M., 98
   on combined system, 26
   on deaf clannishness, 26
   on education of teachers of deaf,
      83–85
   on origin of manualism, 7–8
   on practical vs. classical education,
      90, 107
   on sign language, 26, 121
Gallaudet, Thomas H., 85, 118,
   119
   and American Asylum, 3, 7, 15
   and *Amistad,* 114–15
   on beauty of sign language, 89
   on education, 18–20, 163
   and evangelicalism, 15, 17–20,
      55
   on oratory, 93
   on sign language, 17–19, 53, 55
   on sign language as natural lan-
      guage, 110, 113–14
   on sign language as natural lan-
      guage of deaf, 123, 125
Gallaudet College, 64, 84
   and training of teachers, 25, 185n.
      18, 197n. 46
   oralist dislike of, 98
Garretson, Mervin, 160–61
Garrett, Emma, 74, 75
   on beauty, 105
   on college education for deaf,
      98
   on evolution and speech, 43
   and Home for Training in Speech
      of Deaf Children, 57–58, 65
   on low wages of women teachers,
      62
   and mainstreaming, 152, 157
   and nature/normality, 137–39,
      145–46
   opposed to gesturing, 135

Garrett, Emma (*continued*)
  and practicality movement, 101,
    106
  on spelling reform and Visible
    Speech, 103–4
  and teacher training, 57–58, 95
Garrett, Mary, 62, 157
  Home for Training in Speech of
    Deaf Children, 57–58, 65
  and nature/normality, 138, 143,
    146
  and passing, 146
  on peculiarity, 32
  and practicality movement, 101
Genesis, 39, 125
Germany, prestige of, 106
gesture, 111–12
  Condillac on, 38–39
  of Italian immigrants, 42
  in oratory, 92–93, 106
  and original language, 38–44
  and sign language, 107, 134–36
  See also pantomime; sign language
Gillet, Horace, 121, 124
Gillett, Philip G., 47
Gilman, Sander, 183n. 76
Gossett, Suzanne, 76
Graybill, Patrick, 160–61
Greek. *See* ancient languages
Greenburger, David, 137–38
Grimke, Sarah and Angelina, 72

habit, role in education for oralists,
    63–65
Hacking, Ian, 141–42, 210nn. 32, 33
handicapped, origin and use of term,
    101–2, 147
Hanson, Olof, 4, 5, 25, 77
hearing impaired, connotations of,
    158–59
heart
  emphasized by manualists, 18–19,
    88, 170n. 7
  and 1970s neoromanticism, 155–
    56
Heroditus, 127

history, oralist and manualist notions
    of, 40, 44–45, 55
Hofstadter, Richard, 175–76n. 2
home, significance for oralists, 66–
    69
Home for Training in Speech of Deaf
    Children (Philadelphia), 57–58,
    65
home schools, 64–65
  and normality, 138
  See also individual schools
Horace, 85
Howe, David Walker, 19
Howe, Samuel Gridley, 8, 67, 169n.
    25
Hoxie, Frederick E., 29
Hubbard, Gardiner G., 43, 59
Hull, Susanna E., 43
humanity, distinguishing characteris-
    tics of, 48–55
Humphries, Tom, 164n. 6, 171n. 24
Huxley, Thomas H., 48, 50–51

Illinois Institution, 27, 47, 57, 72
immigrants, 103, 156
  deaf compared to, 16, 27–32, 34,
    42
inclusion. *See* mainstreaming
Indiana School for the Deaf, 152
infant schools. *See* home schools
initialized signs, 120–21
Innes, Joseph, 154
innocence of deaf, 21–23, 117, 130
insanity, 54–55, 183n. 76
isolation
  as metaphor (*see* metaphors of
    deafness, isolation/outsider)
  as result of mainstreaming, 152–
    54

Jacobs, Leo, 160–61
Johnson, Paul E., 18
Jordan, David Starr, 97

Keeler, Sadie, 138
Keep, John R., 89, 117, 121

Kimball, Bruce, 106
Kinney, R. H., 110
Kirkhuff, J. D., 28, 43, 137
Kisor, Henry, 165n. 11

Lane, Albert G., 147
Lane, Harlan, 118, 166n. 16, 167n. 19,
    169n. 25, 204n. 29
language
    as distinguishing characteristic of
        humanity, 48–49
    natural, as defined by manualists,
        108–23, 127–31, 142
    natural, as defined by modern lin-
        guists, 108
    natural vs. artificial/arbitrary,
        108–31, 132–35
    original, 9, 38–45, 116, 117, 127–
        30
    See also American Sign Language,
        English language; nature/natu-
        ral; sign language; speech
language criticism, 90–91
Latin. *See* ancient languages
Lease, Mary Clyens, 75
Levine, Daniel, 176n. 3
linguistic Darwinism, 40
linguists
    on gesture, 40
    modern, 108, 112
lip-reading, limitations of, 18, 59, 76,
    89
Livy, 85
Locke, John, 38, 126

mainstream
    and concept of normality, 155
    and outsider metaphor, 35
mainstreaming, 35, 65
    differences from oralism, 155–
        56
    made possible by sign language,
        157
    objections to, 152–54, 160–63
    similarity to oralism, 154–55

for students with disabilities other
    than deafness, 159
Mallery, Garrick, 41–42, 43–44, 73,
    105–6
Mann, Horace, 8, 169n. 25
manualism
    defined, 4, 14
    establishment of, 6–9
manualists
    classical education of, 83–85,
        94
    and community, 9, 15–16, 21, 25,
        33
    conception of history, 39–40,
        44
    and deaf community, 163
    as evangelical Protestants, 9, 15–
        16, 18–22, 33, 39–40, 63, 110,
        126
    faulted, 163
    and gender, 63–64, 70–71, 82
    as liberally educated gentlemen,
        83–94
    as missionaries, 15–20, 71
    and natural language, 108–31
    and original language, 9, 38–45,
        116, 117, 127–30
    See also education, manualist view
        of; teachers of deaf, male
manually coded English, 35, 108, 119,
    163
    criticisms of, 157, 169n. 29
    defined, 13, 156–57
    and mainstreaming, 152, 168n. 20
    See also American Sign Language;
        methodical sign language; sign
        language
Marsh, Margaret, 67
Martha's Vineyard, 3, 13
Massieu, Jean, 7
materialism, nineteenth-century
    debate over, 124
McCowen, Mary, 52
McCowen Oral School for Young
    Deaf Children, 65
McGregor, Robert P., 6

men. *See* manualists, and gender;
teachers of deaf, male
metaphors of deafness, 11, 20, 23, 34,
161
and analogy, 23–24
ethnicity, 158–60
foreignness, 26–35
innocence and ignorance, 21–24
isolation/outsider, 16, 20–21, 24–
25, 28, 31–35
light and darkness, 20–22, 24–25,
33
mainstream, 35, 154–55
and paternalism, 11
silence, 22–24, 171n. 24
similarity of manualist and oralist,
150
methodical sign language, 13, 35,
118–21, 156, 204n. 29
middle landscape, 121–22
Milton, John, 128–29
mother, image of
and concepts of nature/normality,
138–39
significance for oralists, 66–67,
80–81
Mott, Lucretia, 72
"Must the Classics Go?" (West), 90, 107
"Must the Sign-Language Go?" (Gallaudet), 90
mute, use of term, 24

National Association of the Deaf
film project of, 12
positions taken on deaf education,
77, 149–50, 152, 161
nativism, 29, 158. *See also* community; metaphors of deafness,
foreignness
nature/natural
as both prescription and description, 142–43
and cultivation, 113–16, 118, 119,
122–23
disputed meaning of, 132–36
God as author of, 124–25

language (*see* language, natural;
sign language, as natural language)
meaning of, for manualists,
109–22, 127–31, 124, 140,
142–43
meaning of, for oralists, 132,
136–40
order of thought, 116–17
remedies, 124
signs (*see* sign language, as natural
language)
as synonym for normal, 136–42
Nebraska School for the Deaf, 25
newspapers and periodicals, deaf
community, 24, 29, 34
New York Evening Post, 42
New York Institution, 59, 64, 85, 139
New York Times, 139, 153–54
noble language of signs, 86, 88
normal, as synonym for hearing, 147
normality, concept of, 9, 110, 131
and day schools, 138
as end result of progress, 210n. 33
and equality, 146–48
as evolutionary concept, 143–44
history of, 141–43
as merely average, 210n. 32
as naturalness, 136–40
for oralists, 136–48
and peculiarity, 145
as prescription and description,
142–44, 147
North Carolina Institution, 45–47
Noyes, J. L., 135

Ohio Institution, 83–84
Oklahoma Industrial Institution for
the Deaf, Blind, and Orphans
of the Colored Race, 45–46
oral failures, 25–26, 171n. 31
oralism
dangers of, 151
deaf people's views of, 4–6, 10,
76–78, 80, 149–51
defined, 4, 13–14, 35

growth of, 3–4, 25, 165n. 8
historians' views of, 6
as progress, 5
See also manualism; manualists;
   oralists
oralists
   business values of, 96–101
   and commuity, 9, 16, 27–34
   conception of history, 44–45
   education of, 94–96
   and efficiency, 96–97, 102–4
   on employment of deaf people,
      99–101
   on equality, 159–60
   and evolutionary theory, 40–48,
      50–55
   and gender, 57–82
   and Germany, 106
   and image of deaf child, 78–80
   and natural, 132, 136–40
   and normality, 140–48
   and practicality movement, 96–
      100, 104
   and professionalization, 94–96
   and science, 96
   See also education, oralist concep-
      tion of; manualism; manualists;
      oralism
oratory, and sign language, 92–93
Oregon School, 77
Origin of Species, The (Darwin), 36
outsider, image of. See metaphors of
   deafness, isolation/outsider

Padden, Carol, 164n. 6, 171n. 24
pantomime
   Roman, 44, 86–88, 94
   and sign language, 44, 86–88, 108,
      112–13, 115, 134–35
   See also gesture
Paradise Lost (Milton), 128–29
Paris Institute for Deaf Mutes, 7, 39
passing as hearing, 146
paternalism, 11, 81, 150
Patterson, Robert, 121, 123–24
peculiarity, oralist concern with, 32,
   145

Peet, Harvey P.
   on definition of humanity, 49
   on education, 125–26
   on Latin's resemblance to sign lan-
      guage, 90
   on methodical signs, 119
   on original language, 127–30
   on progress, 44
   on religion, 19
   on Rome, 87–88
   on sign language as natural,
      127–30
Peet, Isaac Lewis, 140
Pennsylvania Institution, 28, 47,
      68–69
   and oralist education, 28, 57, 58,
      188n. 37
   visited by American Indians, 43
Pettingill, Benjamin D., 52
   on sign language as natural,
      111–12, 114, 125, 133–34
Porter, Sarah, 52–53, 162
practicality movement, 84, 96–100
Principles of Scientific Management, The
   (Taylor), 97
professionalization of teachers, 94–96
progress, 37–38, 40–45, 105–6, 126
progressive, oralists as, 149, 32
Protestantism. See evangelical Protestantism
Psammetichus (ancient king of
   Egypt), 127

Quintilian, 92, 112

race
   Africans/African Americans, 41,
      43, 45–48, 179n. 35, 180n. 38,
      42
   American Indians, 43–45, 73, 109,
      114, 156
   and sign language, 9, 40–48, 132,
      155–56
   See also American Indians; deaf
      people, African-American
Rae, Luzerne, 20, 48, 110–11, 125

Ramsey, Claire, 157
refinement. *See* decorum, refinement, taste
religion. *See* evangelical Protestantism
Rochester Method, 175n. 73, 208n. 4
romanticism, 9, 16, 106, 126
  and innocence, 21
  and nature, 115
  new, 156
Rome, 92
  and art of pantomime, 86–88, 94
  and gesture in oratory, 92–93
  importance to manualists, 85–86, 90, 105
  as model for historical explanation, 122
  See also ancient languages; manualists, classical education of
Roscius, 86, 94
Ryan, Mary, 78–79

Sacks, Oliver, 151
sameness, oralist emphasis of, 79, 144–48. *See also* difference
Sarah Fuller Home School for Little Deaf Children, 65
schools for deaf
  boarding schools criticized, 31–32, 65–68
  and cottage plan, 68–69
  day schools, 66, 67–68, 99–100, 138, 153
  first established, 3–4, 164n. 3
  lowering of admission age, 62–66, 70, 188n. 37
  principals of, 85, 194n. 6
  segregated, 45–48, 179n. 35, 180nn. 38, 42
  today, 152
  and transmission of sign language, 2
  See also education, deaf; teachers, deaf; teachers of deaf, female; teachers of deaf, male; *and specific school names*
Science, 42

science, popular esteem for, 96
scientific management, 96–97, 102
scientific naturalism. *See* evolutionary theory
Second Great Awakening, 15–16. *See also* evangelical Protestantism
sentimentalism, 67, 69, 80–81
Sheridan, Laura, 73–74
Sicard, Abbé, 7
Sidranski, Ruth, 151
signed English. *See* manually coded English
sign language
  of aboriginal peoples, 41–45, 73, 109, 156, 177n. 18
  American (*see* American Sign Language)
  as art, 86–88
  attitudes toward in 1970s, 155–56
  beauty of, 88–89, 94, 104–5
  and cultivation, 113–16, 118–22
  defined, 12–13, 17
  and emotion, 18–19, 88, 155–56, 170n. 7
  and evolutionary theory, 38–45, 52–55, 105–6
  and facial expression, 53–54, 91–92, 182n. 72
  as foreign language, 27–29
  grammar, supposed lack of, 116, 121
  and iconicity, 112–15
  and initialized signs, 120, 124
  as language of animals, 52–55
  as natural language, 108–23, 127–31, 142
  as natural language of deaf, 123–27, 129–30, 169n. 26
  and order of thought, 116–17
  as original language, 9, 38–45, 116, 117, 128, 130
  as pantomime, 44, 86–88, 108, 112–15, 134–35
  as primitive language, 38, 40–43, 44–45
  similarity to ancient languages, 44, 89–90, 105, 117

transmission of, 10, 12, 150, 163
as un-American, 27–28
as universal language, 12, 108–15, 142
as unnatural language, 132–35, 144
See also American Sign Language; manually coded English; methodical sign language
silence, metaphor of, 22–24, 171n. 24
soul, 19, 20
as distinguishing characteristic of humanity, 48–51
and evolutionary theory, 51
and facial expression, 53–54
and language, 40, 48–51, 55, 124, 128
See also animals; evangelical Protestantism
species. See animals
speech
and beauty, 89
as distinguishing characteristic of humanity, 49, 50, 51–52, 55
natural elements of, 129–30
natural method of teaching, 136–39
and sentimentalism, 80–81
as universal means of communication, 32, 142, 143
as unnatural to deaf, 89, 123–24, 125, 129–30
spelling reform movement, 103–4
Stanton, Elizabeth Cady, 72, 75
Stone, Collins
on education and the soul, 49–50
and metaphors of deafness, 20
on natural order of thought, 116–17
on natural vs. arbitrary language, 110, 116
on Roman pantomime, 86
on sign language as natural language of deaf, 123, 125
Stone, Lucy, 72
Strober, Myra, 56–57, 69

Talbot, Benjamin, 83–84, 117
Taylor, Frederick Winslow, 97
teachers, deaf, 2, 25, 149
excluded from oralist schools, 81
low pay of, 61, 185n. 21
percentages of in schools for deaf, 60–61, 81, 149
teachers of deaf, female, 57–62, 64–82
and age of students, 62–66, 70
and decline of deaf teachers, 60–61
lacking classical education, 84
low pay of, 59, 61–62, 65–66, 68
and nature of education, 64, 69–71
and oralism, 9, 57–82
percentages of, 58, 60–61
and voice, importance of, 72–76
and woman's sphere, 66, 82
See also oralists, and gender
teachers of deaf, male, 56, 82
and age of students, 63–64, 70
and Civil War, 59
and classical education, 84
and nature of education, 64, 69–71
See also manualists, and gender
Texas Deaf, Dumb, and Blind Institute for Colored Youths, 46, 179n. 35
Trask, Cornelia, 72, 84
Truth, Sojourner, 72
Turner, Charles P., 53
Turner, William, 90
Tuskegee Institution, 98
Tyack, David, 56–57
Tyler, John M., 26–27, 36–38
Tylor, Edward B., 41, 42

vacations, home schools, 65
Van Cleve, 167n. 18, 214n. 9
Veditz, George, 10, 150
Virginia State School for Colored Deaf and Blind Children, 45–46, 179n. 35
Visible Speech, 103–4
vocational education, 97–100
voice, as metaphor for power, 72–76
Volta Review. See Association Review

Washington, Booker T., 98
Weber, Max, 84
Weld, Lewis, 91, 113, 119, 121
West, Andrew, 90, 107
Westervelt, Z. F., 134–35, 144, 175n. 73, 208n. 4
Whitney, William Dwight, 40
Winefield, Richard, 166n. 17
Wisconsin Phonological Institute, 95
woman's sphere. *See* oralists, and gender; teachers of deaf, female, and woman's sphere

women. *See* oralists, and gender; teachers of deaf, female
Woodbridge, William C., 83
Woodruff, Lucius, 21, 50, 88
Woodward, James, 11–12
Worcester, Alice E., 103
World Congress of the Deaf, 78, 147
Wright, Frances, 72
Wright, John Dutton, 102
Wright Oral School, 102

Yale, Caroline, 47
Yale College, 85